EXPLORING CONTENT 2

Reading
for
Academic
Success

ALCI

LORRAINE C. SMITH

Adelphi University

Longman

CONTENTS

UNIT 1   HOW DO ORGANISMS INTERACT WITH THE WORLD AROUND THEM?   1

CHAPTER 1   BEHAVIOR   2

Understanding Behavior   8

The actions of all animals are essential in helping them survive and reproduce. Many animal behaviors, such as caring for their young, may seem to have the same motivations as human behavior, but in fact do not.

Instinctive Behavior and Learned Behavior   20

Behavior may be instinctive or learned. Several factors determine whether a specific animal's behavior is more often instinctive or learned. Learning itself can be categorized into several types.

CHAPTER 2   UNDERSTANDING INSTINCT AND LEARNING   33

Instinct and Learning Compared   36

Instinctive behavior is typical of simple animals, and is genetically determined, whereas learned behavior is characteristic of more complex animals, and involves experience and practice.

Instinct and Learning in the Same Organism   43

Complex animals such as mammals display some instinctive behavior. They also demonstrate a wide range of learned behaviors which help them and their species survive. Complex behaviors may be learned in a variety of ways and have value because they enable a species to adapt successfully within its ecological niche.

SCOPE AND SEQUENCE

UNIT AND CHAPTERS	CONTENT	READING/STUDY SKILLS	CRITICAL THINKING SKILLS
UNIT 1			
HOW DO ORGANISMS INTERACT WITH THE WORLD AROUND THEM? CHAPTER 1: *Behavior* CHAPTER 2: *Understanding Instinct and Learning*	• the nature of instinctive behavior • the nature of learned behavior • different types of learned behavior • instinctive behavior and learned behavior • behavior and the importance of allocating resources • dominance hierarchy • territorial behavior	• preview key vocabulary • use titles and headings to predict content • scan and skim to find main ideas and specific information • highlight important information • monitor reading comprehension • use font styles, context, and the dictionary to learn key vocabulary • use context to learn the meaning of new vocabulary • learn and use word forms • use text organization and graphic organizers to facilitate understanding of text • use referents to aid in understanding text	• predict • evaluate • organize • define • decide • categorize • infer • make generalizations
UNIT 2			
HOW IS OUR WORLD VIEW SHAPED BY OUR CULTURE? CHAPTER 3: *Defining and Exploring Culture* CHAPTER 4: *Nature Shaping Culture*	• cultural and noncultural behaviors • the characteristics of cultural behavior • cultural systems • the concept of world view • the basis for religious systems • polytheistic and monotheistic beliefs • people's relationships with the supernatural • processes underlying culture change	• review skills from unit 1 • annotate text • identify text organization • analyze contrast in sentences and ideas • understand metaphors • write main ideas • identify author's probable intention in presenting information • recognize definitions • analyze complex sentences	• compare • define • predict • organize • contrast • propose • arrange • explain

UNIT AND CHAPTERS	CONTENT	READING/STUDY SKILLS	CRITICAL THINKING SKILLS
UNIT 3			
HOW DOES OUR PLACE IN HISTORY INFLUENCE WHAT WE BELIEVE? CHAPTER 5: *The Birth of Modern Science* CHAPTER 6: *Science and a New World View*	• Aristotle's concept of science • the origin of Western scientific beliefs • how ways of understanding the world changed in seventeenth-century Europe • the work of Galileo Galilei, Johannes Kepler, and Sir Isaac Newton • the conflict between Galileo and the Church	• review skills from units 1 and 2 • write a summary • understand less common uses of common words and expressions • understand language from primary sources, translations, or archaic texts • analyze the author's use of questions in readings	• predict • organize • summarize • critique • synthesize • relate • evaluate
UNIT 4			
HOW DO CULTURE AND HISTORY INFLUENCE ART? CHAPTER 7: *The Rise of the Western Artist* CHAPTER 8: *The Foundations of Chinese Art*	• changing attitudes toward artists in ancient Greece and Rome, in Medieval Europe, and in seventeenth-century Europe • the influence of classical Greek and classical Roman art and architecture on European art and architecture • the development of perspective in European art • Renaissance art in Italy and in Flanders • the significance of calligraphy in Chinese art • Chinese aesthetic theory • the concept of realism in Chinese landscape painting	• review skills from units 1–3 • recognize and understand the passive voice • understand use of prepositional phrases • analyze writing about art • understand author's use of *we*	• compare • predict • generalize • interpret • summarize • evaluate • infer • contrast • contextualize information • organize
UNIT 5			
HOW DO WE EXPLAIN OUR SIMILARITIES AND DIFFERENCES? CHAPTER 9: *Understanding People Across Cultures* CHAPTER 10: *Theories of Human Motivation*	• the nature of cross-cultural psychology • psychological diversity and psychological universals • cross-cultural approaches to studying human behavior • Abraham Maslow's hierarchy of needs • universal mechanisms of human motivation • cognitive theories underlying human motivation	• review skills from units 1–4 • understand the use of dashes • recognize clues to text organization • critique information in textbooks • recognize author critiques and opinions in a text • distinguish between a theory and research supporting a theory	• hypothesize • predict • define • critique • determine • organize • examine • summarize • relate • analyze

ABOUT *EXPLORING CONTENT*

Exploring Content: Reading for Academic Success, Book Two, is the second of two reading texts geared primarily toward incoming college English language learners who need to improve their reading proficiency, develop effective critical thinking and study skills, and build background knowledge and vocabulary essential to their understanding of specific content areas in required core college courses.

Exploring Content has been designed to give students an introduction to a number of content areas, while at the same time fostering reading and study skills so essential to success in postsecondary education. The subject areas are represented by excerpts from college textbooks. The readings are shorter than a complete textbook chapter, but they have not been simplified, in order to help students develop proficiency in reading unmodified material from a college text. Students are provided with illustrations, diagrams, and charts designed to facilitate understanding of text and non-text information (Hyerle, 1996). The questions and activities in each chapter help the students read, write, think about, organize, analyze, and understand the concepts and information in the chapters in a manner similar to what they will experience in college courses. While they are developing understanding of ideas, vocabulary, and information, they are working on their reading, writing, and study skills, and developing their speaking and listening skills as well.

Content-Based Instruction (CBI)

Content-based instruction is "the integration of content learning with language teaching aims. More specifically, it refers to the concurrent study of language and subject matter, with the form and sequence of language presentation dictated by content material" (Brinton, Snow, & Wesche, 1989, p. vii). Content-based instruction is multi-purpose. It involves helping students simultaneously develop their English proficiency and learn subject matter (Kasper, Babbitt, Mlynarczyk et al, 2000). Students use English to build background knowledge, and, through critical thinking, make connections and develop concepts. Students work together to construct knowledge and develop their ideas. Many activities involve purposeful listening and speaking. Writing is also an integral component in content-based instruction. The writing tasks in the books are "low stakes," i.e., informal, ungraded assignments whose purpose is to help students reflect in writing on what they are learning and to make visible their emerging understanding of new content (Elbow, 1997).

Because content-based instruction is multi-faceted, assessment in CBI must be as well. Consequently, as students progress through a content-based curriculum, content knowledge and understanding, development and use of content-specific vocabulary, and improved English proficiency are assessed through formative and summative evaluations.

Critical Thinking Skills

The conceptual framework of the book incorporates Benjamin Bloom's taxonomy of educational objectives (Bloom, 1956; Anderson, Krathwohl, Airasian, Cruikshank, Mayer, Pintrich, Raths, & Wittrock, 2001). Bloom places cognitive skills into two general categories. The first involves learners in remembering and organizing; the second involves learners in analyzing and synthesizing. For students to develop critical thinking skills, they need to move beyond the first three levels of knowledge, comprehension, and application in the first category, and engage in the more active processes of analysis, synthesis, and evaluation in the second category. One of the goals of *Exploring Content* is to help students develop critical thinking skills, in part by incorporating analysis, synthesis, and evaluation throughout every chapter. Specific questions and activities at the prereading, reading, and postreading stages have been designed to take the students beyond Bloom's first three levels of cognitive skills. The development of all these essential skills takes place within the context of college-level academic reading.

TO THE TEACHER

How to Use This Book

Exploring Content contains five units of two chapters each, for a total of 10 chapters. Each chapter in Exploring Content consists of the following:

A List of Chapter Goals
An Introductory Reading section which includes:
Activate Your Knowledge
Preview Key Vocabulary
Reading and Study Skill Strategies
Introductory Reading
Checking Comprehension
Learning Vocabulary
A Main Reading section which includes:
Activate Your Knowledge
Main Reading
Checking Comprehension
Learning Vocabulary
Follow-up Assignments which include:
Writing Activities
Extension Activities

List of Chapter Goals

The Chapter Goals section in each chapter lists reading and study skill strategies presented and practiced, as well as content-specific goals. This list, and the list of content-specific vocabulary in the Preview Key Vocabulary, provide a focus for each chapter, and serve as review guides once the class has completed the chapter.

Introductory Section

ACTIVATE YOUR KNOWLEDGE

This section includes a range of activities designed to help the students become engaged in the topic, and to evaluate what they may or may not already know about it. Students work alone, in pairs, or in small groups. Once individuals or groups have completed an activity, the whole class can be brought together to pool their knowledge through whole-class discussion, and by recording groups' information and ideas on the blackboard. Throughout the process, students should be encouraged to think about the questions and to make reasonable guesses when they are unsure. They can return to their answers before beginning the main reading, and check whether their answers were accurate and whether they now know the answers to questions they were unsure of initially. The process of thinking about, discussing, and making reasonable guesses is at the heart of this activity.

PREVIEW KEY VOCABULARY

The Preview Key Vocabulary section shows students what content-specific vocabulary will be presented in the chapter and gives them the opportunity to examine and rank the vocabulary according to how familiar they are with each word or term. The purpose of the list is not to have students look up the words in a dictionary before they begin reading. Not only is doing so a laborious chore, it defeats the purpose of having students learn vocabulary from context, which is an essential reading strategy.

READING AND STUDY SKILL STRATEGIES

A range of reading and study skill strategies are presented in this section. Several strategies are introduced in the first chapter because they are so essential to understanding. From the first reading, students need to preview key vocabulary, to scan titles and headings and to skim through a reading to gain an overview of a passage, and to predict content. While they are reading, students need to highlight important information, monitor their comprehension, and use illustrations and other graphics as aids to comprehension. Furthermore, they need to begin learning how text is organized, and to understand new vocabulary from context and from a dictionary.

Once a strategy is introduced, students use that strategy throughout the book. New strategies are introduced in subsequent units. These strategies include those mentioned in the previous paragraph as well as using font styles to identify key vocabulary, identifying referents, creating diagrams, outlines, and flow charts, annotating text, and analyzing sentence structure. By the end of the book, the students will be on their way to making these strategies an integral part of their reading, which is one of the main goals of the text.

INTRODUCTORY READING

Students should be encouraged to read the passage more than once, each time with a specific purpose. During the first reading, for example, students might highlight essential ideas and the vocabulary they consider important, including key vocabulary, and respond to the Before You Continue Reading items as they read. The Before You Continue items always asks about the key point, topic, or main idea of the previous section, and helps students monitor their comprehension before they have gone too far in the reading. If a student is unsure of the answer, rereading a few paragraphs will not take long, and will help ensure understanding before the student moves on to the rest of the passage.

Students should be encouraged to highlight whenever they read, and to use the wider margin to write questions and comments they may have as they read. This practice helps keep the students' attention focused on the reading. In addition, by writing questions in the margin as they read, they will not forget them, and will be able to ask them in class, either of their classmates or the teacher.

The readings are accompanied by illustrations which are designed to facilitate understanding of the text. Consequently, students should develop the habit of examining them carefully, relating them to the reading, and writing questions and comments about them as well.

CHECKING COMPREHENSION

This section begins with an activity that asks students to consider how a reading has been organized. This section also includes questions the students guessed about in the prereading activity and asks students to review those questions and check the accuracy of their knowledge prior to reading. Beginning in Chapter 3, a Sentence Focus activity is included. This activity focuses on various aspects of sentence structure, such as the author's use of transition words or words of contrast, the passive voice, metaphors, or prepositional phrases. The Checking Comprehension section may also contain multiple choice and short answer questions designed to assess students' comprehension of the main ideas and details of the reading. Students may answer these questions individually first, then compare their answers with a classmate, in a small group, or together as a class.

LEARNING VOCABULARY

The Learning Vocabulary section includes learning vocabulary in context and using the dictionary.

Students often have great difficulty figuring out the meaning of vocabulary in context. Even when they do so in an exercise such as this one, which provides them with multiple choice answers, they still have trouble transferring the skill to the reading in general. The purpose of this exercise is to provide a scaffold for students to learn how to figure out the meaning of unfamiliar words in a supportive activity. When students ask about other vocabulary that is not in this exercise or the Dictionary activity, they should be encouraged to try to figure out the meaning themselves, thus extending this exercise to more realistic circumstances.

Students all too often look up a word in their dictionary, and select the first entry, without regard for the context in which the unknown word was read. What makes this activity more complex is that sometimes more than one entry is a reasonable choice. In such situations, both choices should be accepted. Here, too, once the students complete this activity, they can review the Key Vocabulary at the beginning of the chapter and check the words they have learned.

In college textbooks, new terms and vocabulary frequently appear in boldface or italics. Students do not always see these font changes as indicators of important vocabulary. Activities call out such conventions and help students learn vocabulary in this way.

ACTIVATE YOUR KNOWLEDGE

This section serves the same purpose as the Activate Your Knowledge section in the Introductory section. It also includes a range of activities designed to help the students become engaged in the topic, and to evaluate what they may or may not already know about it. Again, students will work in pairs or small groups, think about and discuss possible answers, and make reasonable guesses when they are unsure. They can return to their answers after completing the Main Reading, and check whether their answers were accurate and whether they now know the answers to questions they were unsure of initially. The process of thinking about, discussing, and making reasonable guesses is more important than "getting the right answer."

READING AND STUDY SKILL STRATEGIES

The reading and study skill strategies that were introduced in the Introductory section are presented for the Main Reading as well. In this manner, students are provided with ample opportunities for practice. A new strategy will be introduced and scaffolded in each unit, and utilized for the remainder of the book.

MAIN READING

Because this passage is a longer reading than the Introductory Reading, students need to understand that they cannot expect to understand and to remember what they read after only one or two readings. Students should be encouraged to read the passage more than once, each time with a specific purpose. During the first reading, for example, students might highlight essential ideas and the vocabulary they consider important, including key vocabulary, and respond to the Before You Continue Reading items. During a second reading, they might focus on key vocabulary.

Students should also be encouraged to use the same strategies they used during the Introductory Reading, including highlighting, writing questions in the margins, and responding to the Before You Continue items, and examining the illustrations accompanying the passage. These strategies need to be practiced in every chapter so they become an integral part of students' reading and study repertoire.

CHECKING COMPREHENSION

This section includes text analysis, sentence focus, short answer, and multiple choice questions designed to assess students' comprehension of text organization, sentence structure, main ideas, and details of the reading. Students may do the activities and answer the questions individually first, then compare their work with a classmate, in a small group, or together as a class.

LEARNING VOCABULARY

These exercises provide students with further practice in developing their vocabulary-learning skills. Word forms are yet another means for learning vocabulary, one which needs to be explicitly demonstrated to students, and in which they need ongoing, consistent practice. This activity is included in the Learning Vocabulary section of the Main Reading. As students become accustomed to doing these vocabulary exercises, they might also explain their rationale for their choice of answer. Very often, an explanation of a wrong choice can be very helpful in understanding why a student continues to have difficulty learning meanings from context and determining the appropriateness of a definition in a dictionary entry.

Once the students complete this activity, they can review the Key Vocabulary at the beginning of the chapter and check the words they learned in both readings. At this point, any key vocabulary that a student has not checked off can be looked up in the relevant passage and discussed, so that all the key vocabulary items are learned.

Follow-up Assignments

WRITING ACTIVITIES

One of the main goals of the writing section is to provide students with opportunities for meaningful use of the vocabulary they learn in the chapter. A chart of key content-specific and academic vocabulary from both chapter readings is always listed at the beginning of the exercise, and serves as a reference. Students should be encouraged to use the vocabulary as they respond to the writing activities and to the extension activities. The writing section also gives the students practice in writing to clarify their understanding of the topics presented in the chapter, and to develop their ideas in writing.

EXTENSION ACTIVITIES

This section incorporates a range of activities. Students may be instructed to complete or create a flowchart, a time line, or a chart, or to label or describe illustrations, and then to draw conclusions from these various formats. In the last activity in this section, students are given a list of key words so they can use the Internet for further research.

Assessment

Content-based assessments should not simply target isolated elements of language nor factual information, but should provide tasks that require students to integrate information and to form and articulate their own opinions about the subject matter.

Kasper, Babbitt, Mlynarczyk, Brinton, Rosenthal, Master, Myers, Egbert, Tillyer, & Wood, 2000, p. 20

Assessment of student learning forms an integral component of this book, and reflects the objectives of content-based instruction: (a) enhanced language proficiency, (b) improved study skills, and (c) knowledge of content and vocabulary. Assessment in *Exploring Content: Reading for Academic Success* is both formative and summative. Ongoing assessment of learning takes place while students are reading and at the end of each chapter as students answer questions about the content and the vocabulary in the reading. Tests provided in the Tests and Answer Keys 2 consist of passages related to those presented in the chapters, which the students are asked to read. Students demonstrate their understanding of a reading by answering questions about the content, the vocabulary, and the strategies they use to work through the text and the test questions, and as they engage in a range of culminating activities.

Bibliography

Adamson, H. D. (1993). *Academic competence—Theory and classroom practice: Preparing ESL students for content courses*. White Plains, NY: Longman.

Anderson, L. W., Krathwohl, D. R., Airasian, P. W., Cruickshank, K. A., Mayer, R. E., Pintrich, P. R., Raths, J., & Wittrock, M. C. (2001). *A taxonomy for learning, teaching, and assessing: A revision of Bloom's taxonomy of educational objectives, abridged edition*. White Plains, NY: Longman.

Black, M. C., & Kiehnhoff, D. M. (1992). Content-based classes as a bridge from the EFL to the university classroom. *TESOL Journal, 1*, 27–28.

Bloom, B. S., Ed. (1956). *Taxonomy of educational objectives: The classification of educational goals, handbook 1: Cognitive domain*. White Plains, NY: David McKay.

Brinton, D. M., Snow, M. A., & Wesche, M. B. (1989). *Content-based second language instruction*. New York: Newbury House.

Crandall, J. (1995). Content-based ESL: An introduction. In J. Crandall (Ed.). *ESL through content-area instruction*. (pp. 1–8). McHenry, IL: The Center for Applied Linguistics/Delta Systems.

Dubin, F., Eskey, D. E., & Grabe, W. (1986). *Teaching second language reading for academic purposes*. Reading, MA: Addison-Wesley.

Elbow, P. (1997). High stakes and low stakes in assigning and responding to writing. In M. D. Sorcinelli and P. Elbow (Eds.) *Writing to learn: Strategies for assigning and responding to writing across the disciplines*. New Directions for Teaching and Learning, Number 69, Spring, 1997. San Francisco: Jossey-Bass.

Eskey, D. E. (1992). Syllabus design in content-based instruction. *The CATESOL Journal, 5*(1), 11–23.

Hyerle, D. (1996). *Visual tools for constructing knowledge*. Alexandria, VA: Association for Supervision and Curriculum Development.

Kasper, L. F. (1995). Theory and practice in content-based ESL reading instruction. *English for Specific Purposes, 14*(3), 223–230.

Kasper, L. F., Babbitt, M., Mlynarczyk, R., Brinton, D. M., Rosenthal, J. W., Master, P., Myers, S. A., Egbert, J., Tillyer, D. A., & Wood, L. S. (2000). *Content-based college ESL instruction*. Mahwah, NJ: Lawrence Erlbaum.

Maaka, M. A., & Ward, S. M. (2000). Content area reading in community college classrooms. *Community College Journal of Research and Practice, 24*(2), 107–125.

Manzo, A. V., Manzo, U. C., & Estes, T. (2001). *Content area literacy: Interactive teaching for active learning* (3rd ed.). New York: John Wiley & Sons.

Nist, S. L., & Simpson, M. L. (2001). *Developing vocabulary for college thinking*. Boston: Allyn and Bacon.

Schleppegrell, M. J., Achugar, M., & Oteíza, T. (2004). The grammar of history: Enhancing content-based instruction through a functional focus on language. *TESOL Quarterly, 38*(1), 67–93.

Schleppegrell, M. J., & Colombi, M. C. (Eds.). (2002). *Developing advanced literacy in first and second languages: Meaning with power*. Mahwah, NJ: Lawrence Erlbaum.

Snow, M. A., & Brinton, D. M. (Eds.). (1997). *The content-based classroom: Perspectives on integrating language and content*. White Plains, NY: Longman.

Valentine, J. F., & Repath-Martos, L. M. (1992). How relevant is relevance?: An examination of student needs, interests, and motivation in the content-based university classroom. *The CATESOL Journal, 5*(1), 25–42.

Zamel, V., & Spack, R. (Eds.). (1998). *Negotiating academic literacies: Teaching and learning across languages and cultures*. Mahwah, NJ: Lawrence Erlbaum.

TO THE STUDENT

Exploring Content is not a text about getting the right answers. Rather, the goal is to engage you in thinking, talking, reading, and writing about college subjects. In other words, the process is as important as—sometimes more important than—a product: a right answer. At times you will have more questions than the text, the teacher, or a fellow student, may be able to answer. That is the nature of learning. Unanswered questions may challenge you to do some research in other books or online. Perhaps your curiosity will stimulate your interest in a semester-long course in a particular subject. Keep in mind that you are getting a brief introduction to each subject. What you learn in this book is like the tip of an iceberg—there is so much more beneath the surface!

At times the material—both the text and the illustrations—may be difficult to understand, and you may not grasp it on your first, or even your second, reading. Keep in mind that your goal is not to learn every new word, but to learn key content-related vocabulary, and to gain an understanding of the concepts integral to that content area. Rereading, carefully examining illustrations, asking questions, making notes, and creating outlines, flowcharts, diagrams—are all strategies that will help you develop your understanding of the content in these chapters. Be patient; be persistent. The skills you develop as you work with the book, your teacher, and your classmates will serve you well in your future college classes.

Each chapter in *Exploring Content* includes excerpts from chapters in current college textbooks. On average, the chapters in *Exploring Content* are 25 pages in length. In a class that meets four to six hours a week, a chapter will generally take about a week to work with. You need to understand that, if you try to learn every word, you will not be able to complete a typical class assignment within the time an instructor gives. Consequently, one of the goals of *Exploring Content* is to help you develop skills and strategies for reading fluently. Proficient readers do not stop and consider every unfamiliar word. They read for general knowledge, then review for the specifics they feel are essential. This proficiency is what *Exploring Content* is designed to help you achieve.

ABOUT THE AUTHOR

Lorraine C. Smith holds a doctorate in Curriculum and Teaching from Teachers College, Columbia University. She has taught ESL for 25 years on all levels, particularly the college level. She has co-authored six ESL reading skills texts and has presented at local, national, and international conferences. Professor Smith teaches in the M.A. TESOL/BE Program at Adelphi University in Garden City, New York.

Author's Acknowledgments

I wish to express my gratitude to my editor, Laura LeDréan, for her continuing support and enthusiasm for this project. I thank Paula Van Ells, my development editor, whose comments and suggestions helped me improve and polish the material.

My special thanks go to Nancy Nici Mare of the English Language Institute at Queens College. She and her ESL students field tested many chapters and gave me valuable suggestions for revision. My thanks also go to Regina A. Rochford of Queensborough Community College, who gave me useful insights and feedback. I am very grateful to my former ESL students at Queensborough, who willingly worked with early drafts of the chapters. Their questions and comments were invaluable to me as I developed the book. Finally, I acknowledge my husband, Joseph, who always said I could do it.

HOW DO ORGANISMS INTERACT WITH THE WORLD AROUND THEM?

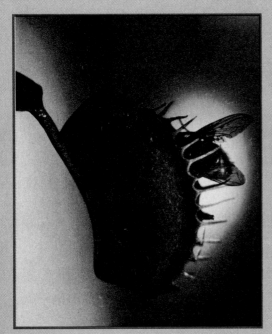

Venus flytrap with trapped insect

Lobsterman with lobster trap

CHAPTER 1

BEHAVIOR

Skills Goals

- *Preview key vocabulary.*
- *Use titles and headings to predict content.*
- *Scan and skim to find main ideas and specific information.*
- *Highlight important information.*
- *Monitor reading comprehension.*
- *Use font styles, context, and the dictionary to learn key vocabulary.*
- *Learn and use word forms.*
- *Use text organization and graphic organizers to facilitate understanding of text.*

Content-Specific Goals

- *Understand the nature of instinctive behavior.*
- *Understand the nature of learned behavior.*
- *Study the different types of learned behavior.*
- *Distinguish between instinctive behavior and learned behavior.*

Fig. 1.0   A bird building a nest

Chapter Readings

Understanding Behavior

Instinctive Behavior and Learned Behavior

INTRODUCING THE READING

Activate Your Knowledge

The following activities will help you prepare for the Introductory Reading. They will help you focus on the topic and discover what you already know about it. Do not worry if you do not know something. You will learn more as you work with the chapter.

A Work alone or in a small group. Read the following excerpt from the Introductory Reading, and then do the task that follows.

> **THE VALUE OF BEHAVIORS**
>
> **Behavior** is how an organism acts, what it does, and how it does it. When we think about the behavior of an animal, we should keep in mind that behavior is like any other characteristic displayed by an animal. Behavior has a value or significance to the animal as it goes about exploiting resources and reproducing more of its own species. Many behaviors are inherited; consequently, they evolved just like the structures of animals. In this respect, behavioral characteristics are no different from structural characteristics.

List two animals. List two of each animal's behaviors. Describe the value of the behaviors for that kind of animal. How does the behavior help it?

ANIMAL	BEHAVIORS	VALUE OF EACH BEHAVIOR
	1.	
	2.	
	1.	
	2.	

B Answer the following questions.

1. What is **behavior**?
   a. everything an animal does or thinks
   b. all of an animal's characteristics
   c. all of an animal's actions

2. Many behaviors are inherited. What types of behaviors are these?
   a. learned
   b. instinctive
   c. structural

3. Many behaviors are not inherited. What types of behavior are these?
   a. learned
   b. instinctive
   c. structural

C **Label the following behaviors *instinctive* (I) or *learned* (L).**

1. ___ A bird flies away as you approach.

2. ___ A person is afraid of snakes.

3. ___ A newborn baby nurses or sucks milk from a bottle.

4. ___ A dog comes when it is called.

5. ___ You blink your eyes when something passes close to your face.

6. ___ Squirrels collect and store nuts.

7. ___ A person runs away from an approaching dog.

8. ___ A child begins to walk.

9. ___ A bird builds a nest.

D **As a class, discuss your responses. Keep in mind that you may not agree.**

Reading and Study Skill Strategies

Using strategies and skills when you work with a reading passage will help you understand and remember what you have read. This chapter introduces several strategies and skills that you will find effective in all your reading, regardless of the subject matter. Some of the strategies or skills may be unfamiliar or difficult to use at first. However, if you persevere, they will get easier. Eventually, they will become an automatic part of your reading and study habits. You will find that your comprehension is improving and your vocabulary is increasing.

PREVIEW KEY VOCABULARY

Before you begin reading a passage, examine the content-specific vocabulary that you will encounter. This practice helps you focus on the topic and judge the difficulty of the text you will read.

Read the content-specific vocabulary below and determine how well you know each one. Use a scale of 1 to 4, where:

1 = I have never seen or heard this vocabulary before.

2 = I have seen or heard this vocabulary before, but I do not know what it means.

3 = I recognize the vocabulary, but I cannot define it accurately or use it with confidence.

4 = I can give an accurate definition or explanation of this vocabulary, and I can use it appropriately in a sentence.

___ adaptability	___ instinctive behavior
___ associative learning	___ irreversible learning
___ conditioned response	___ learned behavior
___ critical period	___ organism
___ genetically determined	___ predator
___ habituation	___ response
___ imprinting	___ species
___ innate	___ stimulus (*plural* stimuli)
___ insight	

Do not try to learn the unfamiliar items before you begin reading. You will learn them as you work with the chapter.

SCANNING AND SKIMMING

Scanning and skimming are useful reading strategies. Scanning involves reading quickly to find specific information. For example, you might scan a page in a telephone book to find a friend's phone number. Clearly, in doing so your eyes move quickly down the page, and you do not read every name and number while you look for the one you want. Scanning for the title and headings before reading an entire passage gives you an overview of the material because the title introduces the topic of a passage, and the headings introduce the topic of each section.

Skimming involves reading quickly to find main ideas or information. For instance, you might scan a chapter to find a particular section you are especially interested in reading, then read that section quickly to get the main idea or to answer a question you may have. You do not read each sentence carefully because you are only trying to understand the general idea, not all the details.

A Scan the Introductory Reading on pages 8–11 for headings and write them on the lines below.

<u>**Understanding Behavior**</u>

_____

_____

_____

B Read the following question, then skim through the section of the Introductory Reading under the first heading to find the answer. Read quickly. Compare your answer with a classmate's.

Is fear of an animal something we are born with, or do we have to learn this fear?

_____

C Based on the title, headings, and your brief skimming, what do you think you are going to read about in the Introductory Reading?

1. In a few sentences, write your predictions.

_____

_____

_____

2. Write one or two questions that you expect to have answered in the Introductory Reading.

_____

_____

3. Go to page *ii* of the Contents. Read the brief summary of this passage, then decide whether to make any changes to your predictions.

4. Compare your predictions and questions with a classmate's. Keep in mind that you may not agree.

MONITOR READING COMPREHENSION

Another useful strategy is to monitor (check) your comprehension as you read by pausing after each section and asking yourself what that section was about. For example, what did it tell you about the heading? This strategy is effective because it helps ensure that you understand a reading passage while you are reading. This practice makes it easier for you to review parts of the text that may have been difficult to comprehend on first reading.

Read the following selection from the Introductory Reading. Monitor your comprehension by completing the *Before You Continue Reading* statement that follows. Then compare your response with a classmate's.

UNDERSTANDING BEHAVIOR

When you watch a bird or squirrel, its activities appear to have a purpose. Birds search for food, take flight as you approach, and build nests in which to raise young. Usually the nests are inconspicuous or placed in difficult-to-reach spots. Likewise, squirrels collect and store nuts and acorns, "scold" you when you get too close, and learn to visit sites where food is available. All of these activities are adaptive and help the species survive. Birds that do not take flight at the approach of another animal will be eaten by predators. Squirrels that do not remember the location of sources of food will be less likely to survive, and birds that build obvious nests on the ground will be more likely to lose their young to predators. However, we need to take care not to attach too much meaning to what animals do. They may not have the same "thoughts" and "motivations" we do.

BEFORE YOU CONTINUE READING

Many animal behaviors seem to have a thoughtful purpose ___.

a. *but the animals may not actually be thinking about what they are doing*

b. *because the animals understand why their actions are important*

c. *and the animals know they need these behaviors to survive*

HIGHLIGHT IMPORTANT INFORMATION

Highlighting the most important ideas of a passage as you read helps you maintain your focus. This practice also makes it easier for you to review the material. As you read, remember to highlight the most important ideas. Important ideas explain the title and headings, and give you specific information about the topic. The sentences that have the most important ideas will include essential vocabulary that you need to know in order to understand the passage.

Reread the following selection from the Introductory Reading.

UNDERSTANDING BEHAVIOR

¹When you watch a bird or squirrel, its activities appear to have a purpose. ²Birds search for food, take flight as you approach, and build nests in which to raise young. ³Usually the nests are inconspicuous or placed in difficult-to-reach spots. ⁴Likewise, squirrels collect and store nuts and acorns, "scold" you when you get too close, and learn to visit sites where food is available. ⁵All of these activities are adaptive and help the species survive. ⁶Birds that do not take flight at the approach of another animal will be eaten by predators. ⁷Squirrels that do not remember the location of sources of food will

(continued)

be less likely to survive, and birds that build obvious nests on the ground will be more likely to lose their young to predators. 8However, we need to take care not to attach too much meaning to what animals do. 9They may not have the same "thoughts" and "motivations" we do.

EXPLANATION OF HIGHLIGHTING

- Sentence 1 has been highlighted because it helps to explain the title, *Understanding Behavior*. Sentence 1 states that we can observe animals' behavior and understand that their behavior may be purposeful.

- Sentence 5 explains the value of the animals' behavior.

- Sentences 2 and 6 give birds' behavior as an example of purposeful activities, and sentences 4 and 7 give squirrels' behavior as a second example of purposeful activities, too.

- Highlight just one example of an animal's behaviors, in this case either sentences 2 and 6 or sentences 4 and 7. It is unnecessary to highlight the entire paragraph.

- Sentences 8 and 9 have been highlighted because they, too, help to explain the title and give us an idea of what the next paragraphs will be about.

We can examine the highlighted sentences for essential vocabulary. For example, the words *purpose, take flight, adaptive, species, survive, predators, thoughts,* and *motivations* help us understand these sentences, so they are important to know.

The entire Introductory Reading has been highlighted. As you read, note which highlighted sentences contain the most important ideas and which contain details.

INTRODUCTORY READING

The following reading is from Concepts in Biology. *As you read, pay attention to the highlighting. Monitor your comprehension by completing the* Before You Continue Reading *statements. If you have trouble, reread the section before you continue reading.*

Understanding Behavior

1   1When you watch a bird or squirrel, its activities appear to have a purpose. 2Birds search for food, take flight as you approach, and build nests in which to raise young. 3Usually the nests are inconspicuous or placed in difficult-to-reach spots. 4Likewise, squirrels collect and store nuts and acorns, "scold" you when you get too close, and learn to visit sites where food is available. 5All of these activities are adaptive and help the species survive. 6Birds that do not take flight at the approach of another animal will be eaten by predators. 7Squirrels that do not remember the location of sources

of food will be less likely to survive, and birds that build obvious nests on the ground will be more likely to lose their young to predators. [8]However, we need to take care not to attach too much meaning to what animals do. [9]They may not have the same "thoughts" and "motivations" we do.

HUMAN BEHAVIOR

2   [1]Why are most people afraid of snakes? [2]Is this a behavior we are born with or do we learn it? [3]Why do you blink when an object rapidly approaches your face? [4]Why do you find it more difficult to communicate with someone on the phone or by computer than face to face? [5]Fear of snakes (many are poisonous) and the blinking of eyes can protect you from injury. [6]It appears that fear of snakes is a learned behavior in humans because little children do not react to snakes any differently than to other small moving objects. [7]The automatic blinking of eyes is a behavior that is programmed into your nervous system. [8]You probably find it more difficult to communicate when you cannot see the person because you rely on facial expression and gestures to communicate part of the message.

Fig. 1.1 A baby girl playing with a harmless Indigo snake

BEFORE YOU CONTINUE READING

1. In humans, ___.

a. *all behavior is learned*

b. *all behavior is automatic*

c. *behavior can be automatic or learned*

THE VALUE OF BEHAVIORS

3   [1]**Behavior** is how an organism acts, what it does, and how it does it. [2]When we think about the behavior of an animal, we should keep in mind that behavior is like any other characteristic displayed by an animal. [3]Behavior has a value or significance to the animal as it goes about

exploiting resources and reproducing more of its own species. [4]Many behaviors are inherited; consequently, they evolved just like the structures of animals. [5]In this respect, behavioral characteristics are no different from structural characteristics. [6]The evolution of behavior is much more difficult to study, however, because behavior is transient and does not leave fossils like the structures do.

4   [1]Behavior is a very important part of the ecological role of any animal. [2]It allows animals to escape predators, seek out mates, gain dominance over others of the same species, and respond to changes in the environment. [3]Plants, for the most part, must rely on structures, physiological changes, or chance to accomplish the same ends. [4]For example, a rabbit can run away from a predator, a plant cannot. [5]But the plant may have developed thorns or toxic compounds in its leaves that discourage animals from eating it. [6]Mate selection in animals often involves elaborate behaviors that assist them in identifying the species and sex of the potential mate. [7]Most plants rely on a much more random method for transferring male gametes to the female plant. [8]Dominance in plants is often achieved by depriving competitors of essential nutrients or by inhibiting the development of the seeds of other plants. [9]As we will read later in this chapter, animals have a variety of behaviors that allow them to exert dominance over members of the same species.

BEFORE YOU CONTINUE READING

2. Behavior is very important to animals because it helps them ___.

a. *survive and reproduce*

b. *dominate many other animals*

c. *evolve over time*

Fig. 1.2 A honey bee on a flower

THE SIGNIFICANCE OF BEHAVIOR

5   [1]It is not always easy to identify the significance of a behavior without careful study of the behavior pattern and the impact it has on other organisms. [2]For example, a hungry baby herring gull pecks at a red spot on its parent's bill. [3]What possible value can this behavior have for either the chick or the parent? [4]If we watch, we see that when the chick pecks at the spot, the parent regurgitates food onto the ground, and the chick feeds. [5]This looks like a simple behavior, but there is more to it than meets the eye. [6]Why did the chick peck to begin with? [7]How did it know to peck at that particular spot? [8]Why did the pecking cause the parent to regurgitate food? [9]These questions are not easy to answer. [10]Many people assume that the actions have the same motivation and direction as similar human behaviors, but this is not necessarily a correct assumption. [11]For example, when a human child points to a piece of candy and makes appropriate noises, it is indicating to its parent that it wants some candy. [12]Is that what the herring gull chick is doing? [13]We don't know. [14]Although both kinds of young may get food, we don't know what the baby gull is thinking because we can't ask it.

■ ■ ■

Fig. 1.3 An adult herring gull feeding its chick

Checking Comprehension

TEXT ANALYSIS

Most good paragraphs are organized in a way that helps the reader understand the text. Elements common to most paragraphs are: a main idea, supporting details, detail development, transitions, and conclusions. For example, in paragraph four, the text begins with a main idea. However, keep in mind that the main idea is not always at the beginning of a paragraph. The next sentence gives an explanation of the main idea, followed by supporting examples. The paragraph ends with a transition.

A Reread paragraph 4. Use the chart below to organize the information in the paragraph. Part of the chart has been completed as an example.

Main Idea	Behavior is very important to animals.
Explanation	Behavior helps animals escape predators, _____, _____, and _____.
Supporting Details	• •
Transition	

B Work with a partner or in a small group. Reread paragraph 1. Use the chart below to organize the information in the paragraph. Some of the chart has been filled in.

FIRST MAIN IDEA	Animal activities appear to have a purpose.	
Supporting Details		• •
	birds' behavior	• Birds build nests in which to raise their young. Nests are inconspicuous, or placed in difficult or hard-to-reach spots.
Supporting Details	squirrels' behavior	• • •
SECOND MAIN IDEA	Animal activities are adaptive and help the species survive.	
Supporting Detail	birds	
Supporting Detail	squirrels	Squirrels that do not remember the location of sources of food will be less likely to survive
Conclusion		

C Label the following behaviors *instinctive* (I) or *learned* (L).

1. ___ A bird flies away as you approach.

2. ___ A person is afraid of snakes.

3. ___ A newborn baby nurses or sucks milk from a bottle.

4. ___ A dog comes when it is called.

5. ___ You blink your eyes when something passes close to your face.

6. ___ Squirrels collect and store nuts.

7. ___ A person runs away from an approaching dog.

8. ___ A child begins to walk.

9. ___ A bird builds a nest.

How accurate were your guesses on page 4? ___

D Answer the following questions in complete sentences.

1. What is the main purpose of plant and animal behavior?

   _____

   _____

2. The parent and baby gulls both demonstrate instinctive behaviors. What is the value of these behaviors to the baby gull and to the gull species?

   _____

   _____

3. If the baby herring gull does not peck at the red spot on the parent's bill, what will happen?

   _____

   _____

Learning Vocabulary

Three effective strategies for building vocabulary involve using context to figure out the meaning, using a dictionary to learn the definition, and learning the different forms of a word.

VOCABULARY IN CONTEXT

When you encounter new vocabulary that you need to know, you can often use the context and your knowledge of the world to figure out the meaning. In the following excerpts, the meanings of the words in italics can be understood in context.

A **Read the example. Then read the explanations.**

EXCERPT ONE

When you watch a bird or squirrel, its activities appear to have a purpose. Birds search for food, *take flight* as you approach, and build nests in which to raise young. Usually the nests are *inconspicuous* or placed in difficult-to-reach spots. Likewise, squirrels collect and store nuts and acorns, "scold" you when you get too close, and learn to visit sites where food is available. All of these activities are adaptive and help the species survive. Birds that do not *take flight* at the approach of another animal will be eaten by *predators*. Squirrels that do not remember the location of sources of food will be less likely to survive, and birds that build obvious nests on the ground will be more likely to lose their young to predators.

1. From the context and from the meaning of the antonym for *inconspicuous*, we can understand that an *inconspicuous* nest is _____.
   (a.) difficult to see
   b. easy to see
   (It would not make sense for birds to build their nests in places that are easy to see, so *inconspicuous* must mean *difficult to see*.)

2. This section contains an antonym for the word *inconspicuous*. The antonym is _____.
   a. difficult to reach
   b. available
   (c.) obvious
   (The opposite of *difficult to see* is *easy to see*. The word *obvious* means *easy to see*, so it must be an antonym of *inconspicuous*. Please note that you needed to read the entire paragraph in order to locate and identify the antonym.)

3. When a bird *takes flight*, it _____.
   (a.) flies away
   b. searches for food
   c. becomes frightened
   (Birds usually fly away when people get too close, so *take flight* must mean *fly away*. Choice b does not make sense. Choice c is possible, but if a bird becomes frightened, it will fly away to protect itself.)

4. A *predator* is an animal that _____.
   a. is hunted and killed for food by other animals
   (b.) hunts and kills other animals for food
   (If a bird does not fly away, it will be eaten. A *predator* must mean *an animal that hunts and kills other animals for food*.)

B Read the following excerpts. Circle the best choice to complete the sentences.

EXCERPT TWO

It is not always easy to identify the *significance* of a behavior without careful study of the behavior pattern and the impact it has on other organisms. For example, a hungry baby herring gull pecks at a red spot on its parent's bill. What possible value can this behavior have for either the chick or the parent?

From the context, we can understand that *significance* means _____.
   a. complexity
   b. difficulty
   c. importance

EXCERPT THREE

Behavior allows animals to escape predators, seek out mates, gain *dominance* over others of the same species, and respond to changes in the environment. *Dominance* in plants is often achieved by depriving competitors of essential nutrients or by inhibiting the development of the seeds of other plants.

From the context, we can understand that *dominance* means _____.
   a. power or control
   b. size or number
   c. fear or intimidation

USING THE DICTIONARY

You can also use a dictionary to learn new words. Dictionary entries often have several definitions for a word, so you need to consider the context in order to figure out the most appropriate definition.

A Read the following example. Then read the explanation.

EXCERPT ONE

Behavior has a value or significance to the animal as it goes about *exploiting* resources (such as food, water, territory) and reproducing more of its own species.

> **ex•ploit** \ik-'sploit, 'ek-,\ *vt* (1838) **1 :** to make productive use of : UTILIZE ⟨*~ing* your talents⟩ ⟨*~* your opponent's weakness⟩ **2 :** to make use of meanly or unjustly for one's own advantage ⟨*~ing* migrant farm workers⟩ — **ex•ploit•able** \-'sploi-tə-bəl\ *adj* — **ex•ploit•er** *n*

(Entry 2 involves behavior that is mean or unjust. Animals do not behave justly or unjustly. These are human motives. If entry 1 is used to complete the sentence below, it will have the same meaning as the original text. That is, the animal will make productive use of resources such as food, water, and territory.)

1. In this context, the most appropriate definition of *exploit* is number ___1___.

2. Animals _____ in order to gain an advantage.
　(a.) make productive use of resources
　b. use resources unjustly or meanly

B **Read the following excerpt and dictionary entry. Select the most appropriate entry for the context, and choose the best answer to complete the sentence that follows. If you choose an entry that includes subentries (for example *1a, 1b, 1c*), indicate the letter as well as the number.**

EXCERPT TWO

Behavior allows animals to escape predators, seek out *mates*, gain dominance over others of the same species, and respond to changes in the environment.

> **mate** *n* [ME, prob. fr. MLG *māt;* akin to OE *gemetta* guest at one's table, *mete* food — more at MEAT] (14c) **1 a** (1) : ASSOCIATE, COMPANION (2) *chiefly Brit* : an assistant to a more skilled worker : HELPER (3) *chiefly Brit* : FRIEND, BUDDY — often used as a familiar form of address **b** *archaic* : MATCH, PEER **2 :** a deck officer on a merchant ship ranking below the captain **3 :** one of a pair: as **a :** either member of a couple and esp. a married couple **b :** either member of a breeding pair of animals **c :** either of two matched objects

1. In this context, the most appropriate definition of *mate* is number _____.

2. Animals seek out _____ of the same species in order to reproduce.
　a. associates or companions
　b. friends
　c. a member of the opposite sex

INTRODUCING THE MAIN READING

Activate Your Knowledge

Before you begin reading, think about what you may already know about the topic. If you cannot answer all the questions, do not worry about it. You will learn more when you read the passage.

A **Work in pairs or in a small group. Answer the following questions.**

1. What is *instinctive behavior*? Give a brief description or definition.

_____

_____

_____

2. What is *learned behavior*? Give a brief description or definition.

_____

_____

_____

B Think of two animals. For each animal, give an example of instinctive behavior and an example of learned behavior. Use the diagram below to help you organize your information.

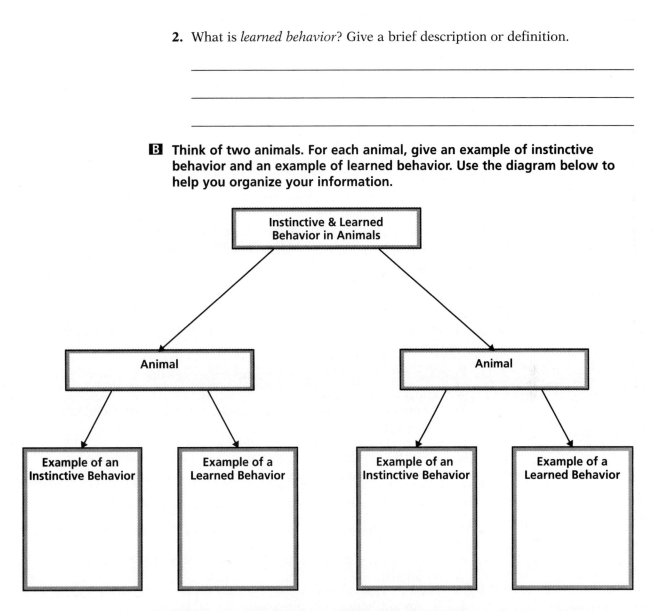

C Put each pair's or group's definitions of *instinctive behavior* and *learned behavior* from Exercise A on the board. Create a class definition for each term. Then review each pair's or group's examples of instinctive and learned behavior for the animals they chose in Exercise B. Decide whether the example behaviors fit the class's definitions for *instinctive* and *learned behaviors*.

Reading and Study Skill Strategies

SCANNING AND SKIMMING

Remember that scanning a passage for the headings and subheadings before reading the entire passage gives you an overview of the material because the title introduces the topic of a passage, and the headings introduce the topic of each section. Skimming for some main ideas will help give you a clearer idea of what the passage is about.

A Before you work with the Main Reading on pages 20–24, scan it and write down the headings on the lines below.

<u>   **Instinctive Behavior and Learned Behavior**   </u>

_____

_____

_____

B Scan through two sections of the Main Reading—the one with the heading *Instinctive Behavior* and the one with the heading *Learned Behavior*—to find the author's definition of *instinctive behavior* and of *learning*. Remember to read quickly. Write the definitions below.

instinctive behavior: _____

learning: _____

C Based on the title, headings, and your brief skimming, what do you think you are going to learn?

1. Read the following statements and check the ones that you predict are correct.

   a. ___ Instinctive behavior is automatic, but it can be modified in a new situation.

   b. ___ Instinctive behavior is automatic and cannot be modified in a new situation.

   c. ___ Instinctive behaviors are genetically determined (inherited).

   d. ___ Instinctive behaviors are not genetically determined (inherited).

   e. ___ Sometimes an instinctive behavior does not have value for an animal.

   f. ___ An instinctive behavior always has value for an animal.

   g. ___ A goose will roll its egg back into its nest in order to protect it from harm.

   h. ___ A goose will roll its egg back into its nest because it has been genetically programmed to do so.

   i. ___ Spiders can always repair a damaged web.

   j. ___ Spiders cannot repair a damaged web; they must build a new one.

2. Write one or two questions that you expect to have answered in the Main Reading.

_____

_____

3. Go to page _ii_ of the Contents. Read the brief summary of this passage, then decide whether to make any changes to your predictions.

4. Compare your predictions and questions with a classmate's. Keep in mind that you may not agree.

USE FONT STYLES TO IDENTIFY AND LEARN KEY VOCABULARY

Font styles such as _italics_ and **boldface** are used in text for a variety of reasons. For example, every content area has specific vocabulary, so when these key words are introduced, they are often put in _italics_ or **boldface** and are usually defined so the reader can understand them right away.

A **Read the following excerpt from the Main Reading, and pay attention to the words in italics and boldface.**

> Both instinct and learning are involved in the behavior patterns of most organisms. We recognize **instinctive behavior** as behavior that is inborn, automatic, and inflexible, whereas **learning** requires experience and produces behaviors that can be changed. Most animals have a high proportion of instinctive behavior and very little learning; some, like many birds and mammals, are able to demonstrate a great deal of learned behavior.
>
> **Instinctive behaviors** are automatic, preprogrammed, and genetically determined. Such behaviors are found in a wide range of organisms from simple one-celled protozoans to complex vertebrates. These behaviors are performed correctly the first time without previous experience when the proper stimulus is given. A _stimulus_ is some change in the internal or external environment of the organism that causes it to react. The reaction of the organism to the stimulus is called a _response_.

B **Define or describe each of the following terms:**

1. instinctive behavior: _____

2. learning: _____

3. _stimulus:_ _____

4. _response:_ _____

MAIN READING

The following reading is also from Concepts in Biology. *As you read, highlight the important ideas and details. Monitor your comprehension by answering the* Before You Continue Reading *questions. If you have trouble answering the question, reread the section before you continue reading.*

Instinctive Behavior and Learned Behavior

1   Before we go much further, we need to discuss how animals generate specific behaviors and the two major kinds of behaviors: instinctive and learned. Both instinct and learning are involved in the behavior patterns of most organisms. We recognize **instinctive behavior** as behavior that is inborn, automatic, and inflexible, whereas **learning** requires experience and produces behaviors that can be changed. Most animals have a high proportion of instinctive behavior and very little learning; some, like many birds and mammals, are able to demonstrate a great deal of learned behavior.

<table>
<tr>
<td>

BEFORE YOU

CONTINUE

READING

</td>
<td>

1. What are the major differences between instinctive behavior and learned behavior?

_____

</td>
</tr>
</table>

INSTINCTIVE BEHAVIOR

2   **Instinctive behaviors** are automatic, preprogrammed, and genetically determined. Such behaviors are found in a wide range of organisms from simple one-celled protozoans to complex vertebrates. These behaviors are performed correctly the first time without previous experience when the proper stimulus is given. A *stimulus* is some change in the internal or external environment of the organism that causes it to react. The reaction of the organism to the stimulus is called a *response*.

3   In our example of the herring gull chick on page 11, the red spot on the bill of the adult bird serves as a stimulus to the chick. The chick responds to this spot in a genetically programmed way. The behavior is innate—it is done correctly the first time without prior experience. The pecking behavior of the chick is in turn the stimulus for the adult bird to regurgitate food. It is obvious that these behaviors have adaptive value for the gull species because they leave little to chance. The young will get food from the adult automatically. Instinctive behavior has great value to a species because it allows correct, appropriate, and necessary behavior to occur without prior experience.

4   The drawback of instinctive behavior is that it cannot be modified when a new situation presents itself, but it can be very effective for the survival of a species if it is involved in fundamental, essential activities that rarely require modification. Instinctive behavior is most common in animals that have short life cycles, simple nervous systems, and little contact with parents. Over long periods of evolutionary time, these genetically determined behaviors have been selected for and have been useful to most of the individuals of the species. However, some instances of inappropriate behavior may be generated by unusual stimuli or unusual circumstances in which the stimulus is given.

BEFORE YOU CONTINUE READING

2. For many species, what is the major advantage of instinctive behavior?

_____

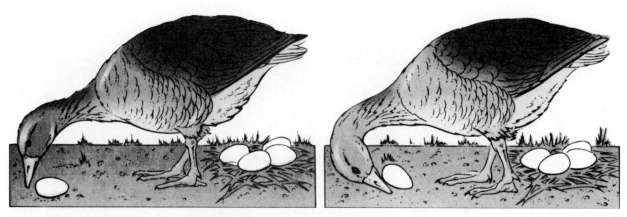

Fig. 1.4 A goose displaying egg-rolling behavior

5   Certain species of geese display a behavior that involves rolling eggs back into the nest. Eggs may roll out of the nest as the parents get on and off the nest during incubation. If the developing young within the egg are exposed to extremes of heat or cold they will be killed. Thus the egg-rolling behavior has a significant adaptive value. If, however, the egg is taken from the goose when it is in the middle of egg-rolling behavior, the goose will continue its egg rolling until it gets back to the nest, even though there is no egg to roll. This is typical of the inflexible nature of instinctive behaviors. It was also discovered that many other somewhat egg-shaped structures would generate the same behavior. For example, beer cans and baseballs were good triggers for egg-rolling behavior. So not only was the bird unable to stop the egg-rolling behavior in midstride, but several nonegg objects generated inappropriate behavior because they had approximately the correct shape.

6   Some activities are so complex that it seems impossible for an organism to be born with such abilities. For example, you have seen spiderwebs in fields, parks, or vacant lots. You may have even watched a spider spin its web. This is not just a careless jumble of silk threads. A web is

so precisely made that you can recognize what species of spider made it. But web spinning is not a learned ability. A spider has no opportunity to learn how to spin a web because it never observes others doing it. Furthermore, spiders do not practice several times before they get a proper, workable web. It is as if a "program" for making a particular web is in the spider's "computer." Many species of spiders appear to be unable to repair defective webs. When a web is damaged they typically start from the beginning and build an entirely new web. This inability to adapt as circumstances change is a prominent characteristic of instinctive behavior. It is one of the major characteristics which differentiate it from learned behavior.

BEFORE YOU CONTINUE READING

3. What characteristics of instinctive behavior do the examples of the goose and the spider both demonstrate?

Fig. 1.5 An orb weaver spider and its web

LEARNED BEHAVIOR

7   The alternative to preprogrammed, instinctive behavior is learned behavior. **Learning** is a change in behavior as a result of experience. Learning becomes more significant in long-lived animals that care for their young. Animals that live many years are more likely to benefit from an ability to recognize previously encountered situations and modify their behavior accordingly. Furthermore, because the young spend time with their parents they can imitate their parents and develop behaviors that are appropriate to local conditions. These behaviors take time to develop but have the advantage of adaptability. In order for learning to become a dominant feature of an animal's life, the animal must also have a large brain to store the new information it is learning. This is probably why learning is a major part of life for only a few kinds of animals like the

vertebrates. In humans, it is clear that nearly all behavior is learned. Even such important behaviors as walking, communicating, and feeding oneself must be learned. In fact, many organisms display such a wide range of learned behaviors that scientists have categorized them in order to understand them better.

KINDS OF LEARNING

8   Scientists recognize different kinds of learning that can be subdivided into several categories: habituation, association, imprinting, and insight.

9   **Habituation** is a change in behavior in which an animal ignores a stimulus after repeated exposure to it. There are many examples of this kind of learning. Many kinds of animals will flee humans, but after repeated exposure to humans they may "learn" to ignore them. Many wild animals such as the deer, elk, and bears in parks have been habituated to the presence of humans and behave in a way that would be totally inappropriate in areas near the park where hunting is allowed. Similarly, loud noises will startle humans and other animals. However, constant exposure to such sounds results in the individual ignoring the sound. As a matter of fact the sound may become so much a part of the environment that the cessation of the sound will evoke a response.

10   **Association** occurs when an animal makes a connection between a stimulus and an outcome. There are several kinds of association learning. Classical conditioning is one of them. In **classical conditioning** the animal modifies its behavior by transferring an involuntary response from a specific natural stimulus to a new stimulus. During the period when learning is taking place the new stimulus is given *before* the normal stimulus and the animal learns to associate the new stimulus with the response it once gave to a different stimulus. An example will help explain this concept.

11   A Russian physiologist, Ivan Pavlov (1849–1936), was investigating the physiology of digestion when he discovered that dogs can associate an unusual stimulus with a natural stimulus. He was studying the production of saliva by dogs and he knew that a natural stimulus, such as the presence or smell of food, would cause the dogs to start salivating. Then he rang a bell just prior to the presentation of the food. After a training period, the dogs would begin to salivate when the bell was rung even though no food was presented. This kind of learning, in which a "new" stimulus (the sound of a bell) is associated with a "natural" stimulus (the taste of food), is called classical conditioning. The response produced by the new stimulus is called a *conditioned response*.

12   **Associative** learning takes place in the natural environment of animals as well. If certain kinds of fruits or insects have unpleasant tastes, animals will learn to associate the bad tastes with the colors and shapes of the offending objects and avoid them in the future. The ability to form an association between two events is extremely valuable to an animal. If this kind of learning allows the animal to get more food, avoid predators, or protect its young more effectively it will be advantageous to the species. The association of certain shapes, colors, odors, or sounds with danger is especially valuable.

Fig. 1.6 Konrad Lorenz. The baby geese following him have imprinted on him.

13   **Imprinting** is a special kind of irreversible learning in which a very young animal is genetically primed to learn a specific behavior in a very short period during a specific time in its life. The time during which the learning is possible is known as the *critical period*. This type of learning was originally recognized by Konrad Lorenz (1903–1989) in his experiments with geese and ducks. Lorenz determined that, shortly after hatching, a duckling would follow an object if the object was fairly large, moved, and made noise.

14   Ducklings will follow only the object on which they were originally imprinted. Under normal conditions, the first large, noisy moving object newly hatched ducklings see is their mother. Imprinting ensures that the immature birds will follow her and learn appropriate feeding, defensive tactics, and other behaviors by example. Because they are always near their mother, she can protect them from enemies or bad weather. If animals imprint on the wrong objects, they are not likely to survive. Since these experiments by Lorenz in the early 1930s, we have discovered that many young animals can be imprinted on several types of stimuli and that there are responses other than following.

15   **Insight** is a special kind of learning in which past experiences are reorganized to solve new problems. When you are faced with a new problem, whether it is a crossword puzzle, a math problem, or any one of a hundred other everyday problems, you sort through your past experiences and locate those that apply. You may not even realize that you are doing it, but you put these past experiences together in a new way that may give the solution to your problem. Because this process is internal and can be demonstrated only through some response, it is very difficult to understand what goes on during insight learning. Behavioral scientists have explored this area for many years, but the study of insight learning is still in its infancy.

■ ■ ■

Checking Comprehension

A Reread paragraphs 3–6. Use the chart below to analyze the main ideas about the advantages and drawbacks of instinctive behavior and the examples that illustrate these ideas.

INSTINCTIVE BEHAVIOR	
Advantages of Instinctive Behavior • • 	**Drawbacks of Instinctive Behavior** • •
Examples • • • 	**Examples** • • •

B Read the following statements, and check the ones that are correct based on the reading. Then compare these responses with your responses on page 18. Discuss your answers as a class.

a. ___ Instinctive behavior is automatic, but it can be modified in a new situation.

b. ___ Instinctive behavior is automatic and cannot be modified in a new situation.

c. ___ Instinctive behaviors are genetically determined (inherited).

d. ___ Instinctive behaviors are not genetically determined (inherited).

e. ___ Sometimes an instinctive behavior does not have value for an animal.

f. ___ An instinctive behavior always has value for an animal.

g. ___ A goose will roll its egg back into its nest in order to protect it from harm.

h. ___ A goose will roll its egg back into its nest because it has been genetically programmed to do so.

i. ___ Spiders can always repair a damaged web.

j. ___ Spiders cannot repair a damaged web; they must build a new one.

How many of your predictions on page 18 were correct? _____

C Read and label each of the following child behaviors. Discuss your answers as a class.

association	habituation	imprinting	insight

1. _____: A newborn infant hears its mother's voice and turns its head towards her.

2. _____: A child wants a box of cookies in a kitchen cabinet. She figures out that if she pulls a chair close to the wall, she can step up and reach the shelf to get the box of cookies.

3. _____: A child who is watching TV pays no attention to his mother when she tells him to turn off the TV or she will not buy him a toy. She always buys him a toy when they go to the store.

4. _____: A child sees her father take her stroller out to the sidewalk. She knows she is going for a walk, and runs for her coat.

D Answer the following questions in complete sentences.

1. What types of animals would be most likely to find instinctive behavior advantageous? Why do you think so?

_____

_____

2. For some animals, why is the ability to learn more advantageous than instinctive behavior?

_____

_____

3. Most of human beings' behavior is learned. If we had more instinctive behaviors, what would be some of the drawbacks? Why do you think so?

_____

_____

_____

4. Of the four types of learning, which do you think is the most advantageous for humans? Explain your reasons for your choice.

_____

_____

_____

5. Under what conditions would habituation be advantageous to a college student? To other people? Give at least two examples, and explain your choices.

_____

_____

_____

_____

_____

E Refer to your diagram on page 17, and recall your class discussion. What revisions do you want to make to your diagram after reading the passage?

Learning Vocabulary

VOCABULARY IN CONTEXT

Read the following excerpts. Circle the best choice to complete the sentences.

EXCERPT ONE

In our example of the herring gull chick on page 11, the red spot on the bill of the adult bird serves as a stimulus to the chick. The chick responds to this spot in a genetically programmed way. The behavior is _innate_—it is done correctly the first time without prior experience.

From this context we can understand that innate behavior is _____.
  a. behavior that only birds can do
  b. very simple behavior that is easy
  c. behavior that an animal is born with

EXCERPT TWO

The drawback of instinctive behavior is that it cannot be _modified_ when a new situation presents itself, but it can be very effective for the survival of a species if it is involved in fundamental, essential activities that rarely require _modification_.

From this context we can understand that _modify_ means _____.
  a. learn
  b. change
  c. understand

USING THE DICTIONARY

Read the following excerpts and dictionary entries. Select the most appropriate entry for the context, and choose the best answer to complete the sentence that follows. If an entry includes subentries (for example *1a, 1b, 1c*), indicate the letter as well as the number.

EXCERPT ONE

Instinctive behavior has great _value_ to a species because it allows correct, appropriate, and necessary behavior to occur without prior experience. Certain species of geese display a behavior that involves rolling eggs back into the nest. Eggs may roll out of the nest as the parents get on and off the nest during incubation. If the developing young within the egg are exposed to extremes of heat or cold they will be killed. Thus the egg-rolling behavior has a significant adaptive *value*.

> **val•ue** \'val-(,)yü\ *n* [ME, fr. MF, fr. (assumed) VL *valuta*. fr. fem. of *valutus*, pp. of L *valēre* to be worth, be strong — more at WIELD] (14c) **1 :** a fair return or equivalent in goods, services, or money for something exchanged **2 :** the monetary worth of something : marketable price **3 :** relative worth, utility, or importance ⟨a good ∼ at the price⟩ ⟨the ∼ of base stealing in baseball⟩ ⟨had nothing of ∼ to say⟩ **4 a :** a numerical quantity that is assigned or is determined by calculation or measurement ⟨let *x* take on positive ∼s⟩ ⟨a ∼ for the age of the earth⟩ **b :** precise signification ⟨ ∼ of a word⟩ **5 :** the relative duration of a musical note **6 a :** relative lightness or darkness of a color: LUMINOSITY **b :** the relation of one part in a picture to another with respect to lightness and darkness **7 :** something (as a principle or quality) intrinsically valuable or desirable ⟨sought material ∼s instead of human ∼s — W. H. Jones⟩ **8 :** DENOMINATION 2 — **val•ue•less** \-(,)yü-ləs, -yə-\ *adj* — **val•ue•less•ness** *n*

1. In this context, the most appropriate definition for *value* is number _____.

2. Because instinctive behavior allows correct, appropriate, and necessary behavior to occur without prior experience, _____.
   a. it is a fair return for goods, services, or money
   b. it is marketable; it is worth money
   c. it has worth, utility, or importance
   d. it has a precise signification

EXCERPT TWO
Because insight learning is internal and can be demonstrated only through some response, it is very difficult to understand what goes on during insight learning. Behavioral scientists have *explored* this area for many years, but the study of insight learning is still in its infancy.

> **ex•plore** \ik-'splōr, -'splȯr\ *vb* **ex•plored; ex•plor•ing** [L *explorare*, fr. *ex-* + *plorare* to cry out] *vt* (1585) **1 a :** to investigate, study, or analyze : look into ⟨ ∼ the relationship between social class and learning ability⟩ — sometimes used with indirect questions ⟨to ∼ where ethical issues arise — R. T. Blackburn⟩ **b :** to become familiar with by testing or experimenting ⟨ ∼ new cuisines⟩ **2 :** to travel over (new territory) for adventure or discovery **3 :** to examine minutely esp. for diagnostic purposes ⟨ ∼ the wound⟩ ∼ *vi* : to make or conduct a systematic search ⟨ ∼ for oil⟩

1. In this context, the most appropriate definition of *explore* is number ___.

2. Behavioral scientists _____ insight learning for many years.
   a. have tested and become familiar with
   b. have studied and analyzed
   c. have traveled for discovery into
   d. have examined minutely for diagnostic purposes

LEARN AND USE WORD FORMS

A Study the word forms in the chart below. If you are not sure about the meaning of a word, reread the text, highlight the words and any of their forms, and try to understand them from context.

VERB	NOUN	ADJECTIVE	ADVERB
adapt	adaptation adaptability	adaptable adaptive	adaptively
associate	association	associative	associatively
dominate	dominance	dominant dominated/dominating	
habituate	habituation	habituated/habituating	
imitate	imitation	imitative	imitatively
modify	modification	modified/modifying	
motivate	motivation	motivated/motivating	
react	reaction	reactive	
respond	response	responsive	responsively
stimulate	stimulus (*plural* stimuli)	stimulated/stimulating	

B Read the sentences. Choose the appropriate word from the following sets and complete each sentence. Refer to the word form chart for the correct form of each word. Be sure to use the correct tense of verbs in either the affirmative or the negative and use the singular or plural of nouns. Use each word only once.

associate	motivate	stimulate
habituate	respond	

1. In every part of the world, humans become _____ to a broad range of situations in order to survive.

2. If an animal _____ quickly to danger, it may be killed.

3. Simple animals exhibit preprogrammed responses to a variety of _____.

4. Behaviorists recognize two types of _____: internal and external.

5. Once a person has developed a strong negative _____ with a stimulus such as a sound or a smell, it is very difficult to overcome the negative response from that stimulus.

adapt	dominate	imitate	modify	react

6. Animals' _____ to particular situations may be either instinctive or learned responses.

7. Animals and plants are not the only organisms to demonstrate _____ behavior. Humans are also able to alter their behavior in a changing environment.

8. Some animals observe other animals and perform the same action. This _____ behavior is a type of learned behavior.

9. Many animals, especially mammals, _____ their behavior in order to adapt to new situations.

10. Some animals gain _____ over other members of their group through fighting, but others do so simply by displaying aggressive behavior.

FOLLOW-UP ASSIGNMENTS

Before you begin any of the assignments, review the content-specific vocabulary and academic vocabulary below, and look over the vocabulary in the word form chart on page 29. If you are still unsure what any words or terms mean, go back through the chapter and review. As you complete the follow-up assignments, be sure to incorporate the appropriate vocabulary.

Content-Specific Vocabulary

adaptability	habituation	organism
associative learning	imprinting	predator
conditioned	innate	response
response	insight	species
critical period	instinctive behavior	stimulus (*plural*
genetically	irreversible learning	stimuli)
determined	learned behavior	

Academic Vocabulary

automatic	inflexible	significance
characteristic	mate	survival
dominance	modify	value
exploit	motivation	
explore	preprogrammed	

Writing Activities

1. The following diagram illustrates the distribution of instinctive behavior and learned behavior in a range of animals. Study the diagram carefully, then write three paragraphs. In the first paragraph, describe instinctive behavior and learned behavior. In the second paragraph, explain what the diagram shows. In the third paragraph, discuss your conclusions about the proportion of instinctive and learned behavior in animals.

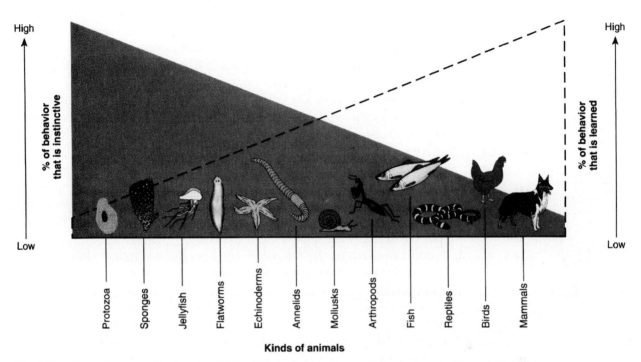

High

% of behavior that is instinctive

Low

High

% of behavior that is learned

Low

Protozoa
Sponges
Jellyfish
Flatworms
Echinoderms
Annelids
Mollusks
Arthropods
Fish
Reptiles
Birds
Mammals

Kinds of animals

Fig. 1.7 Different groups of animals exhibit different proportions of instinctive and learned behavior

2. Think about the four types of learned behavior: habituation, association, imprinting, and insight. Write four paragraphs. In the first paragraph, describe the kind of learning that you think is the most useful to humans. In the second paragraph, give several examples to support your point of view. In the third paragraph, describe the kind of learning that you think is the least useful to humans. In the fourth paragraph, give several examples to support your point of view.

3. Write three paragraphs. In the first paragraph, describe the process of classical conditioning. In the second paragraph, describe how you would train a dog to come when you call it. In the third paragraph, support your use of behaviorist theory in training your dog.

4. Think about training a child to put away his toys without your having to tell him to do so. Write three paragraphs. In the first paragraph, identify and describe the type of learning you would use for this training. In the second paragraph, describe how you would train the child to put away his toys voluntarily and without supervision. In the third paragraph, support your use of the type of learning you employed for the training.

Extension Activities

1. Choose an animal that you are able to observe. For example, you may have a cat or a dog, or live near a park where you can observe squirrels or birds. Spend time observing the animal's behavior, and write your observations in a notebook. Then write a three-paragraph paper. In the first paragraph, describe the animal, where you observed it, and for how long. In the second paragraph, describe the behaviors you observed, including the conditions under which the behaviors occurred and how frequently they occurred. In the third paragraph, give your conclusions about which behaviors were instinctive and which were learned. Support your conclusions with your observations and information on instinctive and learned behavior that you learned in Chapter 1. Present your paper and your findings to the class.

2. Spend some time with a small child (about one to four years old). Observe how the child learns to do something on his or her own. Then write a three-paragraph paper. In the first paragraph, describe the child, where you observed the child, and for how long. In the second paragraph, describe what the child learned to do and how the child learned to do it. In the third paragraph, describe the type of learning that was involved. Support your conclusion with your observations and information on learned behavior that you learned in Chapter 1. Present your paper and your findings to the class.

3. Conduct research on the Internet. Go online. Use a search engine such as Google, AltaVista, Yahoo, About, or Dogpile. Investigate a topic related to the information you read about in Chapter 1. Choose a topic that especially interests you. Use key words such as *conditioned response, habituation, instinctive behavior, associative learning, operant conditioning, B. F. Skinner,* and *Ivan Pavlov*. Prepare an oral report, a written report, or a poster, and present your findings to the class.

Chapter 2

UNDERSTANDING INSTINCT AND LEARNING

Fig. 2.0a Wild stallions fighting

Fig. 2.0b Horse act at the Moscow Circus

Chapter Readings

Instinct and Learning Compared

Instinct and Learning in the Same Organism

INTRODUCING THE READING

Activate Your Knowledge

Work alone or in a small group. Think about the behavior of bees, dogs, and human beings. Give examples of each organism's behavior, and categorize each example as an instinctive or a learned behavior.

TYPES OF BEHAVIOR		
Organism	Examples of Instinctive Behavior	Examples of Learned Behavior
bee		
dog		
human		

Reading and Study Skill Strategies

PREVIEW KEY VOCABULARY

Read the content-specific vocabulary below and determine how well you know each one. Use a scale of 1 to 4, where:

1 = I have never seen or heard this vocabulary before.
2 = I have seen or heard this vocabulary before, but I do not know what it means.
3 = I recognize the vocabulary, but I cannot define it accurately or use it with confidence.
4 = I can give an accurate definition or explanation of this vocabulary, and I can use it appropriately in a sentence.

___ associative learning   ___ innate

___ bonding   ___ insight

___ critical period   ___ instinct

___ dominance hierarchy   ___ invertebrates

___ ecological niche   ___ reflexes

___ ecosystem   ___ resource allocation

___ hereditary   ___ territorial behavior

___ imprinting   ___ vertebrates

Do not try to learn the unfamiliar items before you begin reading. You will learn them as you work with the chapter.

SCANNING AND SKIMMING

A Scan the Introductory Reading on pages 36–37 for headings and write them on the lines below. Include any headings that appear in charts.

Instinct and Learning Compared

_____

_____

B Read the following questions, then skim through the appropriate sections of the Introductory Reading to find the answers. Read quickly. Compare your answers with a classmate's.

1. Which types of animals rely most on instinctive behavior, and which types of animals rely most on learned behavior?

_____

_____

2. What are one or two main differences between instinctive and learned behavior?

_____

_____

C Based on the title, headings, and your brief skimming, what do you think you are going to read about in the Introductory Reading?

1. In a few sentences, write your predictions.

_____

_____

_____

2. Write one or two questions that you expect to have answered in the Introductory Reading.

_____

_____

3. Go to page *ii* of the Contents. Read the brief summary of this passage, then decide whether to make any changes to your predictions.

4. Compare your predictions and questions with a classmate's. Keep in mind that you may not agree.

INTRODUCTORY READING

The following reading, is from Concepts in Biology. *As you read, highlight the important ideas and details. Monitor your comprehension by completing the* Before You Continue Reading *statement.*

Instinct and Learning Compared

1   It is important to recognize that all animals have both learned and instinctive behaviors and that one behavior may have elements that are both instinctive and learned. For example, biologists have raised song sparrows in the absence of any adult birds so there was no song for the young birds to imitate. These isolated birds would sing a series of notes similar to the normal song of the species, but not exactly correct. Birds from the same nest that were raised with their parents developed a song nearly identical to that of their parents. If bird songs were totally instinctive, there would be no difference between these two groups. It appears that the basic melody of the song was inherited by the birds and that the refinements of the song were the result of experience. Therefore, the characteristic song of that species was partly learned behavior (a change in behavior as a result of experience) and partly unlearned (instinctive). This is probably true of the behavior of many organisms; they show complex behaviors that are a combination of instinct and learning. It is important to note that many kinds of birds learn most of their songs with very few innate components. For example, mockingbirds are very good at imitating the songs of a wide variety of bird species found in their local region.

BEFORE YOU CONTINUE READING

In an animal such as a bird, a certain behavior ____.

a. *can only be instinctive because it does not have prior experience*

b. *can only be learned because it needs other birds to imitate*

c. *may be a combination of instinct and learning*

INTEGRATION OF INSTINCT AND LEARNING IN ANIMALS

2   This mixture of learned and instinctive behavior is not the same for all species. Many invertebrate animals (e.g., insects) rely on instinct for the majority of their behavior patterns, whereas many of the vertebrates (particularly birds and mammals) use a great deal of learning. Typically the learned components of an animal's behavior have particular value for the animal's survival. Most of the behavior of a honeybee is instinctive, but it is able to learn new routes to food sources. The style of nest built by a bird is instinctive, but the skill with which it builds may improve with experience. The food-searching behavior of birds is probably instinctive, but the ability to modify the behavior to exploit unusual food sources such as bird feeders is learned. The following table compares instinctive behaviors and learned behaviors.

A COMPARISON OF INSTINCT AND LEARNING	
Instinct	**Learning**
animal is born with the behavior	animal is not born with the behavior
it is hereditary (genetic memory)	learned behavior is not hereditary, but the way in which learning occurs is at least partly hereditary
behavior is done correctly the first time	behavior requires practice
no experience is required	performance improves with experience
behavior cannot be changed	behavior can be changed
memory is not important	memory is important
instinct is typical of simple animals that have short lives and little contact with their parents	learning is typical of more complex animals that have long lives and extensive contact with parents

∎ ∎ ∎

Fig. 2.1   Leaf-cutting ants carry sections of leaves in the rain forest

Checking Comprehension

TEXT ANALYSIS

A paragraph often includes a sentence (often the first sentence) that helps you understand the topic and sometimes the main idea of a paragraph. For example, read the first sentence in paragraph 1:

> It is important to recognize that all animals have both learned and instinctive behaviors and that one behavior may have elements that are both instinctive and learned.

In this example, the reader learns the topic—animals have learned and instinctive behaviors—as well as the main idea—behaviors can have elements of both instinct and learning. The second sentence begins with *for example*, so we know that this sentence will give us details about the statement introduced in the first sentence.

A Reread paragraph 1. Use the chart below to organize the information about the topic and main idea presented in the first sentence.

Topic	Animals have instinctive and learned behaviors.
Main Idea	
Supporting Details	• • •
Conclusion	
Transition	This is probably true of the behavior of many organisms; they show complex behaviors that are a combination of instinct and learning.

B Work with a partner or in a small group. Reread paragraph 2. Use the chart below to organize the information in the paragraph.

Topic	The mix of learning and instinct is different for different animals.		
Main Idea			
	Animal	**Instinctive Behavior**	**Learned Behavior**
Example	honeybee		
Example	bird		
Transition			

C **Answer the following questions in complete sentences.**

1. What are the major differences between instinctive behavior and learned behavior?

   _____

   _____

   _____

2. Review the chart comparing instinct and learning. Which two or three components of each kind of behavior have the most value for an organism's survival? Why do you think so?

   Instinct: _____

   _____

   Learning: _____

   _____

D **Read the following sentences. Circle the best choice to complete the sentences.**

1. The research on song sparrows demonstrates that birds raised in isolation ___.
   a. can never learn the song of their species by themselves
   b. can only learn the songs of other species because they are imitators
   c. might be able to sing a song similar to that of other song sparrows

2. The example of the mockingbird indicates that some birds ___.
   a. can learn the songs of many other bird species
   b. instinctively know the songs of many other bird species
   c. imitate the songs of other mockingbirds

Learning Vocabulary

VOCABULARY IN CONTEXT

Read the following excerpts. Circle the best choice to complete the sentences.

EXCERPT ONE

It is important to recognize that all animals have both learned and instinctive behaviors and that one behavior may have *elements* that are both instinctive and learned. For example, biologists have raised song sparrows in the absence of any adult birds so there was no song for the young birds to imitate. These *isolated* birds would sing a series of notes similar to the normal song of the species, but not exactly correct. However, birds from the same nest that were raised with their parents developed a song nearly identical to that of their parents. It appears that the basic melody of the song was inherited by the birds and that the *refinements* of the song were the result of experience.

1. From this context, we can understand that *elements* are ___.
   a. notes
   b. songs
   c. components

2. From this context, we can understand that the *isolated* birds ___.
   a. lived by themselves, with no other birds around
   b. lived only with other young birds, with no adult birds around

3. From this context, we can understand that *refinements* are ___.
   a. melodies
   b. improvements
   c. similarities

EXCERPT TWO

It is important to note that many kinds of birds learn most of their songs with very few *innate* components. For example, mockingbirds are very good at imitating the songs of a wide variety of bird species found in their local region.

From this context, we can understand that *innate* refers to components that ___.
   a. an animal is born with
   b. an animal learns with experience

EXCERPT THREE

This mixture of learned and instinctive behavior is not the same for all species. Many *invertebrate* animals rely on instinct for the majority of their behavior patterns, *whereas* many of the *vertebrates* (particularly birds and mammals) use a great deal of learning.

1. Birds and mammals are types of *vertebrates*. Basically, this means they ___.
   a. have backbones
   b. do not have backbones

2. The word *whereas* indicates ___.
   a. a similarity
   b. a contrast

3. Examples of *invertebrates* are ___.
   a. reptiles and amphibians
   b. fish
   c. worms and insects

USING THE DICTIONARY

Read the following excerpt and dictionary entry. Select the most appropriate entry for the context, and choose the best answer to complete the sentence that follows. If you choose an entry that includes subentries (for example *1a, 1b, 1c*), indicate the letter as well as the number.

EXCERPT

Instinctive behavior is *hereditary* (genetic memory). Learned behavior is not *hereditary*, but the way in which learning occurs is at least partly *hereditary*.

he•red•i•tary \hə-'re-də-ˌter-ē\ *adj* [L *hereditarius,* fr. *hereditas*] (15c)
1 a : genetically transmitted or transmittable from parent to offspring
b : characteristic of or fostered by one's predecessors **2 a :** received or passing by inheritance or required to pass by inheritance or by reason of birth
b : having title or possession through inheritance or by reason of birth **3 :** of a kind established by tradition <~ enemies> **4 :** of or relating to inheritance or heredity *syn* see INNATE—**he•red•i•tar•i•ly** \-,re-də-'ter- ə-lē\ *adv*

1. In this context, the most appropriate definition for *hereditary* is number ___.

2. Learned behavior is not ___, but instinctive behavior is.
   a. genetically transmitted from parent to offspring
   b. received or passed by inheritance or reason of birth
   c. of a kind established by tradition

INTRODUCING THE MAIN READING

Activate Your Knowledge

Before you begin reading, think about what you may already know about the topic. If you cannot answer all the questions, do not worry about it. You will learn more when you read the passage.

Work alone or in a small group. Answer the following questions.

1. What are some instinctive behaviors that humans have? Make a list.

   _____   _____

   _____   _____

   _____   _____

2. Humans learn in a variety of ways. For example, we learn to dance by watching others and then practicing. What are some other ways that humans learn? Make a list.

_____   _____

_____   _____

_____   _____

3. Normally, all children learn the language spoken by the people around them. How do they learn it?

_____

_____

_____

Reading and Study Skill Strategies

SCANNING AND SKIMMING

A Scan the Main Reading on pages 43–49 for headings and subheadings, and write them on the lines below.

Instinct and Learning in the Same Organism

_____

_____

_____

_____

_____

B Read the following questions, then skim through the appropriate sections of the Main Reading to find the answers. Read quickly. Compare your answer with a classmate's.

1. What is territorial behavior?

_____

_____

2. What is one advantage of dominance hierarchy within a group?

_____

_____

C **Based on the title, headings, and your brief skimming, what do you think you are going to read about in the Main Reading?**

1. In a few sentences, write your predictions.

   _____

   _____

   _____

2. Write one or two questions that you expect to have answered in the Main Reading.

   _____

   _____

3. Go to page *ii* of the Contents. Read the brief summary of this passage, then decide whether to make any changes to your predictions.

4. Compare your predictions and questions with a classmate's. Keep in mind that you may not agree.

MAIN READING

The following reading is also from Concepts in Biology. *As you read, highlight the important ideas and details. Highlight all boldfaced and italicized words. Monitor your comprehension by answering the* **Before You Continue Reading** *questions.*

Instinct and Learning in the Same Organism

1   We tend to think of ourselves as being different from other animals, and we are. However, it is important to recognize that we are different only in the degree to which we employ these different kinds of behavior. Humans have few behaviors that can be considered instincts. We certainly have reflexes that cause us to respond appropriately without thinking. Newborns grasp objects and hang on tightly with both their hands and feet. This kind of grasping behavior in our primitive ancestors would have allowed the child to hang onto its mother's hair as the mother and child traveled from place to place. But do we have more complicated instinctive behaviors?

2   Although nearly all behavior other than reflexes is learned, newborn infants display several behaviors that could be considered instinctive. If you stroke the side of an infant's face, the child will turn its head toward the side touched and begin sucking movements. This is not a simple reflex behavior but rather requires the coordination of several sets of muscles and certainly involves the brain. It is hard to see how this could be a learned behavior because the child does the behavior without prior experience. Therefore it is probably instinctive.

BEFORE YOU CONTINUE READING

1. What is the proportion of instinct and learning in humans?

a. *a high degree of instinct and a low degree of learning*

b. *a high degree of instinct and a high degree of learning*

c. *a low degree of instinct and a high degree of learning*

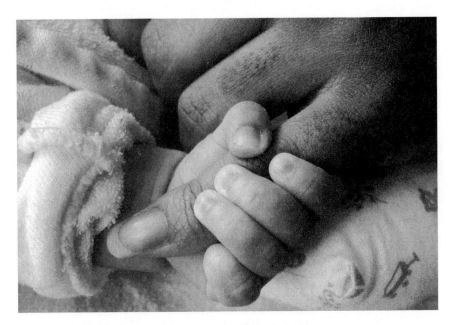

Fig. 2.2   A three-week-old baby's hand grasping its mother's finger

TYPES OF LEARNED BEHAVIOR

3   As we saw in Chapter One, scientists separate learned behavior into several categories, including association, imprinting, and insight.

4   **Associative learning** is extremely common in humans. We associate smells with certain kinds of food, sirens with emergency vehicles, and words with their meanings. Much of the learning that we do is by association. We also often use positive and negative reinforcement as ways to change behavior. We seek to reward appropriate behavior and punish inappropriate behavior. Much of the positive and negative reinforcement can be accomplished without having the actual experience because we can visualize possible consequences of our behavior. Adults routinely describe consequences for children so that children will not experience particularly harmful effects.

5   **Imprinting** in humans is more difficult to demonstrate, but there are some instances in which imprinting may be taking place. *Bonding* between mothers and infants is thought to be an important step in the development of the mother-child relationship. Most mothers form very

strong emotional attachments to their children and, likewise, the children are attached to their mothers, sometimes literally, as they seek to maintain physical contact with their mothers. However, it is very difficult to show what is actually happening at this early time in the life of a child.

6   Another interesting possibility is the language development of children. All children learn whatever languages are spoken where they grow up. If multiple languages are spoken they will learn them all and they learn them easily. However, adults have more difficulty learning new languages, and they often find it impossible to "unlearn" previous languages, so they speak new languages with an accent. This appears to meet the definition of imprinting. Learning takes place at a specific time in life (a *critical period*), the kind of learning is preprogrammed, and what is learned cannot be unlearned. Recent research using tomographic images of the brain shows that those who learned a second language as adults use two different parts of the brain for language: one part for the native language or languages they learned as children, and a different part for their second language.

7   **Insight** is what our species prides itself on. We are thinking animals. *Thinking* is a mental process that involves memory, a concept of self, and an ability to reorganize information. We come up with new solutions to problems. We invent new objects, new languages, new cultures, and new challenges to solve. However, how much of what we think is really completely new, and how much is imitation? As mentioned earlier, association is a major core of our behavior, but we are also able to use past experiences, stored in our large brains, to provide clues to solving new problems.

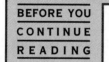

BEFORE YOU CONTINUE READING

2. Which type of learned behavior is the most characteristic of humans?

_____

BEHAVIOR AS A PART OF AN ANIMAL'S ECOLOGICAL NICHE

8   Of the examples used so far in this unit, some involved laboratory studies, such as Pavlov's experiments with dogs, and the experiment with song birds. Some were field studies, such as the observations of web-building in spiders and egg-rolling behavior in geese. Some studies included aspects of both, for example the studies of imprinting among baby ducks and geese. Now that we have some understanding of how organisms generate behavior, we can look at a specific behavior in several kinds of animals and see how it is useful to the animals in their ecological niches.

9   For an animal to be successful, it must receive sufficient resources to live and reproduce. Therefore, organisms have many kinds of behaviors that divide, or allocate, the available resources so that the species as a whole is benefitted, even though some individuals may be harmed.

Territorial Behavior

10   One kind of behavior pattern that is often tied to successful reproduction is territorial behavior. A territory is the space used for food, mating, or other purposes, that an animal defends against others of the same species. The behaviors involved in securing and defending the territory are called **territorial behaviors**. A territory has great importance because it reserves exclusive rights to the use of a certain space for an individual.

11   When territories are first being established, there is much conflict between individuals. This eventually gives way to the use of a series of signals that define the territory and communicate to others that the territory is occupied. The male redwing blackbird has red shoulder patches, but the female does not. The male will perch on a high spot, flash his red shoulder patches, and sing to other males that happen to venture into his territory. Most other males get the message and leave his territory; those that do not leave, he attacks. He will also attack a stuffed, dead male redwing blackbird in his territory, or even a small piece of red cloth. Clearly, the spot of red is the characteristic that stimulates the male to defend his territory. Once the initial period of conflict is over, the birds tend to respect one another's boundaries. All that is required is to frequently announce that the territory is still occupied. This is accomplished by singing from some conspicuous position in the territory. After the territorial boundaries are established, little time is required to prevent other males from venturing close. Thus the animal may spend a great deal of time and energy securing the territory initially, but doesn't need to expend much to maintain it.

12   With many kinds of animals the possession of a territory is often a requirement for reproductive success. In a way, then, territorial behavior has the effect of allocating breeding space and limiting population size to that which the ecosystem can support. This kind of behavior is widespread in the animal kingdom and can be seen in such diverse groups as insects, spiders, fish, reptiles, birds, and mammals.

13   Many carnivorous mammals like foxes, weasels, cougars, coyotes, and wolves use urine or other scents to mark the boundaries of their territories. One of the primary values of the territory for these animals is the food contained within the large space they defend. These territories may include several square kilometers of land. Many other kinds of animals are territorial but use other signaling methods to maintain ownership of their territories. For example, territorial fish use color patterns and threat postures to defend their territories. Crickets use sound and threat postures. Male bullfrogs engage in shoving matches to displace males who invade their small territories along the shoreline.

BEFORE YOU CONTINUE READING

3. **Why are gaining and maintaining territory so important to an animal?**

   a. *because they demonstrate an animal's strength and power over others of the same species*

   b. *because they are essential in providing an animal the opportunity to reproduce*

   c. *because they give an animal enough space to live and to exercise*

Fig. 2.3   An American badger confronting a rattlesnake at the entrance to its den

Dominance Hierarchy

14   Another way of allocating resources is by the establishment of a **dominance hierarchy**, in which a relatively stable, mutually understood order of priority within the group is maintained. A dominance hierarchy is often established in animals that form social groups. One individual in the group dominates all others. A second-ranking individual in the group dominates all but the highest-ranking individual, and so forth, until the lowest-ranking individual must give way to all others within the group. This kind of behavior is seen in barnyard chickens, where it is known as a *pecking order*.

15   A dominance hierarchy allows certain individuals to get preferential treatment when resources are scarce. The dominant individual will have first choice of food, mates, shelter, water, and other resources because of its position. Animals low in the hierarchy may be malnourished or fail to mate in times of scarcity. In many social animals, like wolves, only the dominant males and females reproduce. This ensures that the most favorable genes will be passed on to the next generation. Poorly adapted animals with low rank may never reproduce. Once a dominance hierarchy is established, it results in a more stable social unit with little conflict, except perhaps for an occasional altercation that reinforces the knowledge of which position an animal occupies in the hierarchy. Such a hierarchy frequently results in low-ranking individuals emigrating from the area. Such migrating individuals are often subject to heavy predation. Thus the dominance hierarchy serves as a population-control mechanism and a way of allocating resources. Territorial behavior and dominance hierarchy are important behaviors essential to the survival of many species. In addition to these two types of behavior, animals have other behaviors which enable them to survive when resources are scarce or are unavailable.

4. What are some of the advantages of dominance hierarchy for species that form social groups?

_____

_____

Fig. 2.4   A herd of cows displaying dominance hierarchy

Avoiding Periods of Scarcity

16   Resource allocation (distribution) becomes most critical during periods of scarcity. In some areas, the dry part of the year is the most stressful. In temperate areas, winter reduces many sources of food and forces organisms to adjust. Animals have several ways of coping with seasonal stress. Some animals simply avoid the stress. For instance, in areas where drought occurs, many animals become inactive until water becomes available. Frogs, toads, and many insects remain inactive (estivate) underground during long periods and emerge to mate when it rains. Hibernation in warm-blooded animals is a response to cold, seasonal temperatures in which the body temperature drops and there is a physiological slowing of all body processes that allows an animal to survive on food it has stored within its body. Hibernation is typical of bats, bears, and some squirrels. Similarly cold-blooded animals have their

activities slowed because a drop in air temperature causes a corresponding drop in body temperature. Other animals, such as squirrels, have instinctive behavior patterns that cause them to store food during seasons of plenty for periods of scarcity.

■ ■ ■

USE REFERENTS TO AID IN UNDERSTANDING TEXT

Once a word or a phrase has been mentioned in a reading, it is often replaced with a referent. For example, in the previous sentence, *it* replaces *a word or a phrase*. Common referents include subject, object, and possessive pronouns, as well as such words as *this, that,* and *other*. When you come across a referent, you need to know what it refers to if you are to understand the text.

A Read the following selection from the Main Reading.

> ### TERRITORIAL BEHAVIOR
>
> [1]When territories are first being established, there is much conflict between individuals. [2]This eventually gives way to the use of a series of signals that define the territory and communicate to others that the territory is occupied. [3]The male redwing blackbird has red shoulder patches, but the female does not. [4]The male will perch on a high spot, flash his red shoulder patches, and sing to other males that happen to venture into his territory. [5]Most other males get the message and leave his territory; those that do not leave, he attacks. [6]He will also attack a stuffed, dead male redwing blackbird in his territory, or even a small piece of red cloth. [7]Clearly, the spot of red is the characteristic that stimulates the male to defend his territory.

B Identify what each referent replaces. Check your answers with a classmate. The first one has been done as an example.

1. In sentence 2, *this* refers to <u>conflict</u>   .

2. In sentence 2, *others* refers to _____.

3. In sentence 4, *his* (both instances) refers to _____.

4. In sentence 5, *those* refers to _____.

5. In sentence 7, *that* refers to _____.

Checking Comprehension

TEXT ANALYSIS

Text often contains key words that help the reader organize ideas. For example, the header above paragraph three is entitled *Types of Learned Behavior*. The word *types* alerts the reader that more than one kind of learned behavior is going to be discussed. Now that you have an idea of the content of the next few paragraphs, you can organize the information in a way that will help you understand and remember it.

A Reread paragraphs 3–7. Use the chart below to organize the information in the paragraph.

SECTION TOPIC:		
Types	**Description or Explanation**	**Example**

B Answer the following questions. Write complete sentences where appropriate.

1. What are some instinctive behaviors that humans have? Make a list.

   _____   _____

   _____   _____

2. Humans learn in a variety of ways. For example, we learn to dance by watching others and then practicing. What are some other ways that humans learn? Make a list.

   _____   _____

   _____   _____

3. Normally, all children learn the language spoken by the people around them. How do they learn it?

   _____

   _____

   How many of your answers on pages 41–42 were correct? ____

C Read the following questions and circle the correct answers.

1. How much of a newborn infant's behavior is instinctive?
   a. a lot
   b. some
   c. very little

2. What part of an infant's behavior is probably instinctive?
   a. reflexive behavior
   b. eating behavior
   c. head-turning behavior

3. What is a major indicator of instinctive behavior?
   a. behavior that is in response to touching
   b. behavior that does not require previous experience
   c. behavior that involves the coordination of muscles

D **Answer the following questions in complete sentences.**

1. Consider the author's definition of *critical period* in paragraph 6. Aside from language, what other human learning might need to take place during a *critical period*?

_____

_____

_____

2. According to the author's definition of *thinking*, can animals think? Explain your reasons for your answer.

_____

_____

3. Research shows that we use one part of our brain for our first language(s) and another part of our brain for a language we learn as adults. What general conclusion might we draw from this research finding?

_____

_____

_____

4. In humans, most behavior appears to be learned. Of what value is this high proportion of learned behavior?

_____

_____

5. Male redwing blackbirds have red shoulder patches. Female redwing blackbirds do not have red shoulder patches.

   a. Why do you think males have red shoulder patches?

_____

_____

   b. Why do you think females do not need red shoulder patches?

_____

_____

Learning Vocabulary

VOCABULARY IN CONTEXT

Read the following excerpts. Circle the best choice to complete the sentences.

EXCERPT ONE

Now that we have some understanding of how organisms generate behavior, we can look at a specific behavior in several kinds of animals and see how it is useful to the animals in their *ecological niches*. For an animal to be successful, it must receive sufficient resources to live and reproduce. Therefore, organisms have many kinds of behaviors that divide, or allocate, the available resources so that the species as a whole is benefitted, even though some individuals may be harmed.

1. An animal's *ecological niche* is most likely ___.
   a. the specific type of food that the animal likes to eat
   b. the specific part of the environment in which the animal lives

2. In the same surroundings, such as a forest, a bird and a squirrel will have ___.
   a. different ecological niches
   b. the same ecological niche

EXCERPT TWO

Resource *allocation* (distribution) becomes most critical during periods of *scarcity*. In some areas, the dry part of the year is the most stressful. In temperate areas, winter reduces many sources of food and forces organisms to adjust. Animals have several ways of coping with seasonal stress. Some animals simply avoid the stress. For instance, in areas where *drought* occurs, many animals become inactive until water becomes available.

1. From this context, we can understand that the *scarcity* of resources such as food and water means that these resources are ___.
   a. difficult to find
   b. easily available

2. From this context, we can understand that resource *allocation* refers to ___.
   a. how animals are able to find resources in their environment
   b. how animals fight over resources in their environment

3. A period of *drought* occurs when ___.
   a. water is available
   b. water is unavailable

USING THE DICTIONARY

Read the following excerpts and dictionary entries. Select the most appropriate entry for the context, and choose the best answer to complete the sentence that follows. If an entry includes subentries (for example 1a, 1b, 1c), indicate the letter as well as the number.

EXCERPT ONE

Resource allocation becomes most critical during periods of scarcity. In some areas, the dry part of the year is the most stressful. In temperate areas, winter reduces many sources of food and forces organisms to adjust. Animals have several ways of *coping with* seasonal stress. Some animals simply avoid the stress. For instance, in areas where drought occurs, many animals become inactive until water becomes available.

cope *vb* **coped; cop•ing** [ME *copen, coupen,* fr. MF *couper* to strike, cut, fr. OF, fr. *coup* blow, fr. LL *colpus,* alter. of L *colaphus,* fr. Gk *kolaphos* buffet] *vi* (14c) **1** *obs:* STRIKE, FIGHT **2 a :** to maintain a contest or combat usu. on even terms or with success—used with *with* **b :** to deal with and attempt to overcome problems and difficulties—often used with *with* **3** *archaic:* MEET, ENCOUNTER ~ *vt* **1** *obs:* to meet in combat **2** *obs:* to come in contact with **3** *obs:* MATCH

1. In this context, the most appropriate definition for *cope* is number ___.

2. Animals have several ways of ___ seasonal stress.
    a. striking or fighting
    b. maintaining a contest on even terms with
    c. dealing with and attempting to overcome

EXCERPT TWO

Humans have few behaviors that can be considered instincts. We certainly have *reflexes* that cause us to respond appropriately without thinking. Newborns grasp objects and hang on tightly with both their hands and feet.

re•flex \'rē-ˌfleks \ *n* [L *reflexus,* pp. of *reflectere* to reflect] (1508) **1 a :** reflected heat, light, or color **b :** a mirrored image **c :** a copy exact in essential or peculiar features **2 a :** an automatic and often inborn response to a stimulus that involves a nerve impulse passing inward from a receptor to a nerve center and thence outward to an effector (as a muscle or gland) without reaching the level of consciousness—compare HABIT **b :** the process that culminates in a reflex and comprises reception, transmission, and reaction—called also *reflex action* **c** *pl*: the power of acting or responding with adequate speed **d :** a way of thinking or behaving **3 :** a linguistic element (as a word or sound) or system (as writing) that is derived from a prior and esp. an older element or system ⟨*boat* is the ~ of Old English *bāt*⟩

1. In this context, the appropriate definition for *reflex* is number ___.

2. We have ___ that cause us to respond appropriately without thinking.
   a. reflected heat, light, or color
   b. automatic and inborn responses to stimuli
   c. ways of thinking and behaving

LEARN AND USE WORD FORMS

A Study the word forms in the chart below. If you are not sure about the meaning of a word, reread the text, highlight the words and any of their forms, and try to understand them from context.

VERB	NOUN	ADJECTIVE	ADVERB
allocate	allocation	allocated	
associate	association	associative	
dominate	domination dominance	dominant dominated/dominating	
exploit	exploitation	exploited/exploiting	
imitate	imitation	imitative imitated/imitating	imitatively
modify	modification	modified/modifying	
reproduce	reproduction	reproductive	reproductively
stimulate	stimulation stimulus (*plural* stimuli)	stimulated/stimulating	
visualize	visualization	visual	visually
refine	refinement	refined/refining	

B Read the sentences. Choose the appropriate word from the following sets and complete each sentence. Be sure to use the correct tense of verbs in either the affirmative or the negative and the singular or plural of nouns. Use each word only once.

allocate	modify	visualize
dominate	reproduce	

1. When we _____ something that may happen as a result of a particular action, we are demonstrating insightful behavior.

2. Many animals, such as chimpanzees, can make a number of _____ to a tool such as a branch or a piece of grass.

3. Within their social group, humans often _____ resources according to need, but animals will almost always try to gain resources only for themselves and their offspring.

4. An animal that _____ because it cannot gain territory or find a mate may survive, but its genes will not be passed on to the next generation of its species.

5. In some species, such as wolves, only the _____ male and female reproduce.

associate	exploit	imitate	refine	stimulate

6. Although different species may live in the same environment, they often _____ different resources because they inhabit different niches within the same environment.

7. When a person hears a familiar song and it reminds her of a specific event such as a party, the person is experiencing _____ learning.

8. _____ behavior is common among many species. Even organisms that demonstrate considerable learning often copy the behavior of others, especially when young.

9. Complex animals such as mammals will respond to _____ with a wide range of responses.

10. Higher animals such as mammals often demonstrate _____ in their behavior as they develop experience.

FOLLOW-UP ASSIGNMENTS

Before you begin any of the assignments, review the content-specific vocabulary and academic vocabulary below, and look over the vocabulary in the word form chart on page 54. If you are still unsure what any words or terms mean, go back through the chapter and review. As you complete the follow-up assignments, be sure to incorporate the appropriate vocabulary.

Content-Specific Vocabulary

associative learning	ecosystem	invertebrates
bonding	hereditary	reflexes
critical period	imprinting	resource allocation
dominance	innate	territorial behavior
hierarchy	insight	vertebrates
ecological niche	instinct	

Academic Vocabulary

(in)appropriate	exploit	relationship
component	grasping	reward
consequences	isolated	scarcity
diverse	preprogrammed	whereas
element	refinement	

Writing Activities

1. The proportion of instinctive and learned behavior varies among species of animals. Write three paragraphs. In the first paragraph, describe in general the types of animals for whom having a large proportion of instinctive behavior has value in terms of their survival. In the second paragraph, describe in general the types of animals for whom having a large proportion of learned behavior has value in terms of their survival. In the third paragraph, discuss which of the four types of learned behavior might be the most advantageous to certain species, and explain your reasons.

2. Write three paragraphs in which you respond to the following situation. When members of a species, such as redwing blackbirds, compete for territory, some of the animals lose out and have no territory. In the first paragraph, describe how these animals might lose out. In the second paragraph, discuss what might happen to these individuals. What are some of the possible consequences of holding no territory? In the third paragraph, explain how the loss of territory on the part of some individuals benefits the species as a whole.

3. Write three paragraphs. In the first paragraph, describe the meaning of dominance hierarchy. In the second paragraph, discuss at least two advantages of dominance hierarchy to the individuals within a given species. In the third paragraph, give the advantages of dominance hierarchy to the group.

Extension Activities

1. Research two or three different animals, such as birds, snakes, frogs, mice, cats, or dogs. Compare their parenting behaviors. Design a poster or a chart that illustrates each animal's parenting behavior and shows which behaviors appear to be instinctive and which appear to be learned. Present your findings to the class.

2. Think about what you have learned in Chapters 1 and 2. Research the work of Konrad Lorenz, who studied baby geese and ducks, as you read in Chapter 1. How did the baby geese imprint on him? What happened while they were growing to adulthood? Did Lorenz help the geese become independent? If so, how? Prepare a report, and present it to the class.

3. Work with one or more partners. Choose a particular animal to study. Research how the animal is usually trained through classical conditioning or operational conditioning. Then prepare a report on your findings to present to the class.

4. Conduct research on the Internet. Go online. Use a search engine such as Google, AltaVista, Yahoo, About, or Dogpile. Investigate a topic related to the information you read about in Chapter 2. Choose a topic that especially interests you. You may wish to follow up on one of the questions you wrote on page 35 or page 43. Use key words such as *associative learning, human bonding, dominance hierarchy, ecological niche, ecosystem, resource allocation, territorial behavior,* and *classical conditioning.* Prepare an oral report, a written report, or a poster, and present your findings to the class.

HOW IS OUR WORLD VIEW SHAPED BY OUR CULTURE?

Circular medieval map of the Christian World with Jerusalem in the center

View of the Earth from the surface of the moon (Apollo 8 mission, 1968)

CHAPTER 3

DEFINING AND EXPLORING CULTURE

Fig. 3.0a Japanese man teaching his daughter to play baseball

Fig. 3.0b Mayan woman teaching her daughter to weave

Chapter Readings

The Concept of Culture

A Model for the Study of Cultural Systems

INTRODUCING THE READING

Activate Your Knowledge

A Work in a small group. Think about how you would define *culture*. What characteristics would you use to describe cultures? Use the concept map below to help you organize your ideas. Add to the chart as you think of more ways to describe or characterize culture.

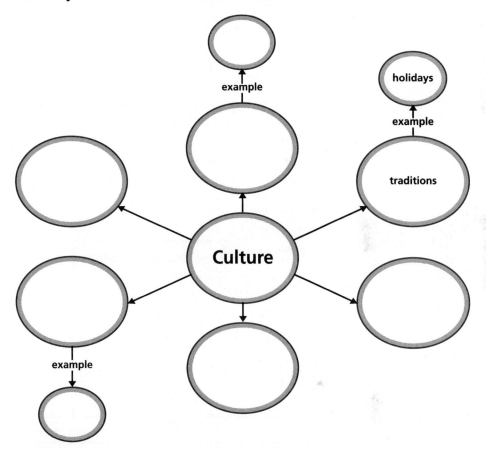

B Put the diagram on the board. Work as a class. Add all the groups' ideas to the diagram. Write a class definition of *culture*.

Reading and Study Skill Strategies

PREVIEW KEY VOCABULARY

Read the content-specific vocabulary below and determine how well you know each one. Use a scale of 1 to 4, where:

1 = I have never seen or heard this vocabulary before.
2 = I have seen or heard this vocabulary before, but I do not know what it means.
3 = I recognize the vocabulary, but I cannot define it accurately or use it with confidence.
4 = I can give an accurate definition or explanation of this vocabulary, and I can use it appropriately in a sentence.

___ abstractions	___ generalizations
___ artifacts	___ ideas
___ codify	___ monotheistic
___ concepts	___ polytheistic
___ culture	___ taboo
___ extragenetic	___ world view

Do not try to learn the unfamiliar items before you begin reading. You will learn them as you work with the chapter.

SCANNING AND SKIMMING

In the previous two chapters, you previewed the title and headings of the readings as they appeared in the text. Another way of previewing the reading is by creating a diagram.

A Scan the Introductory Reading on pages 64–68 and write down the heading in the diagram. Then go to the last paragraph of the Introductory Reading, on page 68, and skim it to find the four characteristics of culture. Write them in the diagram. One of the characteristics has already been filled in.

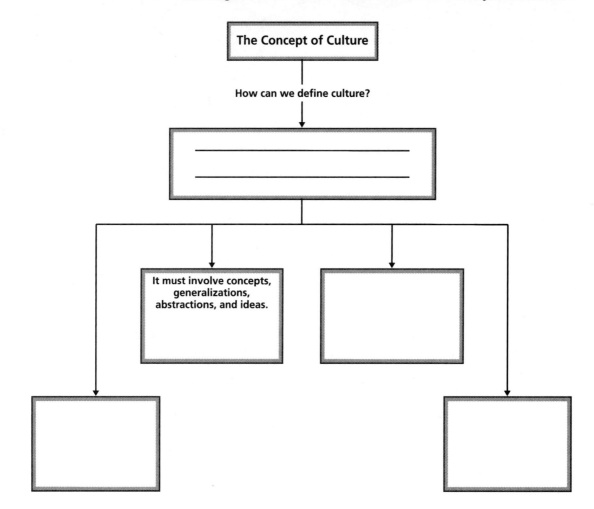

B **Based on the title, headings, and your brief skimming, what do you think you are going to read about in the Introductory Reading?**

1. In a few sentences, write your predictions.

_____

_____

_____

2. Write one or two questions that you expect to have answered in the Introductory Reading.

_____

_____

3. Go to page *iii* of the Contents. Read the brief summary of this passage, then decide whether to make any changes to your predictions.

4. Compare your predictions and questions with a classmate's. Keep in mind that you may not agree.

ANNOTATE TEXT

Annotating text means writing brief notes in the margin. These notes might be a definition of a new word, a simple outline of a paragraph, key words, questions you have about what you have read, or comments you have about the text. Annotating text helps you remember what you have read and makes it easy for you to find important words, phrases, or ideas when you are reviewing.

A **Read the following excerpt from the Introductory Reading and study the annotation in the margin.**

We learn to—

• *make generalizations*

• *adapt generalizations to new situations*

What is an elimination taboo?

dogs can generalize too

elimination taboo—don't go to the bathroom indoors!

Think about having to learn every specific behavior for every situation you encounter in the course of a day. Life as we know it would be impossible. Rather, because we have learned generalizations, or have generated our own generalizations from specific data, we adapt those generalizations to each new situation—more often than not successfully. But even concepts and generalizations don't absolutely define human cultural behavior. My dogs have some concept of the elimination taboo. I don't have to take them into every house and building we may visit and teach them all over again. Rather, I'm confident that they have generalized from their training in my house. They have some concept that says something like "don't go to the bathroom in people's buildings." But that still doesn't make their behavior cultural.

B Annotate the following excerpt from the Introductory Reading.

> Now, if I adopted a new puppy and put her in the house with my present dogs, and if I had no input into the situation and allowed the puppy to leave and enter the house at will, would she learn the elimination taboo? I doubt it. Each dog can learn it independently, but one can't share the information, and certainly not the generalization, with other dogs. ("Hey listen, never, ever go to the bathroom in peoples' houses, OK?") Dogs can and do learn by imitation and, probably, after a while, the new dog would start to behave accordingly. But she would have learned on her own, passively. It is not culture.

C Work with a classmate and compare your annotations. Then compare your annotations with the annotations in paragraph 10 on page 67 when you begin reading. Annotating has been done for you in the entire Introductory Reading, as an example.

INTRODUCTORY READING

The following reading is from Introducing Anthropology: An Integrated Approach. *As you read, highlight the important ideas, details, and boldfaced or italicized words. Monitor your comprehension by answering the* Before You Continue Reading *questions. Study the annotations in the margin.*

The Concept of Culture

1   Among the most amazing builders in the world are weaver ants from the Old World tropics. Colonies of these ants construct nests in trees in the form of tents made from the tree's leaves. To do this, teams of ants form living staples suspended between the leaves and pull the leaves together. Then other ants gently carry larvae along the seam, stimulating them to excrete silk which "sews" the leaves together.

ants built a nest

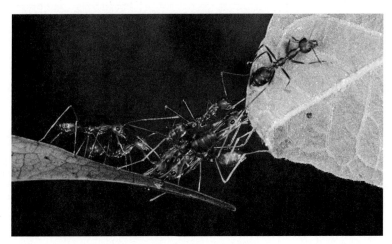

Fig. 3.1 Weaver ants pulling two leaves together

2

A few years ago I decided to build a wall and hang a door in order to create a new room for my study. Having virtually no knowledge of such matters, my first step was to purchase a book about home improvements and digest all the necessary information about partition building, lumber, drywall, and tools. Then I drew up my plans and materials list. Still unsure of myself, I consulted with a colleague who is experienced in carpentry and who came over to look at my proposed construction site. Based on his knowledge, he suggested a few amendments to my plans to take into account my particular situation. Off I went to buy my materials and some shiny new power tools and a few days later, I had my new room, complete with a door that actually swings open and closed. Both these examples are amazing feats of engineering, but they are fundamentally different. My project was cultural. The ants' was not. I had to do all sorts of thinking and analyzing to build my wall. The ants did not think at all about their nest. This distinction should be obvious, and it's fairly easy to decide, in general, whether a behavior is cultural or not.

- *read book*

- *asked for help*

- *building wall was cultural*
- *ants' nest wasn't—no thinking involved*

DEFINING CULTURE

3

We all know what culture is. Or do we? Can you define culture? If you can't, don't worry. You're in good company. For the entire history of anthropology, a continual project has been to try to come up with just such a definition. One reason for the difficulty is simply that the phenomenon of culture is so complex. The second reason is that, until recently, we were trying desperately to define culture in a way that made it our species' unique possession. As you can probably guess, it's not. A concise definition is difficult, if not impossible, but we can list and discuss the characteristics of culture to show, point by point, how cultural behaviors differ from noncultural ones, and to examine in what ways nonhumans exhibit cultural behaviors.

defining culture is difficult

BEFORE YOU CONTINUE READING

1. What is main idea of this section?

  a. *The behavior of ants building a nest is noncultural because it is instinctive, but the behavior of the author building a wall is cultural because it requires thinking and learning.*

  b. *The behavior of the author building a wall is cultural, and the behavior of ants building a nest is cultural, too, even though it is instinctive, because it requires a group effort.*

  c. *The behavior of ants building a nest is noncultural because it is instinctive, and the behavior of the author building a wall is noncultural, too, because he built it by himself.*

THE FOUR CHARACTERISTICS OF CULTURAL BEHAVIOR

cultural behavior—

1. learned

ants' behavior is instinctive

4   Perhaps the easiest characteristic of a cultural behavior to see is that culture is *learned.* The ants clearly didn't learn how to build nests, even as complex as that behavior might be. Rather, the behavior is built into their genes and is expressed by a complex series of stimuli that elicit a complex set of responses. My accomplishment, on the other hand, was only possible through learning, and the skills and information I learned were in turn learned by those who instructed me, who learned it from someone else, and so on.

5   Learning used to be considered the only distinguishing feature between cultural and noncultural behaviors, but a moment's reflection will tell you that learning is not enough. Other

Fig. 3.2 Man learning to use a power saw

creatures learn. My dogs, for example, have learned many things, including, of course, the taboo (prohibition) against eliminating in the house, but these things would not really be considered cultural. Why not? What other differences are there?

animals learn too

eliminating in house???

2. culture
• *concepts*
• *generalizations*
What are generalizations?
• *abstractions*
• *ideas*

concept
• *a conscious plan*

6   A second characteristic of culture is that it involves *concepts, generalizations, abstractions,* and *ideas.* The ants are locked into the specifics of their nest-building behavior. It must work the same all the time. If some important variable is different, the ants cannot make specific adjustments. They don't, in other words, know what they are doing. Their behavior is not part of some larger concept.

7   My wall building, however, certainly involved concepts. No external stimuli elicited a wall-building response in me. Rather, I decided, consciously, to do the project for my own set of reasons. My book didn't relate to my wall in particular but gave general ideas about partition building that I adapted to my specific situation. As I ran into unexpected problems, I was able to use my knowledge of the general principles to solve them. I now should be able to apply what I've learned to other, similar tasks.

We learn to—
• *make generalizations*
• *adapt them to new situations*
What is an elimination taboo?
dogs can generalize too

8   Think about having to learn every specific behavior for every situation you encounter in the course of a day. Life as we know it would be impossible. Rather, because we have learned generalizations, or have generated our own generalizations from specific data, we adapt those generalizations to each new situation—more often than not successfully. But even concepts and generalizations don't absolutely define human cultural behavior. My dogs have some concept of the elimination taboo. I don't have to take them into every house and building we may visit and teach them all over again. Rather, I'm confident that they have generalized

elimination taboo—don't
go to the bathroom
indoors!

from their training in my house. They have some concept that says something like "don't go to the bathroom in people's buildings." But that still doesn't make their behavior cultural.

9

3. active learning /
sharing information

extragenetically—not
under genetic influence

There is another dimension to learning that is important. Learning in most organisms is passive. They learn from imitation or from trial and error. For many birds, for example, singing just the right song is impossible unless they've heard another bird sing it. Singing itself is genetic, but the song must be learned. But learning can also be active, when information is *shared* among organisms, is *transmitted* from one organism to another *extragenetically*, that is, without any direct genetic influence, as in the birdsong example. The ants' basic information about nest-building is solely genetic. The information I acquired about wall-building was shared extragenetically.

10

Now, if I adopted a new puppy and put her in the house with my present dogs, and if I had no input into the situation and allowed the puppy to leave and enter the house at will, would she learn the elimination taboo? I doubt it. Each dog can learn it independently, but one can't share the information, and certainly not the generalization, with other dogs. ("Hey listen, never, ever go to the bathroom in peoples' houses, OK?") Dogs can and do learn by imitation and, probably, after a while, the new dog would start to behave accordingly. But she would have learned on her own, passively. It is not culture.

dogs—don't share
learning with puppy

BEFORE YOU CONTINUE READING

2. What is the main idea of this section?

  a. *Animals are capable of cultural behavior if they can generalize what they learn to other situations, even if their behavior is instinctive.*

  b. *Dogs, birds, and ants all exhibit some genetically determined behavior and some learned behavior.*

  c. *Cultural behavior must be learned actively, it must be generalizable, and it must be shared among members of a group.*

11

4. artifacts—"man made
objects"

The fourth characteristic of culture is the presence of *artifacts*. An **artifact** is defined as any object made intentionally. It is, in other words, not natural but, in the common phrase, "man made." This book is an artifact. To be sure, the ants made their nest, but that nest is natural. The program for it is genetic and so, in a sense, it is like their hormones and bodies—natural and not the result of learned, shared, concepts and generalizations. Although the usual definition of artifact limits it to concrete items—tools, houses, books, pottery—I'd like to expand it a bit here to include cultural institutions and organizational systems—things like religions, governments, educational establishments. These too are "man made." Artifacts—both concrete ones and abstract organizing principles—facilitate the realization of cultural ideas, and human culture is dependent upon them. Without artifacts, there is no way I could have built my wall—which, of course, is an artifact itself.

can be concrete or
abstract

Can there be a culture
without artifacts?

12   So, cultural behavior has these four characteristics:

1. It must be learned.
2. It must involve concepts, generalizations, abstractions, and ideas.
3. It must be shared through extragenetic transmission.
4. It must be realized through the use of artifacts, both concrete and abstract.

■ ■ ■

Checking Comprehension

TEXT ANALYSIS

Paragraph 3 introduces the concept of culture and describes the difficulty in defining it. This paragraph contains specific markers that help us organize the text that follows.

A **Read the last sentence in paragraph 3.**

A concise definition is difficult, if not impossible, but we can list and discuss the characteristics of culture to show, point by point, how cultural behaviors differ from noncultural ones, and to examine in what ways nonhumans exhibit cultural behaviors.

The words *list* and *discuss* and the phrase *point by point* indicate that the text which follows will list, explain, and then show how cultural and noncultural behaviors differ.

B **Reread paragraphs 3–12 and complete the chart below.**

THE FOUR CHARACTERISTICS OF CULTURAL BEHAVIOR		
Characteristics	**Noncultural Behavior**	**Cultural Behavior**
Cultural behavior is learned.	Ants did not learn how to build nests. Their nest-building behavior is built into their genes.	The author learned how to build a wall by learning from books and from other people.

Answer the following questions in complete sentences.

1. What is the biggest difference between the weaver ants building a nest and the author building a wall?

   _____

   _____

2. Refer to the author's example of birds singing, in paragraph 9. What part of the birds' behavior is genetic (instinctive) and what part is learned?

   _____

   _____

3. When humans generalize, what type of learning are they exhibiting? Give an example.

   _____

   _____

   _____

4. In paragraph 8, the author states that "life as we know it would be impossible" if we had to learn "every specific behavior for every situation" we experience in our daily lives. Do you agree with the author? Explain your answer. Refer to a typical day in your life in your response.

   _____

   _____

   _____

   _____

SENTENCE FOCUS

Sometimes a sentence within a paragraph is difficult to understand but it holds important information about the content you are studying. In order to understand the sentence, it is important to look at the parts of the sentence that connect it to other ideas in the paragraph or text. For example, terms such as *rather, on the other hand, but, although,* and *on the contrary* indicate contrast between sentences and ideas.

A **Reread the paragraph excerpt. Pay attention to the italicized words. Read the comprehension item. Then read the explanation.**

PARAGRAPH 4

[1]Perhaps the easiest characteristic of a cultural behavior to see is that culture is learned. [2]The ants clearly didn't learn how to build nests, even as complex as that behavior might be. [3]*Rather*, the behavior is built into

their genes and is expressed by a complex series of stimuli that elicit a complex set of responses. [4]My accomplishment, *on the other hand*, was only possible through learning, and the skills and information I learned were in turn learned by those who instructed me, who learned it from someone else, and so on.

Ants' nest-building behavior is not cultural behavior because _____.

    a. ants teach each other how to build nests, which is a very complex task

    (b.) ants are born with the ability to build nests as they respond to their environment

The word *rather* indicates a contrast between the information in sentence 2 and the information in sentence 3. The author introduces the idea of what ant nest-building is not (i.e., learned) and then tells us what ant building is (built into their genes, an instinctive response). The phrase *on the other hand* indicates a contrast between the information in sentence 3 and the information in sentence 4. The author indicates that a human accomplishment is different from an ant accomplishment because it shows learning.

B **Reread the paragraph excerpts. Pay attention to the italicized words. Then circle the correct choice to complete the sentences.**

PARAGRAPH 8

[1]Think about having to learn every specific behavior for every situation you encounter in the course of a day. [2]Life as we know it would be impossible. [3]*Rather*, because we have learned generalizations, or have generated our own generalizations from specific data, we adapt those generalizations to each new situation—more often than not successfully.

Human beings are successful because ___.

    a. we do not have to learn a new behavior for every new situation

    b. we can learn a new behavior for every new situation

PARAGRAPH 10

[1]Each dog can learn the elimination taboo independently, *but* one can't share the information, and certainly not the generalization, with other dogs. [2]Dogs can and do learn by imitation and, probably, after a while, a new dog would start to behave accordingly. [3]*But* she would have learned on her own, passively. It is not culture.

Dogs are capable of learning new behavior. Their learned behavior ___.

    a. is not cultural behavior because they cannot teach other dogs what they have learned

    b. is cultural behavior because they show they are capable of learning

VOCABULARY IN CONTEXT

Reread the paragraphs indicated from the Introductory Reading to figure out the meaning of the italicized words. Then circle the correct choice to complete the sentences.

Paragraph 5: *feature* and *taboo*

1. From this context, we can understand that a *feature* is a(n) ___.
    a. characteristic
    b. behavior
    c. accomplishment

2. A synonym of *taboo* in this context is ___.
    a. learning
    b. prohibition
    c. behavior

Paragraph 9: *transmitted* and *extragenetically*

1. From this context, we can understand that *transmitted* means ___.
    a. communicated
    b. taught
    c. learned

2. *Extragenetically* means ___.
    a. completely genetic
    b. influenced by genetics
    c. not influenced by genetics

USING THE DICTIONARY

Read the following excerpt and dictionary entry. Select the most appropriate entry for the italicized word, based on the context. Then circle the correct choice to complete the sentences. If you choose an entry that includes subentries (for example *1a, 1b, 1c*), indicate the letter as well as the number.

EXCERPT

Artifacts—both concrete ones and abstract organizing principles—facilitate the *realization* of cultural ideas, and human culture is dependent upon them. Without artifacts, there is no way I could have built my wall.

re·al·i·za·tion \,rē-ə-lə-'zā-shən, ,ri-ə-\ *n* (ca. 1611) **1 :** the action of realizing: the state of being realized **2 :** something realized
re·al·ize \'rē-ə-,līz, 'ri- ə-\ *vt* **-ized; -iz·ing** [F *réaliser*, fr. MF *realiser*, fr. *real* real] (ca. 1611) **1 a :** to bring into concrete existence : ACCOMPLISH ⟨finally *realized* her goal⟩ **b :** to cause to seem real : make appear real ⟨a book in which the characters are carefully *realized*⟩ **2 a :** to convert into actual money ⟨*realized* assets⟩ **b :** to bring or get by sale, investment, or effort : GAIN **3 :** to conceive vividly as real : be fully aware of ⟨did not ∼ the risk she was taking⟩ *syn* see THINK — **re·al·iz·able** \,rē-ə-'lī-zə-bəl, ,ri-\ *adj* — **re·al·iz·er** *n*

1. Read the dictionary entries for both *realization* and *realize*. In the entry for the verb form, the most appropriate definition is number ___.

2. Artifacts make it easier for people to ___.
   a. bring cultural ideas into concrete existence
   b. cause cultural ideas to seem real
   c. convert cultural ideas into money
   d. be fully aware of cultural ideas

INTRODUCING THE MAIN READING

Activate Your Knowledge

Work with one or two classmates who are from a culture that is different from yours or who are familiar with a different culture.

A **Think about the characteristics of culture that you described at the beginning of the chapter on page 61. In what ways are your cultures different (e.g., definitions of family or of educational systems)? Use the chart below to organize your information.**

TYPE OF DIFFERENCE	CULTURE: _____	CULTURE: _____	CULTURE: _____

B Combine all the groups' charts on the board to make a single chart.

C Examine the types of differences. Discuss possible reasons and explanations for the variations among the cultures you have described.

Reading and Study Skill Strategies

SCANNING AND SKIMMING

A Scan the Main Reading on pages 74–80 and write down the headings on the lines below.

A Model for the Study of Cultural Systems

_____

_____

_____

_____

B Read the following questions, then skim through the appropriate sections of the Main Reading to find the answers. Read quickly. Compare your answers with a classmate's.

1. What two definitions of *world view* are given in the reading?

_____

_____

2. What do people do when they **codify** their world view?

_____

C Based on the title, headings, and your brief skimming, what do you think you are going to read about in the Main Reading?

1. In a few sentences, write your predictions.

_____

_____

_____

2. Write one or two questions that you expect to have answered in the Main Reading.

_____

_____

3. Go to page *iii* of the Contents. Read the brief summary of this passage, then decide whether to make any changes to your predictions.

4. Compare your predictions and questions with a classmate's. Keep in mind that you may not agree.

MAIN READING

The following reading is from Introducing Anthropology: An Integrated Approach. *As you read, highlight the important ideas and details. Highlight all italicized and boldfaced vocabulary. Monitor your comprehension by answering the* Before You Continue Reading *questions. Annotate the text.*

A Model for the Study of Cultural Systems

1   This is the story of culture as a species characteristic shared by us all. But there's another level, the level of cultures—the specific systems that characterize the societies within our species. How do we study, describe, and explain all the world's cultural systems? Why do we find such an enormous amount of variation from one culture to the next?

2   If we think of culture as an adaptive mechanism, it's easy to understand some of the cultural variation we observe around the world. Important aspects of people's cultures are geared to the conditions of their habitats. The Netsilik people of the Canadian Arctic have all sorts of cultural ideas and technologies for hunting seals but not for hunting kangaroos. For Native Australians it's just the opposite. Living in New England, I own all manner of clothing and heating devices to keep me warm during the winter. Native Americans in the tropical rain forests of Brazil, however, are concerned very little about warmth.

Fig. 3.3 A Netsilik (Eskimo) hunting seals

3   We begin, naturally, with the biological characteristics of humans. We should never lose sight of the fact that, despite the power of culture, we are still limited by our biological structure, function, and needs. However, because part of our biology includes a brain capable of culture, there is a variety of specific ways we can go about fulfilling our basic needs. There are many possible behavioral patterns and our task as anthropologists is to figure out why, from all the possible patterns, each society exhibits and practices its unique combination, its specific cultural system. I like to visualize all the potential possibilities going into a metaphorical filter, like the filter in a drip coffeemaker. All the unwanted behaviors are filtered out. Those that are wanted, that work for the society in question, pass through and are combined and integrated to form the cultural system. The problem now becomes, what to label the filter? To what single thing may we link all the aspects of a cultural system, as well as the combination that becomes the system itself?

BEFORE YOU CONTINUE READING

1. What is the main idea of this section?

  a. *Cultural systems are completely determined by our biological structure, function, and needs.*

  b. *The variation in cultural systems is due to our biological structure, function, and needs, and the way we go about fulfilling those needs.*

  c. *Cultural systems filter out unwanted behavior that doesn't fulfill our biological needs.*

THE CONCEPT OF WORLD VIEW

4   I think the best label is **world view**. World view is "a set of assumptions about the way things are." What sorts of "things"? Well, as vague as this sounds, just about anything. The nature of the world and its living creatures; the place of humans in the natural world; the proper relationships between humans and nonhumans, between individuals and groups of people; the explanations for why all these are as they are—these and many more items are the "things" with which the world view of a culture concerns itself. World view, as the term implies, must be a view of the world that a group of people knows. It includes their natural world and their cultural world, that is, their cultural system at a point in time as well as the history of that culture, how it got to be the way it is. These two factors, of course, interact as people move around, encounter other peoples, and develop new and different ways to cope with their environments.

5   World view, then, can best be thought of as the collective interpretation of and response to the worlds (natural and cultural) in which a society of people live. All aspects of a cultural system may be seen as derived from, linked to, and supportive of this view of the world. Such a model takes into account both direct adaptive responses that make logical sense as well as the idiosyncratic responses of real people, which may or may not make logical sense to others but which are perfectly reasonable and consistent to the people in question.

6   Obviously, some examples are in order at this point, but not without two words of caution. First, these examples are simplifications. I will be trying to narrow things down as much as possible in order to show what we mean by world view and how it serves as a label for our imaginary filter. In real life, much more would be involved. Second, we must appreciate the difficulty of trying to understand and describe another culture's world view. Remember, world view is not a thing. It is an abstraction, a term we have put on the totality of the collective interpretations and responses of a society of people. One cannot ask members of another culture what their world view is. It is not something people articulate because it is really in the background.

RELIGIOUS BELIEFS AS PART OF A CULTURE'S WORLD VIEW

7   We can, however, open a window onto another group's world view by looking at their religious beliefs. Religion is not the same as world view. Religion is one aspect of a cultural system. But one function of religion in all societies is to allow people to **codify** their world view—to talk about, share, and pass on those assumptions about the way things are. Most, if not all, religions include a creation story (how the world and its people began); the history of a people; stories that indicate a people's relationship to the supernatural, to each other, and to the other species on earth and to the earth itself; and basic rules of behavior. So with these cautions in mind, let's compare two rather distinct world views—that of Arctic peoples with those of certain societies from Southwest Asia (also called the Near East or Middle East) around 10,000 years ago.

8   The peoples of the American Arctic (whom we may collectively refer to as Eskimo, although there is some disagreement over that usage) live in one of the harshest environments of any human group. It's not that the Eskimo are poorly adapted. On the contrary, even before acquiring modern technological items, they were known for their ingenuity and inventiveness at using natural resources cleverly and efficiently to satisfy their needs. They saw themselves not as separate from the land and its

life, but as one with it. As writer Barry Lopez puts it, their relationships with animals, even those they hunt, are "local and personal" and those animals are "part of one's community." But this intimacy with nature comes at a price. The Arctic is never an easy place to live, and the Eskimo saw that world as one over which their control was limited, tenuous, and unstable. They live, says Lopez, with "a fear tied to their knowledge that sudden, cataclysmic events are as much a part of life, of really living, as are the moments when one pauses to look at something beautiful."

Fig. 3.4 Inuit (Eskimo) couple with a seal they have just killed

9   How is this view reflected in Eskimo religion? In other words, how did the Eskimo codify this world view? There are many different Arctic peoples, both in North America and Asia, and so there are many specific individual cultural systems. We may look at a few aspects of one and, because there are certain similarities among peoples of this region, it can represent some generalizations about them all.

10   The Netsilik people live in the Hudson Bay region of Canada. Their name means "people of the seal" because seal hunting in the winter is a major focus of their lives, although they also hunt caribou and fish for salmon in the spring, summer, and fall. The Netsilik express their view of the world by believing that the natural world is under the control of the spirit world and important natural phenomena—as well as all humans and animals—have spirits or souls. There are other spirits with various degrees of control over the world as well. We say technically that the Netsilik, like many hunting peoples, are **polytheistic**—they recognize multiple supernatural beings.

**BEFORE YOU
CONTINUE
READING**

3. The main idea of this section is that a cultural group's religious beliefs ____.

a. *depend on the group's relationship with the animals in its environment, for example, the Netsilik people and seals*

b. *help people systematize their world view, and the description of the Netsilik people's beliefs is an example*

c. *always include the belief that animals and humans have spirits or souls as part of their world view*

THE RELIGIOUS CONCEPTS OF POLYTHEISM AND MONOTHEISM

11   The control of these souls over the physical world helps explain why things are as they are, especially why things can go wrong. Souls are seen as, at best, unreliable and are generally considered evil or capable of becoming evil. Souls that have been wronged can cause misfortunes and thus there are many rules about how they should be treated. A newly killed seal, for instance, must be placed on fresh snow rather than the dirty floor of the igloo. The hunters beg the forgiveness of the spirit. Water is poured in the dead seal's mouth because its soul is still thirsty. Caribou souls are especially sensitive and no work on caribou hides can be done in sight of living caribou. If they see and are offended, their soul will not allow them to be caught. By adhering to these taboos the Netsilik gained at least some sense of influence over their difficult lives. Thus, not only the technology of the Netsilik but more abstract aspects of their culture can be linked to their interpretation of and response to the real world in which they live.

Fig. 3.5 A caribou

12   Contrast this with a second example. In Southwest Asia prior to about 10,000 years ago, people also lived as hunters of wild animals and gatherers of wild plants. The lives of these peoples were not, perhaps, as hard a life as those of the Eskimo, but they were still dependent upon naturally occurring resources in an environment where humans were pretty much at the mercy of nature. Religions in the area were probably also polytheistic, with various supernatural entities controlling important natural phenomena.

13   But about 10,000 years ago, a major cultural event began to take place in the area—the invention of farming. People with this cultural ability had direct control over the most important natural resource, food. Think of how that cultural change would eventually alter the world a people lived in and change their feelings about that world and their place in it. As the long history of farming influenced the physical and cultural worlds of this area, we see a change in world view reflected in three important religious traditions that originated in Southwest Asia—Judaism, Christianity, and Islam.

14   All three of these religious are **monotheistic**, that is, they recognize one supreme supernatural being. That one being, whom we can refer to as God in all three cases, brought about and has control over all natural phenomena, including human affairs. But things are not entirely out of human hands. First, humans are said to have been created in God's image, so humans have a closer connection to the supernatural than do any other living things. In the Judeo-Christian tradition, for example, humans are given dominance over the other creatures of the earth; it is the first human, Adam, who names the animals; and humans are enjoined to multiply and subdue the earth.

15   Second, humans are not so much at the whimsical mercy of the supernatural as they are in Eskimo tradition. In the Judeo-Christian-Islamic tradition, humans may petition God through prayer and action. They can ask God for favors and, if God is pleased and willing, stand a chance of having those requests granted. Humans have some sense of personal control in their dealings with the supernatural, even with an all-powerful being.

16   This is a clear reflection and articulation of a world view in which people are coming to see themselves as having a real ability to know and understand the world around them and to use that knowledge to exercise real control over their world for their own benefit. As humans now have some dominion over the natural world, so God has dominion over humans. As people begin to view the world as clearly divided into the human and the natural, so too is there a division between humans and a single, omnipotent supernatural entity. Gone are the multitude of spirits and souls, fairly equally powerful and able to control aspects of the real world at will and under only minimal influence from people.

ASPECTS OF THE AMERICAN WORLD VIEW

17   Thus, world view is, I think, a useful focus around which we may describe the other aspects of a society's natural and cultural worlds. Doing so allows us to take into account both the practical and the more abstract connections within the integrated whole we call a cultural system. As an exercise, try putting into words some important facets of a modern American world view. Remember that world view is not the same as religion; it's far more abstract. For instance, Americans value individualism. Think about our folk heroes, past, present, real, and fictional. Daniel Boone, Davy Crockett, Paul Bunyan, Harriet Tubman, John Glenn, Muhammad Ali, to name a few, are all embodiments, in their own ways, of the rugged individual we so admire. Still another aspect of the American world view might be the way we value size. We like things big. We have built, at one time or another, the tallest building, the biggest sports stadium, even the

Fig. 3.6 Daniel Boone (1734–1820)

largest shopping mall. We even admire physical size in people. Studies have indicated that taller men are more likely to be hired for some jobs than shorter men, even if height is irrelevant to the work.

18   In summary, a cultural behavior is a concept or idea that is shared among members of a population, transmitted extragenetically through learning, and made possible through artifacts. Culture is the major adaptive mechanism of our species, which we absolutely depend upon for our survival.

▪ ▪ ▪

Checking Comprehension

TEXT ANALYSIS

Sometimes text can be organized visually based on a *metaphor* an author has chosen. Authors often use *metaphors* to help readers understand a new or complex concept. Put simply, a *metaphor* is a comparison of two different concepts in order to make one concept easier to understand or visualize.

A **In paragraph 3 the author has used the metaphor of water passing through a filter in a coffeemaker in order to help the reader understand and visualize how societies select particular behavior patterns. Reread paragraph 3. Check your comprehension of the coffee filter metaphor by labeling the illustration below with the following phrases:**

biological humans

a group's natural environment and cultural environment

metaphorical filter

possible behavior patterns

a specific cultural system

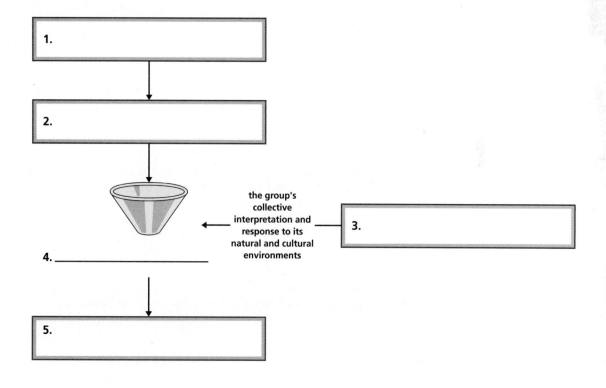

B Refer to the first sentence in paragraph 8 on page 76. Identify the referents.

1. *Whom* refers to _____.

2. *We* refers to _____.

3. *That usage* refers to _____.

C Answer the following questions in complete sentences.

1. What factors help to account for cultural variations among groups of people?

_____

_____

2. What factors might cause a cultural group's world view to change?

_____

_____

3. In what ways does the Netsilik people's view of the world help them survive in their difficult environment?

_____

_____

4. Under what changing conditions might a cultural group's religious beliefs change from a polytheistic to a monotheistic belief?

_____

_____

5. The author approaches religion from a nonreligious viewpoint and describes it as an aspect of a cultural system. What purpose does religion serve, according to the author?

_____

_____

D Review your annotations on pages 74–80. If you have any questions that have not been answered, discuss them now in your class.

SENTENCE FOCUS

As you learned on page 69, it is important to look at the parts of the sentence that connect it to other ideas in the paragraph or text. For example, terms such as *rather, on the other hand, but, although,* and *on the contrary* indicate contrast between sentences and ideas.

Reread the paragraph excerpt. Pay attention to the italicized words. Then circle the correct choice to complete the sentences.

PARAGRAPH 8

¹The peoples of the American Arctic (whom we may collectively refer to as Eskimo, *although* there is some disagreement over that usage) live in one of the harshest environments of any human group. ²It's not that the Eskimo are poorly adapted. ³*On the contrary*, even before acquiring modern technological items, they were known for their ingenuity and inventiveness at using natural resources cleverly and efficiently to satisfy their needs. ⁴They saw themselves not as separate from the land and its life, *but* as one with it. ⁵As writer Barry Lopez puts it, their relationships with animals, even those they hunt, are "local and personal" and those animals are "part of one's community."

1. The use of the term *Eskimo* to describe the peoples of the American Arctic ___.
    a. is acceptable to almost everyone
    b. is not acceptable to everyone

2. The Eskimo live in an extremely harsh environment for which ___.
    a. they are very well adapted
    b. they are not well adapted

3. The Eskimo see themselves ___.
    a. as different from the animals they hunt in their community
    b. and the animals they hunt as part of a single community

Learning Vocabulary

VOCABULARY IN CONTEXT

Reread the paragraphs indicated from the Main Reading to figure out the meaning of the italicized words. Then circle the correct choice to complete the sentences, or write the correct meaning.

Paragraph 1: *variation*

From this context, we can understand that *variation* means ___.
    a. characteristics
    b. mechanisms
    c. diversity

Paragraph 2: *habitat*

From this context, we can understand that *habitat* means ___.
    a. environment
    b. house
    c. climate

Paragraph 7: *codify*

From this context, we can understand that *codify* means ___.
    a. write down
    b. argue about
    c. systematize

USING THE DICTIONARY

Read the following excerpt and dictionary entry. Select the most appropriate entry for the italicized word, based on the context. Then circle the correct choice to complete the sentences. If you choose an entry that includes subentries (for example *1a, 1b, 1c*), indicate the letter as well as the number.

EXCERPT

Most, if not all, religions include a creation story (how the world and its people began); the history of a people; stories that indicate a people's relationship to the *supernatural*, to each other, and to the other species on earth and to the earth itself; and basic rules of behavior.

su·per·nat·u·ral \,sü-pər-'na-chə-rəl, -'nach-rəl\ *adj* [ML *supernaturalis*, fr. L *super-* + *natura* nature] (15c) **1** : of or relating to an order of existence beyond the visible observable universe; *esp* : of or relating to God or a god, demigod, spirit, or devil **2 a** : departing from what is usual or normal esp. so as to appear to transcend the laws of nature **b** : attributed to an invisible agent (as a ghost or spirit) — **supernatural** *n* — **su·per·nat·u·ral·ly** \-'na-chər-ə-lē, -'nach-rə-, -'na-chər-lē\ *adv* — **super·nat·u·ral·ness** *n*

1. In this context, the most appropriate definition for *supernatural* is number ___.

2. Most, if not all, religions include stories that indicate a people's relationship to ___.
   a. God, a god or gods, spirits
   b. a departure from what is normal
   c. things that are attributed to an invisible agent, such as a ghost or spirit

LEARN AND USE WORD FORMS

A Study the word forms in the chart below. If you are not sure about the meaning of a word, reread the text, highlight the words and any of their forms, and try to understand them from context.

VERB	NOUN	ADJECTIVE	ADVERB
adapt	adaptation	adaptive	adaptively
characterize	characteristic	characteristic	characteristically
conceptualize	concept	conceptual	conceptually
express	expression	expressive	expressively
generalize	generalization	generalizable	
interact	interaction	interactive	interactively
interpret	interpretation	interpreted	
invent	invention inventiveness	inventive	
realize	realization	realizable	
stimulate	stimulus (*plural* stimuli)	stimulated/stimulating	
transmit	transmission	transmitted	
vary	variation	variable	variably

B Read the sentences. Choose the appropriate word from the following sets and complete each sentence. Be sure to use the correct tense of verbs in either the affirmative or the negative, and use the singular or plural of nouns. Use each word only once.

adapt	express	invent
characterize	interact	vary

1. The ways in which a cultural group _____ with its environment depends in part on how much control the people feel they have over it.

2. Even cultural groups that live in a similar environment often demonstrate a wide range of _____ in their world view. How can we explain these differences?

3. Cultural groups often _____ successfully to external influences. Sometimes, however, groups find it very difficult to change.

4. Belief in a number of supernatural beings is _____ of a polytheistic religion.

5. Even when natural resources are limited, people can be quite _____ and resourceful.

6. Artists often _____ their cultural beliefs through their artwork.

| conceptualize | interpret | stimulate |
| generalize | realize | transmit |

7. When studying other cultures, we must be cautious about making _____. Even within a cultural group, individuals and their personal beliefs may vary.

8. When people come to a(n) _____ that they have some control over their environment, they tend to develop a monotheistic religion.

9. Cultural groups _____ their supernatural beings in the same way. Some visualize them as human, some as animals, some as part human and part animal

10. One of the defining characteristics of a culture is the _____ of the group's beliefs from one generation to the next.

11. People in different cultural groups may see the same event, for example, a bird flying or a comet ("shooting star"), but they _____ the event the same way. In fact, they may have many different ways of explaining the event.

12. Because of their range of experiences, people may respond differently to the same _____.

FOLLOW-UP ASSIGNMENTS

Before you begin any of the assignments, review the content-specific vocabulary and academic vocabulary below, and look over the vocabulary in the word form chart on page 85. If you are still unsure what any words or terms mean, go back through the chapter and review. As you complete the follow-up assignments, be sure to incorporate the appropriate vocabulary.

Content-Specific Vocabulary

abstractions	culture	monotheistic
artifacts	extragenetic	polytheistic
codify	generalizations	taboo
concepts	ideas	world view

Academic Vocabulary

active	habitat	transmit
characteristic	passive	variation
codify	realization	
feature	supernatural	

Writing Activities

1. In the Introductory Reading, the author expands the concrete concept of an artifact to include abstract artifacts such as religions, governments, and educational institutions. Write three paragraphs. In the first paragraph, review the concept of artifact, and describe both concrete and abstract artifacts. In the second paragraph, describe artifacts that might fit the description of a concrete or an abstract artifact, and explain why you consider them cultural artifacts. In the third paragraph, tell whether you agree with this expanded definition of artifact, and explain your reasons.

2. On pages 76–79 in the Main Reading, the author states that most, if not all, religions include some of the same components. Write three paragraphs. In the first paragraph, describe these components, and state whether you agree or disagree with the author that most religions share them. In the second paragraph, describe at least two religions and give examples to support your position that religions do or do not share these components. In the third paragraph, describe additional components shared by the two religions you have chosen, and state whether you think these components are shared by most other religions as well.

3. Write three paragraphs about your culture's world view. In the first paragraph, identify your cultural group, then describe its environment. In the second paragraph, describe at least one aspect of your cultural group's world view. In the third paragraph, tell whether your cultural group's world view is changing. If it is changing, describe how. If it isn't, explain why you think it is not changing.

Extension Activities

1. Research two cultural groups in different parts of the world. Study their environment, their religious beliefs, and their world view. Compare these characteristics, and create a chart to present and describe to your classmates.

2. Research two cultural groups in the same part of the world, living in the same environment. Study their environment, their religious beliefs, and their world view. Compare these characteristics, and create a chart to present and describe to your classmates.

3. Research one cultural group that particularly interests you. Study the group's environment, religious beliefs, and world view. Compare them to your own. Create a chart to present and describe to your classmates.

4. Conduct research on the Internet. Go online. Use a search engine such as Google, AltaVista, Yahoo, About, or Dogpile. Investigate a topic related to the information you read about in Chapter 3. Choose a topic that especially interests you. You may wish to follow up on one of the questions you wrote on page 63 or page 73. Use key words such as *culture, cultural system, monotheism, polytheism,* and *world view.* Prepare an oral report, a written report, or a poster, and present your findings to the class.

CHAPTER
4

NATURE SHAPING CULTURE

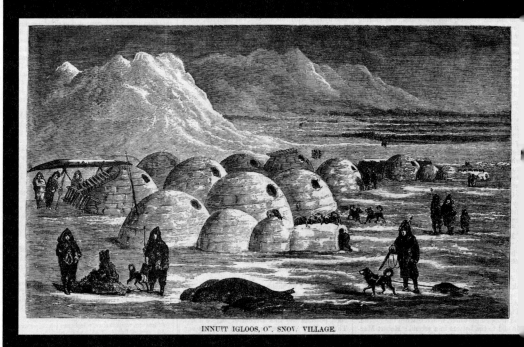

INNUIT IGLOOS, OR SNOW VILLAGE.

Fig. 4.0 Inuit people outside a village of igloos in the Arctic (ca. 1871)

Chapter Readings

Making the World View Real

The Processes of Culture Change

INTRODUCING THE READING

Activate Your Knowledge

A **Work in a small group. Read the following excerpt from the Introductory Reading.**

Religions vary greatly from society to society but the one trait they all have in common is the supernatural. **Religion** is a set of beliefs and behaviors pertaining to the supernatural. By *supernatural* we mean something—a force or power of being—that is outside the known laws of nature.

B **In your group, think of some religions you are familiar with. Make a list of traits these religions have in common. When you are finished, compare your list with those of the other groups. Create a class list.**

supernatural	

Reading and Study Skill Strategies

PREVIEW KEY VOCABULARY

Read the content-specific vocabulary below and determine how well you know each one. Use a scale of 1 to 4, where:

1 = I have never seen or heard this vocabulary before.
2 = I have seen or heard this vocabulary before, but I do not know what it means.
3 = I recognize the vocabulary, but I cannot define it accurately or use it with confidence.
4 = I can give an accurate definition or explanation of this vocabulary, and I can use it appropriately in a sentence.

___ acculturation	___ priest
___ cultural system	___ revolution
___ diffusion system	___ shaman
___ discovery	___ stimulus diffusion
___ egalitarian	___ supernatural
___ hierarchical	___ syncretism
___ invention	

Do not try to learn the unfamiliar items before you begin reading. You will learn them as you work with the chapter.

SCANNING AND SKIMMING

A Before you work with the Introductory Reading on pages 92–94, scan it and write down the headings on the lines below.

Making the World View Real
_____

_____

_____

B Read the following questions, then skim through the appropriate sections of the Introductory Reading to find the answers. Read quickly. Compare your answer with a classmate's.

1. What do all religions have in common?

_____

_____

2. What is one religious difference among cultures?

_____

_____

C Based on the title, headings, and your brief skimming, what do you think you are going to read about in the Introductory Reading?

1. In a few sentences, write your predictions.

_____

_____

_____

2. Write one or two questions that you expect to have answered in the Introductory Reading.

_____

_____

3. Go to page *iii* of the Contents. Read the brief summary of this passage, then decide whether to make any changes to your predictions.

4. Compare your predictions and questions with a classmate's. Keep in mind that you may not agree.

MONITOR READING COMPREHENSION

Most college textbooks do not include **Before You Continue Reading** questions, so being able to monitor your comprehension on your own is important. One way of doing so is to briefly complete a two-part statement such as the following: **The topic is _____, and the main idea is _____**. The first part of the statement focuses on what the passage is about; the second part gives you the opportunity to state the idea, information, or opinion being discussed.

Read the following selection from the Introductory Reading. Monitor your comprehension by circling the correct choice in the *Before You Continue Reading* that follows. Then compare your response with a classmate's.

> **MAKING THE WORLD VIEW REAL**
>
> Beliefs are important, because beliefs are a direct reflection of our world view, our set of assumptions, attitudes, and responses that give rise to and hold together the cultural fabric of our lives. Except for personal survival, nothing is more important or more central to our existence. Religions are our way of making our world view real. They provide us with a means for communicating our assumptions about the world. They give us a medium for formulating values of behavior that correspond to the world view. They provide a framework for putting those values into action in our everyday dealings with one another and with the world around us. Furthermore, they are the way in which we impart our world view to future generations.

BEFORE YOU CONTINUE READING

a. **The topic is** our ability to pass on our world view to our children and grandchildren, **and the main idea is** that our behavior is influenced by the assumptions and attitudes that we have.

b. **The topic is** the importance of religious beliefs as an essential part of our world view, **and the main idea is** that our religious beliefs give us the values we act on in our everyday lives, and which we want to pass on to our children and grandchildren.

c. **The topic is** the importance of personal survival and its effect on our beliefs, **and the main idea is** that our personal survival is important so we can pass on our values to our children and grandchildren.

RECOGNIZING DEFINITIONS

When new vocabulary appears in a textbook, you can often find its definition by looking for certain verbs or expressions. The easiest definitions to see have the expression *defined as* or the verb *be*. For example, in paragraph 2, **religion** is defined as follows:

Religion is a set of beliefs and behaviors pertaining to the supernatural.

Other verbs and phrases such as *mean, is called, is referred to as, is known as, which is*, and *i.e.* are also used to define vocabulary.

Skim paragraphs 2, 8, and 9. Write the definitions of the following words:

1. *supernatural* (paragraph 2): _____

2. **shaman** (paragraph 8): _____

3. **priest** (paragraph 9): _____

INTRODUCTORY READING

The following reading is from Introducing Anthropology: An Integrated Approach. *As you read, highlight the important ideas and details. Highlight all boldfaced and italicized words. Annotate the text. As you read, pay attention to the* Before You Continue Reading *statements, which have been completed as examples.*

Making the World View Real

1   Beliefs are important, because beliefs are a direct reflection of our world view, our set of assumptions, attitudes, and responses that give rise to and hold together the cultural fabric of our lives. Except for personal survival, nothing is more important or more central to our existence. Religions are our way of making our world view real. They provide us with a means for communicating our assumptions about the world. They give us a medium for formulating values of behavior that correspond to the world view. They provide a framework for putting those values into action in our everyday dealings with one another and with the world around us. Furthermore, they are the way in which we impart our world view to future generations.

> **BEFORE YOU CONTINUE READING**
>
> 1. **The topic is** the importance of religious beliefs as an essential part of our world view, **and the main idea is** that our religious beliefs give us the values we act on in our everyday lives, and which we want to pass on to our children and grandchildren.

RELIGION AND RELIGIOUS SYSTEMS

2   Religions vary greatly from society to society but the one trait they all have in common is the supernatural. **Religion** is a set of beliefs and behaviors pertaining to the supernatural. By *supernatural* we mean something—a force or power of being—that is outside the known laws of nature. Thus, one difference among societies is in which phenomena are dealt with by religion—a belief system—and which are dealt with using scientific knowledge.

3   Some natural phenomena are within the intellectual grasp of a group of humans, but others are not. These, however, also need to be explained— which is where forces outside of nature come in. For example, our species has had a science of making stone tools for millions of years. The abilities of the human brain were brought to bear on the problem of selecting and modifying natural objects into artifacts, and the efforts that resulted were quite successful. But what about a phenomenon like the weather? Or the movement of stars? Relatively speaking, we have only recently begun to understand these things scientifically because such understanding requires groundwork in the form of data, experimentation, the generation of theory, and the technology to acquire the data and conduct the experiments.

4   But all these phenomena are important to all people—including our remote ancestors—who seek to explain them. People need to feel some control over the facets of their worlds, even if only in the form of

understanding those facets. So, when some natural phenomenon was beyond the reach of a people's scientific know-how, the supernatural was invoked. If the phenomenon seemed to be beyond the laws of nature, so then was the explanation. Thus, all aspects of their world were put into concrete terms that could be communicated. The world view, in other words, was made real.

BEFORE YOU
CONTINUE
READING

2. **The topic is** <u>religious belief in the supernatural</u> , **and the main idea is** <u>that all people have the need to understand the world around them, either through their own knowledge or, if they don't have an explanation, through belief in supernatural powers.</u>

DIFFERENCES IN RELIGIOUS EXPRESSION AMONG CULTURES

5   Let's look at the ways in which religious expression differs among cultures. Like any cultural expression, religion varies in how it is geared to individual culture systems and in how it changes to keep pace with them. There are, of course, as many specific religious systems as there are cultures, but we can get an overview by noting the variation in some general aspects of religion.

6   In Chapter 3, we discussed the distinction between monotheistic and polytheistic religions and the connection between these and some general types of world view. Polytheism tends to be found in societies like the Eskimo, that interact with their environments on a more personal level, where the people see themselves as one of many natural phenomena. Groups practicing polytheism tend not to have political systems with formal leadership. The supernatural reflects the natural in terms of social organization as well. Monotheistic systems are found in groups that have gained distinct control over their habitats—groups like the early agriculturalists of Southwest Asia. Such groups tend to have a hierarchical political system with formal leadership and full-time labor specialists.

7   Also showing variation is the degree to which the supernatural intervenes in the daily affairs of people. Generally, the more important scientific knowledge is to a people, the less direct is the influence of the gods. Natural phenomena, including human actions, are attributed to natural forces. The degree and kind of intervention may also be related to the complexity of the social order. Especially where there are inequalities in wealth and power, rules for human behavior that are said to come directly from the supernatural may help to maintain the existing order (and, thus, the wealth and power of those who have it).

BEFORE YOU
CONTINUE
READING

3. **The topic is** <u>the ways that religious beliefs vary from culture to culture, depending on their world view</u> , **and the main idea is** <u>that religious beliefs and world views are linked to how a cultural group sees its relationship with, and control over, nature.</u>

8   The kind of person who specializes in taking care of the religious knowledge and welfare of a people varies as well. Here, we may define two basic categories. The first are part-time specialists, usually called on only in times of crises like illnesses. They are often referred to as **shamans**. Shamans receive their powers directly from the supernatural; they are "chosen" for this position. This type of religious specialist is found in egalitarian or less complex horticultural societies where there are no full-time specialists in anything and where religious knowledge, so vital to survival, is known and practiced by everyone. Only special situations, like curing, require the extra help of shamans.

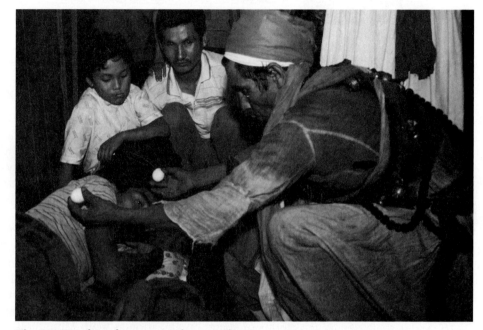

Fig. 4.1 Nepalese shaman treating a patient

9   More complex cultures have **priests**. In anthropological terminology, priests are full-time specialists who train for their profession, learning what is passed down by their predecessors. They are the repositories (holders) of religious knowledge and thus are the persons who know best what the gods say, how best to interpret their words, and how best to get in touch with the gods. Where shamans have real supernatural power, priests have knowledge of the supernatural. Put another way, priests tell us what to do on behalf of the supernatural and shamans tell the supernatural what to do on behalf of us. Priests in the Catholic Church would be an example of priests in the anthropological sense.

10   With priests' knowledge often comes power of a more down-to-earth nature—political power. In some cultures it can be difficult to separate the political system from the religious system and political leaders from the religious ones. This was true among the ancient Aztecs of Mexico, for instance, and to a great extent in medieval and Renaissance Europe.

11   This, then, is what religion is and some of the general ways in which it varies from culture to culture. The richness of this variation, and the explanations for individual expressions within particular cultures, is a broad and complex field.

■ ■ ■

Checking Comprehension

TEXT ANALYSIS

Sometimes text is organized on the basis of similarities and differences. This is the case with the Introductory Reading.

A Reread paragraphs 5–11. Use the diagram on the next page to organize your information.

B Refer to paragraph 6 on page 93. Identify the referents.

1. In the first sentence, *these* refers to _____.

2. In the second sentence, *that* refers to _____.

3. In the second sentence, *their* refers to _____.

C According to paragraphs 5–7, certain societies are more likely to be monotheistic, others to be polytheistic. For each society below, write *M* (monotheistic) or *P* (polytheistic).

1. ___ an organized agricultural society

2. ___ an industrialized society

3. ___ a cooperative society, without labor specialists

4. ___ a society that depends on the environment

D Answer the following questions in complete sentences.

1. What is the *supernatural*?

   _____

2. What are two common needs among all people, regardless of their environment or culture?

   _____

   _____

3. What are the major differences between shamans and priests?

   _____

   _____

4. According to the text, why have priests sometimes gained political power in addition to religious influence?

   _____

   _____

   _____

E Review your annotations on pages 92–94. If you have any questions that have not been answered, discuss them now in your class.

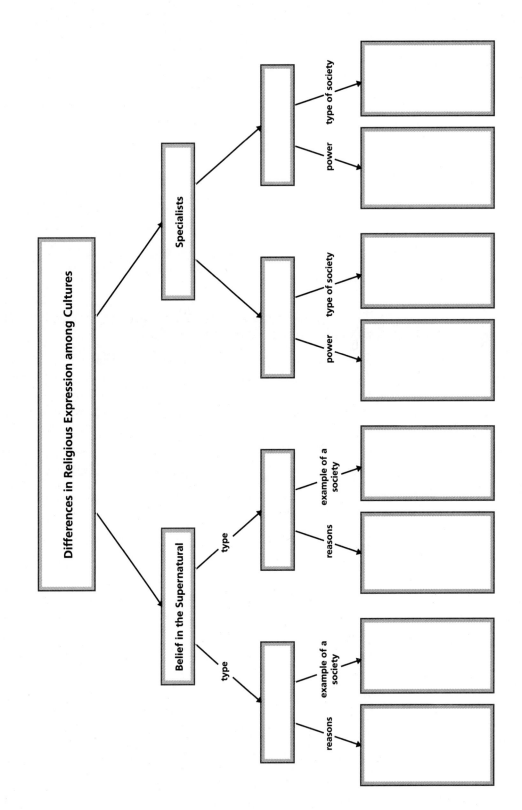

Differences in Religious Expression among Cultures

Specialists

type of society

power

type of society

power

Belief in the Supernatural

type

type

example of a society

reasons

example of a society

reasons

SENTENCE FOCUS

Sometimes sentences may be difficult to understand because of the use of such words as *even if*, or *if . . . then*. Depending on the context, *if* can have different meanings.

A **Read the following examples and explanations.**

1. I have just begun studying Italian. When I go to Italy, I will try to speak Italian, *even if* I can only say a few words such as "hello," "good-bye," and "thank you."

    Explanation: I can only say a few words in Italian, but I will try to speak it anyway.

2. *If* John can save enough money for a vacation next year, *then* he will travel to Southeast Asia.

    Explanation: John's trip to Southeast Asia depends on his ability to save enough money. He needs to save money in order to be able to travel to Southeast Asia.

B **Reread the paragraph excerpts. Pay attention to the italicized words. Then circle the correct choice to complete the sentences.**

PARAGRAPH 4

¹People need to feel some control over the facets of their worlds, *even if* only in the form of understanding those facets. ²So, when some natural phenomenon was beyond the reach of a people's scientific know-how, the supernatural was invoked. ³*If* the phenomenon seemed to be beyond the laws of nature, so *then* was the explanation.

1. People need to feel some control over the facets of their worlds, and ___.
    a. understanding the facets of their worlds is often sufficient control
    b. understanding the facets of their worlds is not sufficient control
    c. understanding the facets of their worlds gives them complete control

2. If a phenomenon seemed to be beyond the laws of nature, ___.
    a. the explanation was never beyond the laws of nature
    b. the explanation was, therefore, beyond the laws of nature
    c. the explanation was a law of nature

Learning Vocabulary

VOCABULARY IN CONTEXT

Reread the paragraphs indicated from the Introductory Reading to figure out the meaning of the italicized words. Then circle the correct choice to complete the sentences.

Paragraph 2: *trait* and *supernatural*

1. From this context, we can understand that a *trait* is a ___.
    a. law
    b. characteristic
    c. advantage

2. *Supernatural* refers to ___.
- **a.** a force not explained by science
- **b.** a conscious, or thinking, power
- **c.** a natural phenomenon

Paragraph 7: *intervene*

From this context, we can understand that *intervene* means ___.
- **a.** interfere, either positively or negatively
- **b.** provide wealth or power
- **c.** maintain order

USING THE DICTIONARY

Read the following excerpts and dictionary entries. Select the most appropriate entry for the italicized word, based on the context. Then circle the correct choice to complete the sentences. If you choose an entry that includes subentries (for example, *1a, 1b, 1c*), indicate the letter as well as the number.

EXCERPT ONE

Groups practicing polytheism tend not to have political systems with formal leadership. The supernatural reflects the natural in terms of social organization as well. Monotheistic systems are found in groups that have gained distinct control over their habitats—groups like the early agriculturalists of Southwest Asia. Such groups tend to have a *hierarchical* political system with formal leadership and full-time labor specialists.

> **hi•er•ar•chy** \'hī-(ə-),rär-kē *also* 'hi(- ə)r-,är-\ *n, pl* **-chies** (14c) **1 :** a division of angels **2 a :** a ruling body of clergy organized into orders or ranks each subordinate to the one above it; *esp* : the bishops of a province or nation **b :** church government by a hierarchy **3 :** a body of persons in authority **4 :** the classification of a group of people according to ability or to economic, social, or professional standing: *also* : the group so classified **5 :** a graded or ranked series ⟨a ∼ of values⟩

1. The definition for *hierarchy* that is most related to *hierarchical* in the excerpt is number ___.

2. A hierarchical political system is based on ___.
- **a.** a group of angels
- **b.** a ruling body of clergy organized into orders or ranks
- **c.** a body of persons in authority
- **d.** groups of people classified according to ability or to economic, social, or professional standing

EXCERPT TWO

Some natural *phenomena* are within the intellectual grasp of a group of humans, but others are not. These, however, also need to be explained—which is where forces outside of nature come in. For example, our species has had a science of making stone tools for millions of years. The abilities of the human brain were brought to bear on the problem of selecting and modifying natural objects into artifacts, and the efforts that resulted were quite successful. But what about a *phenomenon* like the weather? Or the movement of stars?

phe•nom•e•non \fi-'nä-mə-,nän, -nən\ *n, pl* **-na** \-nə, -,nä\ *or* **-nons**
[LL *phaenomenon,* fr. Gk *phainomenon,* fr. neut. of *phainomenos,* prp. of *phainesthai* to appear, middle voice of *phainein* to show — more at FANCY]
(1605) **1** *pl phenomena* : an observable fact or event **2** *pl phenomena* **a :** an object or aspect known through the senses rather than by thought or intuition **b :** a temporal or spatiotemporal object of sensory experience as distinguished from a noumenon **c :** a fact or event of scientific interest susceptible of scientific description and explanation **3 a :** a rare or significant fact or event **b** *pl phenomenons* : an exceptional, unusual, or abnormal person, thing, or occurrence *usage* see PHENOMENA

In the context of this paragraph, *phenomena* may best be described as ___.
    a. facts or events that are observable through the senses
    b. objects that are known from sensory experiences
    c. rare or significant facts or events

INTRODUCING THE MAIN READING

Activate Your Knowledge

Work alone or with a partner.

1. What are some components of a culture in addition to religious beliefs? Make a list.

    _____religious beliefs_____   _____

    _____   _____

    _____   _____

    _____   _____

2. What are some factors that might cause a culture to change? Make a list.

    _____   _____

    _____   _____

    _____   _____

    _____   _____

Reading and Study Skill Strategies

RECOGNIZING DEFINITIONS

As you learned on page 91, writers use various ways of alerting readers to definitions. These include writing *defined as,* using the verb *be,* and using such words and abbreviations as *mean, is called, is referred to as, is known as, which is,* and *i.e.*

Skim the Main Reading. Write the definitions of the following words:

1. *world view* (paragraph 2): _____

2. *syncretism* (paragraph 11): _____

3. *stimulus diffusion* (paragraph 15): _____

SCANNING AND SKIMMING

A Scan the Main Reading on pages 101–105 and list the five processes of culture change in the chart below.

THE PROCESSES OF CULTURE CHANGE		
Process	**Definition**	**Examples from Your Own Culture or a Culture You Are Familiar With**

B Skim the reading for the definition of each process, and write it under Definition in the chart above. Recall from pages 91 and 99 that definitions may be recognized by the use of such words as: *mean, is called, is referred to as, is known as, which is,* and *i.e.*

C As a class, draw the chart on the board. Give an example of each process, from your own culture or from another culture. Be sure to identify the culture you draw on.

D Based on the title, headings, and your brief skimming, what do you think you are going to read about in the Main Reading?

1. In a few sentences, write your predictions.

_____

_____

_____

2. Write one or two questions that you expect to have answered in the Main Reading.

_____

_____

3. Go to page *iii* of the Contents. Read the brief summary of this passage, then decide whether to make any changes to your predictions.

4. Compare your predictions and questions with a classmate's. Keep in mind that you may not agree.

MAIN READING

The following reading is also from Introducing Anthropology: An Integrated Approach. *As you read, highlight the important ideas and details. Highlight all boldfaced and italicized words. Monitor your comprehension by completing the* Before You Continue Reading *statements. Annotate the text.*

The Processes of Culture Change

1   It should be obvious by now that cultures are anything but static and unchanging. Although we can try to describe the interrelationships among the features of a cultural system at any given point in time, many of those features are changing as we're studying and analyzing them. Culture change is the norm, not the exception. Some cultures change slowly. Many change rapidly. But they all change. Think of the changes you've witnessed in your culture.

2   We have already noted some major changes and their effects—things like the beginning of domestication and the change in religious beliefs. But culture change involves smaller changes as well. And any change acts to alter the cultural system of which it is a part, because culture works *as* a system, with all its facets operating together and interacting with one another. All those facets, in turn, are related to the society's *world view*, which is the collective interpretation and response of the people to their natural and cultural environment.

3   How do cultures change? Are there any specific processes that account for changes in cultural systems? The answers to these questions can help us explain changes in the past, understand changes that are going on now, and give us some guidelines for thinking about changes in the future as the rate of culture change accelerates in the modern world.

BEFORE YOU CONTINUE READING	**1. The topic is** _____ , **and the main idea is** _____ _____ .

THE PROCESSES OF DISCOVERY AND INVENTION

4   Every cultural alteration—every new idea or new artifact—must start somewhere. Thus, at the base of all culture change are the related processes of **discovery** and **invention**. Discovery is the realization and understanding of some set of relationships—anything from the nature of fire to the reaction of the people of a society to some aspect of their environment. Invention refers to the creation of artifacts, whether concrete (tools) or abstract (institutions), that put the discovery to use. Discovery is knowledge; invention is application.

5   For example, discovery of the nature of fire was necessary before fire could be used for cooking, light, heat, and scaring away animals. The fact that flint struck with another rock would produce a spark or that wood rubbed against wood would produce heat had to be discovered before fire could be purposely made. Discoveries, of course, may be intentionally sought after (since, as the saying goes, "necessity is the mother of invention"), or they may be accidental. Nor need discoveries—additions to knowledge—be concrete. One may, for example, "discover"—in the sense of proposing an idea—that societies should be based on the premise that each person possesses the right to life, liberty, and the pursuit of happiness. Then one can invent a social system that implements that idea, that puts it into action in the complex, everyday, real world.

6   A discovery may not always lead to all the inventions that outsiders would think of as its obvious applications. The applications of a discovery must fit within the existing cultural system. As a classic example, consider the wheel in Mesoamerica. The properties of the wheel—contrary to the common misconception—*were* discovered in the New World. The idea was just never put to use as it had been in the Old World, where it was used for wheeled vehicles and for making pottery. The only known use of the wheel in the New World prior to European contact was for children's toys—clay animals with axles and wheels. Without domestic draft animals, there was no need to invent wheeled vehicles, and perfectly usable pottery was already being produced without potter's wheels.

Fig. 4.2   Clay toys, Vera Cruz, Mexico (800–1250)

7   Sometimes a discovery is not accepted if it appears inconsistent with some aspect of a cultural system. The discovery by Copernicus, later verified by Galileo, that the earth was not the center of the universe violated mainstream religious interpretations of the Bible, which were said to indicate that the earth did not move. The telescope, however, the instrument Galileo used to gather supporting data for this idea, was readily adopted for acceptable uses such as keeping track of the comings and goings of merchant vessels in the port of Venice.

8   Finally, it is important to understand that, once adopted, a new discovery and its initial applications become part of a cultural system, where their presence brings about changes in the system. Think about such things as the domestication of the horse, the invention of wheeled vehicles, and more recent innovations such as the production and harnessing of electricity; the understanding of the energy within the atom.

BEFORE YOU CONTINUE READING

2. The topic is _____,
   and the main idea is _____
   _____.

THE PROCESS OF DIFFUSION

9   Each society can only discover and invent so much. Thus, the second basic process of culture change is the **diffusion** of discoveries and artifacts, i.e., the giving and taking of culture among different societies. This is thought to be responsible, on average, for 90 percent of a society's cultural inventory. Though we are, by our very nature, an inventive, creative species, we nonetheless rely heavily on borrowed items for stimulating and bringing about change. Societies isolated from outside contact change slowly. Those with greater opportunity for contact—and thus for borrowing—change more rapidly. This emphasis on diffusion is sometimes hard to grasp because once an item is borrowed it is modified and adapted to the borrowing culture and becomes a part of its cultural system. It becomes so firmly a part of that system that we don't think about the fact that it may not have originated within that culture.

10   Cultural ideas and technologies are not, of course, always borrowed intact, nor is everything borrowed that *could* be borrowed. If, to take a hypothetical example, a Native American people from before European contact had seen wheeled vehicles, they may well have rejected the idea of incorporating them since they lacked domesticable large animals to pull them. Other items may be rejected because they conflict with religious or ethical beliefs. Anthropologists Carol and Melvin Ember point out that, although the Japanese borrowed much from the Chinese, they never adopted the idea of binding the feet of women because Japanese culture traditionally abhors any type of body mutilation. Clothing styles seem particularly open to diffusion (American jeans are sought after all over the world), but differences in modesty cause many styles to be rejected. Items that *are* borrowed are usually modified to fit the receiving society's cultural system. So central is wine in French culture that when fast-food restaurants like McDonald's diffused there, wine was added to the menu.

11   Adaptation of borrowed items is often strikingly seen in religion. Because of the cultural and psychological importance of religion, people are obviously reluctant to give up their religious beliefs, even under pressure. Thus, new beliefs are often incorporated into existing ones to produce a synthesis. This is called *syncretism*. Voodoo (or voudou), for example, a religion of Haiti, derives from several West African cultural traditions and is heavily influenced by Catholicism. Part of the explanation for the great variety of specific beliefs and rituals within Christianity is the wide spread of that religion and the synthesis of basic Christian ideas with existing religious traditions of the cultures adopting, or forced to adopt, it. Many non-European expressions of Catholicism still include, at the specific urging of the Vatican, traditional local elements.

BEFORE YOU CONTINUE READING

3. The topic is _____,
   and the main idea is _____
   _____.

ACCULTURATION AND REVOLUTION AS PROCESSES OF CULTURE CHANGE

12   There are two other basic recognized processes of culture change that are, in a sense, extreme forms of invention and diffusion. One is **acculturation,** defined as rapid diffusion under the influence of a dominant society. This may occur voluntarily or by force and with violence. Examples of the latter are all too common. Native Americans, for instance, were quickly acculturated into the European-based society of the colonial powers and later the United States. As just one example, many Indians in the American Southwest still practice Catholicism and have Spanish surnames, a remnant of several hundred years of Spanish presence in the region. Countries conquered during war are forced to take on at least some of the cultural aspects of their conquerors, although the conquerors can also be influenced by the cultures they defeat. For example, when the European Christians conquered and ruled Islamic Spain, from the eleventh through the fifteenth centuries, they found a wealth of written knowledge in science, mathematics, and philosophy, some of it passed down from classical Greece. This knowledge then entered and had a profound effect on Western Europe's history. You will read more about this in Chapters 5 and 6.

13   An example of more voluntary acculturation is the phenomenon of the cargo cults. Peoples of a number of South Pacific island societies, from New Guinea to Fiji, came into brief contact with industrialized technologies during World War II. Liking what they saw, they wanted the benefits of some of that technology, which came to be generally called—borrowing the English word—"cargo." Once the war was over, the islands were left pretty much as they had been. To get the cargo back, peoples of some of these societies took on many of the trappings of Western culture as they remembered them. They began to use English words. They started to dress and mimic the military personnel they had observed, sometimes marching and carrying rifles carved from wood. They worshiped sacred objects—old helmets, dog tags, and other military and personal items the western military had left behind. They created gods to whom they prayed for the return of the cargo.

14   Another process of culture change is **revolution**. Usually thought of in the context of violent overthrow of an existing government—as in the American, French, and Russian revolutions—a revolution can also refer to a radical change in other aspects of society. There are scientific revolutions. The discoveries of Copernicus, Darwin, and Einstein come to mind—discoveries that radically and fairly rapidly changed the very way we think. A revolution in the sense of a process of culture change can, I believe, be thought of as rapid invention—new ideas and applications from within a society (or borrowed and radically adapted from outside) that thoroughly alter that society.

15   These are the processes that bring about changes in cultures. All these processes should not be thought of as independent and separate, of course. They can work together in interaction. For example, the stimulus for an invention can diffuse from another culture, even if the invention itself does not. This, in fact, is known as *stimulus diffusion*. For example, in the early nineteenth century, a Cherokee named Sequoyah invented an alphabetic system for writing his language, stimulated by his knowledge that whites had a means for inscribing their language.

■ ■ ■

Checking Comprehension

TEXT ANALYSIS

A Sometimes text that presents many terms and definitions also presents examples to illustrate them. This technique helps you to remember the terms and definitions, and the differences among them. In the chart below, the names of the processes and definitions from the Main Reading are filled in. Without rereading, try to remember a text example for each. Compare your examples with a partner's, then reread the text to check your answers.

THE PROCESSES OF CULTURE CHANGE	
Processes and Their Definitions	**Examples from the Main Reading**
discovery: the realization and understanding of some set of relationships	
invention: the creation of artifacts (concrete or abstract)	
diffusion: the giving and taking of culture among different societies	
acculturation: rapid diffusion under the influence of a dominant society	
revolution: a radical change in some aspect of society	

B Refer to paragraph 12 on page 104. Identify the referents.

1. In the second sentence, *one* refers to _____.

2. In the third sentence, *this* refers to _____.

3. In the fourth sentence, *the latter* refers to _____.

C Circle the correct answers.

1. What is a defining feature of all cultures?
   a. They change slowly.
   b. They change quickly.
   c. They change.

2. Why is it so difficult to describe features of any culture at a particular point in time?
   a. Because cultures are continuously changing.
   b. Because features of some cultures are difficult to define.
   c. Because features of some cultures are static (unchanging).

D Answer the following questions. Write complete sentences where appropriate.

1. What is the difference between discovery and invention?

   _____

   _____

   _____

2. Why might a discovery or invention not be accepted by a particular culture?

   _____

   _____

   _____

3. What factors help determine whether cultural diffusion takes place?

   _____

   _____

   _____

4. What are some ways that acculturation takes place?

_____

_____

_____

5. Galileo used the telescope to make observations that supported Copernicus's theory that the sun, not the Earth, was the center of our universe.

    a. For what purposes was Galileo's telescope used?

    _____

    _____

    b. Which use of Galileo's telescope was acceptable in the culture of his time? Why?

    _____

    _____

    _____

6. Sequoyah invented an alphabetic system for his language, Cherokee. He based it on the system of writing he had seen for English, even though he could not read it.

Examine Sequoyah's alphabetic system for Cherokee on the next page. Explain why Sequoyah's invented alphabetic system represents an example of stimulus diffusion.

_____

_____

_____

Fig. 4.3 Sequoyah's Cherokee alphabet

E Review your annotations on pages 101–105. If you have any questions that have not been answered, discuss them now in your class.

SENTENCE FOCUS

Sometimes sentences are difficult to understand because they contain a number of clauses and phrases. In such cases, identifying the main subject and main verb, and the direct object if there is one, will help you understand the sentence.

A **Read the sentence below, from paragraph 7.**

> The discovery by Copernicus, later verified by Galileo, that the earth was not the center of the universe violated mainstream religious interpretations of the Bible, which were said to indicate that the earth did not move.

In this sentence, the main subject is *discovery*, the main verb is *violated*, and the direct object is *interpretations*. Now we can add descriptors to the subject and object.

> *The discovery by Copernicus violated mainstream religious interpretations.*

We can add more information to this sentence.

> *The discovery by Copernicus that the earth was not the center of the universe violated mainstream religious interpretations of the Bible.*

Now the sentence is easier to understand.

B **Circle the correct answer.**

Why wasn't Copernicus's discovery accepted even after it had been confirmed by Galileo?
a. It conflicted with a commonly held belief.
b. It did not appear in the Bible.
c. It did not belong to the group's cultural system.

C **Read the following sentence. Underline the subject and main verb.**

Usually thought of in the context of violent overthrow of an existing government—as in the American, French, and Russian revolutions—a revolution can also refer to a radical change in other aspects of society.

D **Circle the correct answers.**

1. What is the subject of this sentence?
   a. context
   b. government
   c. revolution

2. What is the main verb?
   a. thought
   b. existing
   c. can refer

3. According to this sentence, what is a revolution?
   a. the violent overthrow of an existing government
   b. a radical change in some aspect of society

VOCABULARY IN CONTEXT

Reread the paragraphs indicated from the Main Reading to figure out the meaning of the italicized words. Then circle the correct choice to complete the sentences.

Paragraph 2: *alter*

In this paragraph, a synonym for *alter* is ___.
- **a.** change
- **b.** operate
- **c.** interact

Paragraph 3: *account for*

In this paragraph, a synonym for *account for* is ___.
- **a.** understand
- **b.** process
- **c.** explain

Paragraph 5: *intentionally*

1. In this paragraph, a word that has the opposite meaning of *intentionally* is ___.
   - **a.** accidentally
   - **b.** concretely
   - **c.** necessarily

2. From the context, we can understand that *intentionally* means ___.
   - **a.** by accident
   - **b.** on purpose
   - **c.** of necessity

USING THE DICTIONARY

Read the following excerpts and dictionary entries. Select the most appropriate entry for the italicized word, based on the context. If you choose an entry that includes subentries (for example *1a, 1b, 1c*), indicate the letter as well as the number. Then complete the sentences that follow by using the appropriate definition. Make sure your sentence is grammatically correct.

EXCERPT ONE

Invention refers to the creation of artifacts, whether concrete (tools) or abstract (institutions), that put the discovery to use. Discovery is knowledge; invention is *application*.

ap•pli•ca•tion \,a-plə-'kā-shən\ *n* [ME *applicacioun*, fr. L *application-applicatio* inclination, fr. *applicare*] (15c) **1 :** an act of applying: **a** (1) **:** an act of putting to use ⟨~ of new techniques⟩ (2) **:** a use to which something is put ⟨new ~s for old remedies⟩ (3) **:** a program (as a word processor or a spreadsheet) that performs one of the important tasks for which a computer is used **b :** an act of administering or superposing ⟨~ of paint to a house⟩ **c :** assiduous attention ⟨succeeds by ~ to her studies⟩ **2 a :** REQUEST, PETITION ⟨an ~ for financial aid⟩ **b :** a form used in making a request **3 :** the practical inference to be derived from a discourse (as a moral tale) **4 :** a medicated or protective layer or material ⟨an oily ~ for dry skin⟩ **5 :** capacity for practical use ⟨words of varied ~⟩

1. In this context, the appropriate definition for *application* is number _____.

2. Discovery is knowledge; invention _____

_____.

EXCERPT TWO

Each society can only discover and invent so much. Thus, the second basic process of culture change is the *diffusion* of discoveries and artifacts, i.e., the giving and taking of culture among different societies.

dif•fu•sion \di-'fyü-zhən\ *n* (14c) **1 :** the action of diffusing : the state of being diffused **2 :** PROLIXITY, DIFFUSENESS **3 a :** the process whereby particles of liquids, gases, or solids intermingle as the result of their spontaneous movement caused by thermal agitation and in dissolved substances move from a region of higher to one of lower concentration **b** (1) **:** reflection of light by a rough reflecting surface (2) **:** transmission of light through a translucent material: SCATTERING **4 :** the spread of cultural elements from one area or group of people to others by contact **5 :** the softening of sharp outlines in a photographic image — **dif•fu•sion•al** \-'fyü-zhə-nᵊl\ *adj*

1. In this context, the appropriate definition for *diffusion* is number _____.

2. The second basic process of culture change is _____

_____.

LEARN AND USE WORD FORMS

A Study the word forms in the chart below. If you are not sure about the meaning of a word, reread the text, highlight the words and any of their forms, and try to understand them from context.

VERB	NOUN	ADJECTIVE	ADVERB
acculturate	acculturation	acculturated	
adopt	adoption	adopted	
apply	application	applicable/applied	
express	expression	expressive	expressively
incorporate	incorporation	incorporated	
intervene	intervention	intervening	
modify	modification	modified/modifying	
stimulate	stimulus (*plural* stimuli)	stimulated/stimulating	
vary	variation	variable varied/varying	
change	change	changeable changed/changing	
contact	contact		
view	view		

B Read the sentences. Choose the appropriate word from the following sets and complete each sentence. Be sure to use the correct tense of verbs in either the affirmative or the negative and the singular or plural of nouns. Use each word only once.

acculturate	apply	intervene	stimulate	vary

1. In many cultures, people believe that supernatural beings _____ in human affairs. This interference may be positive or negative.

2. The five processes of culture change are _____ when discussing change in any culture, past or present.

3. Anthropologists have recorded many _____ in religious beliefs. At the same time, belief in a supernatural being is always either monotheistic or polytheistic.

4. When exposed to another culture, a group of people may become _____ voluntarily, under pressure, or by force.

5. Inventions, discoveries, and contact with other cultures are all _____ that help effect culture change.

adopt	contact	express	incorporate	modify

6. Whenever a new invention or discovery _____ into a culture, that culture is likely to experience some form of change. The change could be major or minor.

7. When a culture comes into contact with a more complex culture, the _____ of some of the complex culture's ideas and technologies is unavoidable.

8. A culture rarely gives up everything. Instead, a culture makes a range of _____, depending in part on its world view and its environment.

9. Some groups in New Guinea were the last known groups to come into _____ with the outside world. This was in the 1930s.

10. Religious _____ takes many forms. Cultural groups differ in their monotheistic and their polytheistic beliefs.

FOLLOW-UP ASSIGNMENTS

Before you begin any of the assignments, review the content-specific vocabulary and academic vocabulary below, and look over the vocabulary in the word form chart on page 112. If you are still unsure what any words or terms mean, go back through the chapter and review. As you complete the follow-up assignments, be sure to incorporate the appropriate vocabulary.

Content-Specific Vocabulary

acculturation	hierarchical	stimulus diffusion
cultural system	invention	supernatural
diffusion system	priest	syncretism
discovery	revolution	
egalitarian	shaman	

Academic Vocabulary

alter	dominant	intervene
account for	expression	phenomenon
application	influence	(*plural* phenomena)
contact	intentionally	trait
domestication	interact	variation

Writing Activities

1. What have been some culture changes that are a consequence of the production and harnessing of electricity? Write three paragraphs. In the first paragraph, describe what life was like before electricity had been produced and harnessed. In the second paragraph, discuss what became possible as a result of this discovery and invention. In the third paragraph, outline some of the culture changes that are a consequence of the harnessing and production of electricity.

2. Think of an example of a recent discovery or invention that you think will not be accepted in your culture at the present time. Write three paragraphs. In the first paragraph, describe your current culture with regard to the possible use of this discovery or invention. In the second paragraph, outline the changes that might need to occur in your culture before this discovery or invention could possibly be accepted and adopted. In the third paragraph, speculate (guess) how the adoption of this discovery or invention might in itself cause culture changes over time.

3. In this chapter, the concept of revolution does not refer to the violent overthrow of an existing government. Rather, revolution refers to a radical change in aspects of society. Think of a radical change in one aspect of a society that you are familiar with. Write three paragraphs. In the first paragraph, briefly describe the society. In the second paragraph, describe a change or changes that took place. In the third paragraph, explain why this change was radical.

Extension Activities

1. Research Sequoyah and the Cherokee nation online or in books. Find out why his people initially resisted his invention. Investigate the reasons why a culture that had never had a writing system adopted Sequoyah's alphabet.

2. The discoveries of Copernicus, Darwin, and Einstein are examples of discoveries that radically and fairly rapidly changed the very way we think. Research one of these three scientists. Get information about his discoveries. Find out the consequences of these discoveries in effecting culture change. Prepare a report and present it to your class.

3. Several civilizations existed in Mesoamerica prior to European contact, including the Aztecs, the Mayans, and the Incas. Research one of these civilizations or another Mesoamerican civilization that interests you. Find out about that civilization's culture, world view, and religious beliefs. How did each culture change as a result of contact with Europeans? Prepare a report and present it to your class.

4. Research Japanese culture with regard to Chinese influence. Find out what Japanese culture, world view, and religious beliefs were prior to Chinese influence. Find out what the Japanese borrowed from Chinese culture and how this culture diffusion effected culture change among the Japanese. Prepare a report and present it to your class.

5. Conduct research on the Internet. Go online. Use a search engine such as Google, AltaVista, Yahoo, About, or Dogpile. Investigate a topic related to the information you read about in Chapter 4. Choose a topic that especially interests you. You may wish to follow up on one of the questions you wrote on page 90 or page 101. Use key words such as *social organization*, *acculturation*, and *cultural diffusion*. Prepare an oral report, a written report, or a poster, and present your findings to the class.

HOW DOES OUR PLACE IN HISTORY INFLUENCE WHAT WE BELIEVE?

A solar eclipse over Stonehenge, England

117

THE BIRTH OF MODERN SCIENCE

Skills Goals

- *Review skills from Chapters 1–4.*
- *Write a summary.*
- *Understand less common uses of common words and expressions.*

Content-Specific Goals

- *Learn Aristotle's concept of science.*
- *Understand the origin of Western scientific beliefs.*

'They were seen to fall evenly.'

28

Fig. 5.0 Galileo dropping two balls of different sizes from the Tower of Pisa

Chapter Readings

The Aristotelian Origins of Western Scientific Beliefs

The Seventeenth-Century Scientific Revolution

INTRODUCING THE READING

Activate Your Knowledge

Work in pairs or small groups.

A Read the following paragraph about Aristotle.

> Greek philosopher, scientist, and educator, Aristotle (384–322 B.C.) was the son of a physician who personally served the king of Macedonia. At 17, Aristotle entered the Academy of Plato, where he worked and studied for 20 years until Plato's death. He then became the tutor of young Alexander the Great. Eight years later Aristotle formed his own school. Aristotle's aim was to systematize existing knowledge, and to this end he made critical observations, collected specimens, and gathered together, summarized, and classified almost all existing knowledge of the physical world.

Fig. 5.1 Manuscript illumination of Aristotle tutoring Alexander (late Middle Ages)

B Aristotle lived over 2,300 years ago. Consider what people knew about nature, physics, and astronomy at that time. Then read the following statements, and check the ones that you think Aristotle believed.

1. ___ Rocks fall to the ground due to gravity.

2. ___ Rocks fall because their proper place is on the ground.

3. ___ Heavier objects fall faster than lighter objects because they are trying harder to return to their proper place.

4. ___ The Earth revolves around the Sun, and the Sun is at the center of our solar system.

5. ___ The Sun revolves around the Earth, and the Earth is at the center of our solar system.

6. ___ The Earth and the other objects in the universe obey the same natural laws.

7. ___ The Earth and the other objects in the universe obey different natural laws.

C Read the following dictionary entry, which defines the Dark Ages.

> **dark age** *n* (1730) **1 :** a time during which a civilization undergoes a decline: as **a** *pl, cap D&A* : the European historical period from about A.D. 476 to about 1000; *broadly* : MIDDLE AGES **b** *often pl, often cap D&A* : the Greek historical period of three to four centuries from about 1100 B.C. **2 a** *often pl, often cap D&A*: the primitive period in the development of something (in the 1890s, way back in baseball's *Dark Ages* — R. W. Creamer) **b** *often pl, often cap D&A* : a state of stagnation or decline

D What do you know about the European Dark Ages? Use the concept map below to organize your ideas. Add to the concept map as you develop your ideas.

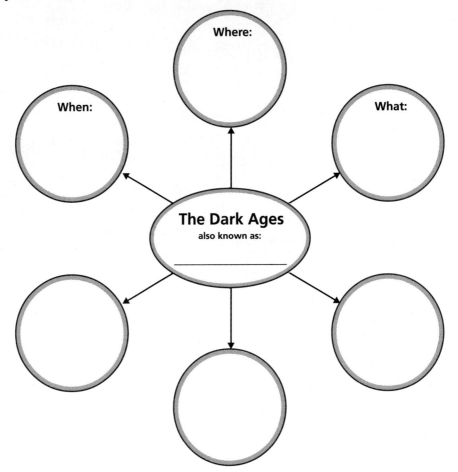

E Put the diagram on the board. Work as a class. Add all the groups' ideas to the diagram.

Reading and Study Skill Strategies

PREVIEW KEY VOCABULARY

Read the content-specific vocabulary below and determine how well you know each one. Use a scale of 1 to 4, where:

1 = I have never seen or heard this vocabulary before.

2 = I have seen or heard this vocabulary before, but I do not know what it means.

3 = I recognize the vocabulary, but I cannot define it accurately or use it with confidence.

4 = I can give an accurate definition or explanation of this vocabulary, and I can use it appropriately in a sentence.

___ Aristotle	___ Galileo
___ astronomy	___ hypothesis
___ the Church	___ Nicolaus Copernicus
___ the Dark Ages	___ revolve
___ eccentric	___ the Scientific Revolution
___ experimentation	___ systematize

Do not try to learn the unfamiliar items before you begin reading. You will learn them as you work with the chapter.

SCANNING AND SKIMMING

A **Before you work with the Introductory Reading on pages 123–125, scan it and write down the headings on the lines below.**

The Aristotelian Origins of Western Scientific Beliefs

_____

_____

_____

B Read the following questions, then skim through the sections of the Introductory Reading under the appropriate headings to find the answers. Read quickly. Compare your answers with a classmate's.

1. What was Aristotle's concept of motion?
   a. Objects are set in motion by an external force, for example, pushing.
   b. Objects move because they are made of Earth, air, water, or fire.
   c. Objects move because they are trying to go where they belong.

2. During the Dark Ages in Western Europe, what happened to Aristotle's ideas?
   a. His ideas were permanently forgotten in Western Europe.
   b. His ideas were eventually adopted and defended by the Church.
   c. His ideas on motion were eventually adopted by Galileo.

3. What was a main reason why science in the seventeenth century was considered new?
   a. Because it involved mathematics, which the old science did not
   b. Because ancient knowledge was too old and uninteresting
   c. Because it challenged people's assumptions and beliefs about the world

C Based on the title, headings, and your brief skimming, what do you think you are going to read about in the Introductory Reading?

1. In a few sentences, write your predictions.

   _____

   _____

   _____

2. Write one or two questions that you expect to have answered in the Introductory Reading.

   _____

   _____

3. Go to page *iii* of the Contents. Read the brief summary of this passage, then decide whether to make any changes to your predictions.

4. Compare your predictions and questions with a classmate's. Keep in mind that you may not agree.

INTRODUCTORY READING

The Introductory Reading is from Conceptual Physical Science *and from* Civilization in the West, Volume B, Fourth Edition. *As you read, highlight the important ideas and details. Monitor your comprehension by completing the* Before You Continue Reading *statement. Annotate the text.*

The Aristotelian Origins of Western Scientific Beliefs

1   Greek philosopher, scientist, and educator, Aristotle (384–322 B.C.) was the son of a physician who personally served the king of Macedonia. At 17, Aristotle entered the Academy of Plato, where he worked and studied for 20 years until Plato's death. He then became the tutor of young Alexander the Great. Eight years later Aristotle formed his own school. Aristotle's aim was to systematize existing knowledge, and to this end he made critical observations, collected specimens, and gathered together, summarized, and classified almost all existing knowledge of the physical world.

Fig. 5.2 Symbols of the four elements: earth, water, air, and fire (seventeenth century)

ARISTOTLE'S BELIEFS

2   Aristotle believed that on Earth all things were changeable and imperfect, while in the heavens all was permanent and unchanging. On Earth the four elements (earth, water, air, and fire) each had its own place, and motion was an attempt to reach that place. Earth was in the center, water above it, air above that, and fire the highest of all the Earthly substances. Therefore an object composed largely of earth, such

as a rock, would, if suspended in air, fall downward, while bubbles of air trapped under water would move upward. Again, rain fell but fire rose. It also seemed to Aristotle that the heavier an object was, the harder it would try to reach its proper place since the heaviness was the manifestation of its eagerness to return. Therefore, a heavier object would fall more rapidly than a lighter one. The motion of heavenly objects, on the other hand, was no attempt to get anywhere. It was a steady, permanent motion, even and circular.

3   Aristotle's systematic approach became the method from which Western science later arose. After his death, his voluminous notebooks were preserved in caves near his home and were later sold to the library at Alexandria.

ARISTOTLE'S IDEAS DURING THE DARK AGES

4   Scholarly activity ceased in most of Europe through the Dark Ages, and the works of Aristotle were forgotten. Scholarship continued in the Byzantine and Islamic empires, and various texts of Aristotle's teachings were reintroduced to Europe during the eleventh and twelfth centuries and translated into Latin. The Church, at that time the dominant political and cultural force in Western Europe, first prohibited the works of Aristotle and then accepted and incorporated them into Christian doctrine. Any attack on Aristotle was an attack on the Church itself. It was in this climate that Galileo effectively challenged Aristotle's ideas on motion, and ushered in a new method of knowing—experimentation.

BEFORE YOU CONTINUE READING

The topic of the first four paragraphs is _____,
and the main idea is _____
_____.

THE SEVENTEENTH-CENTURY SCIENTIFIC REVOLUTION

5   One of the most astonishing yet perplexing moments in the history of Western thought is the emergence of the new science (in the seventeenth century). It was astonishing because it seemed truly new. The discoveries of the stargazers, like those of the sea explorers, challenged people's most basic assumptions and beliefs. Men dropping balls from towers or peering at the skies though a glass claimed that they had disproved thousands of years of certainty about the nature of the universe. But the new science was perplexing because it seemed to loosen the moorings of everything that educated people thought they knew about their world. Nothing could be more disorienting than to challenge common sense. People needed to do

little more than wake up in the morning to know that the Sun moved from east to west while the Earth stood still. But mathematics, experimentation, and deduction were needed to understand that the Earth was in constant motion and that it revolved around the Sun.

6   The scientific revolution was the opening of a new era in European history. After two centuries of classical revival, European thinkers had finally come against the limits of ancient knowledge. Ancient wisdom had served Europeans well, and it was not to be discarded lightly. But one by one, the certainties of the past were being called into question. The explanations of the universe and the natural world that had been advanced by Aristotle and codified by his followers no longer seemed adequate. There were too many contradictions between theory and observation, too many things that did not fit. Yet breaking the hold of Aristotelianism was no easy task. A full century was to pass before even learned people would accept the proofs that the Earth revolved around the Sun. Even then, the most famous of them— Galileo—had to recant those views or be condemned as a heretic.

■ ■ ■

Fig. 5.3 The Grand Orrery by Rowley, London (1715–1728), showing motions of the Earth, Moon, and planets around the Sun

Checking Comprehension

TEXT ANALYSIS

Sometimes text is organized on the basis of a statement that is followed by several examples which explain the statement. However, authors do not always use the words *for example* or *for instance* to introduce an example. You need to develop the habit of looking for explanations. This is the case with the Introductory Reading.

A Reread paragraph 5. Examine part I of the outline of this paragraph, below.

THE SEVENTEENTH-CENTURY SCIENTIFIC REVOLUTION

I. The new science was an astonishing, perplexing time in the history of Western thought.
   A. It was astonishing.
      1. It seemed truly new.
      2. New discoveries challenged people's most basic assumptions and beliefs about the nature of the universe.

   B. It was perplexing.
      1. It upset educated people, who thought they knew about their world through common sense, for instance, that the Sun moved and the Earth stood still.
      2. It required mathematics, experimentation, and deduction to understand that the Earth was in constant motion and that it revolved around the Sun.

II. The scientific revolution was the opening of a new era in European history.
   A. Opening a new era

      1. _____

      _____

      2. _____

      _____

B Now reread paragraph 6 and complete part II of the outline above.

C Which of the following statements did Aristotle believe?

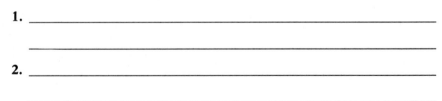

1. ___ Rocks fall to the ground due to gravity.

2. ___ Rocks fall because their proper place is on the ground.

3. ___ Heavier objects fall faster than lighter objects because they are trying harder to return to their proper place.

4. ___ The Earth revolves around the Sun, and the Sun is at the center of our solar system.

5. ___ The Sun revolves around the Earth, and the Earth is at the center of our solar system.

6. ___ The Earth and the other objects in the universe obey the same natural laws.

7. ___ The Earth and the other objects in the universe obey different natural laws.

Check your predictions on pages 119–120. How many of them were accurate? ___

D **Answer the following questions in complete sentences.**

1. Before the Scientific Revolution, why did people believe that the Earth stood still and that the Sun revolved around the Earth?

_____

_____

2. What was needed in order for people to understand that the Sun is at the center of our solar system and the Earth revolves around the Sun?

_____

_____

3. When the new science emerged, what did people rely on in order to understand the world?

_____

_____

4. Why is the new science of the seventeenth century termed a "Scientific Revolution"? In what ways was the new science revolutionary?

_____

_____

E **Review your annotations on pages 123–125. If you have any questions that have not been answered, discuss them now in your class.**

SENTENCE FOCUS

A Sometimes sentences may be difficult to understand because of the use of common words that also have less common meanings or uses. For example, *while* usually means *at the same time* but can also mean *but*. *Again* usually indicates repeated actions but can also signal a reinforcing thought or example.

Reread the paragraph excerpt. Pay attention to the italicized words. Then circle the correct choice to complete the sentences.

PARAGRAPH 2

¹Aristotle believed that on Earth all things were changeable and imperfect, *while* in the heavens all was permanent and unchanging. ²On Earth the four elements (earth, air, water, and fire) each had its own place, and motion was an attempt to reach that place. ³Earth was in the center, water above it, air above that, and fire the highest of all the earthly substances. ⁴Therefore an object composed largely of earth, such as a rock, would, if suspended in air, fall downward, *while* bubbles of air trapped under water would move upward. ⁵*Again*, rain fell but fire rose.

1. In sentences 1 and 4, *while* means ___.
   a. during
   b. at the same time
   c. in contrast

2. In sentence 5, *again* introduces ___.
   a. another example to support the idea in sentence 2
   b. a second description of a type of water found on Earth
   c. a second activity of the same water on Earth

3. According to Aristotle, rain falls because ___.
   a. it is heavy
   b. rain is always in motion
   c. its place is below air

4. According to Aristotle, fire rises because ___.
   a. it is the highest of all the elements
   b. it is lighter than air
   c. fire is always in motion

B Use the concept map below to help you visualize the content of paragraph 2. Part of the concept map has been completed.

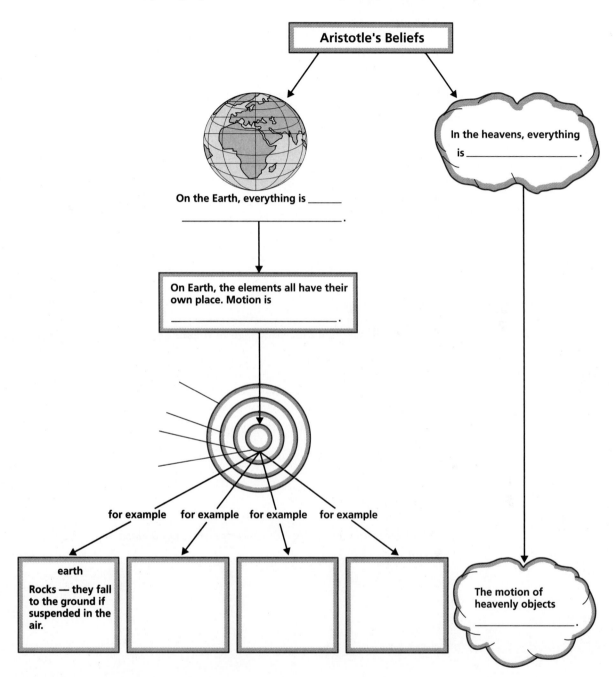

Aristotle's Beliefs

On the Earth, everything is _____ _____.

In the heavens, everything is _____.

On Earth, the elements all have their own place. Motion is _____.

for example   for example   for example   for example

earth

Rocks — they fall to the ground if suspended in the air.

The motion of heavenly objects _____.

Learning Vocabulary

VOCABULARY IN CONTEXT

Reread the paragraphs indicated from the Introductory Reading to figure out the meaning of the italicized words. Then write or circle the correct answer.

Paragraph 1: *aim* and *systematize*

1. In this paragraph, a synonym for *aim* is _____.

2. In this paragraph, *systematize* means _____.

Paragraph 3: *preserved*
Preserved means ___.
   a. sold
   b. written
   c. safeguarded

Paragraph 4: *scholarly, scholarship,* and *ceased*

1. *Scholarship* and *scholarly* refer to ___.
   a. learning
   b. hiding
   c. library work

2. The context makes it clear that *ceased* means _____.

Paragraph 5: *astonishing, perplexing,* and *peering through a glass*

1. *Astonishing* means ___.
   a. complicated
   b. extraordinary
   c. confusing

2. *Perplexing* means ___.
   a. complicated
   b. extraordinary
   c. confusing

3. The context makes it clear that *peering through a glass* is another way of saying _____.

USING THE DICTIONARY

Read the following excerpt and dictionary entries. Then complete the sentences that follow by using the most appropriate definition. Make sure your sentence is grammatically correct.

EXCERPT

The Church was the dominant political and cultural force in Western Europe at the time Galileo Galilei lived (1564–1642). The Church incorporated Aristotle's teachings into Christian *doctrine*. Any attack on Aristotle was an attack on the Church itself. It was in this climate that Galileo effectively challenged Aristotle's ideas on motion, and *ushered in* a new method of knowing—experimentation.

doc·trine \'däk-trən\ *n* [ME, fr. MF & L; MF, fr. L *doctrina*, fr. *doctor*] (14c) **1** *archaic* : TEACHING, INSTRUCTION **2 a** : something that is taught **b** : a principle or position or the body of principles in a branch of knowledge or system of belief: DOGMA **c** : a principle of law established through past decisions **d** : a statement of fundamental government policy esp. in international relations

usher *vb* **ush·ered; ush·er·ing** \'ə-sh(ə-)riŋ\ *vt* (1596) **1** : to conduct to a place **2** : to precede as an usher, forerunner, or harbinger **3** : to cause to enter: INTRODUCE ⟨a new theory ∼ *ed* into the world⟩ ∼ *vi* : to serve as an usher ⟨∼ at a wedding⟩

1. According to the dictionary entry, Christian *doctrine* refers to _____

   _____.

2. Galileo _____ the method of experimentation, which, in the seventeenth century, was a new approach to learning.

WRITE A SUMMARY

A summary gives the main ideas of a text passage. A summary paraphrases, or restates, the information. It should be shorter than the original text. Summaries do not repeat sentences word for word from the passage, and there are few or no details. Summarizing in your own words helps you check how well you have understood what you read. Summary writing is also an important skill for writing essay exams and for explaining ideas from multiple long sources for research papers.

A first step in summarizing a passage is to review your highlighting and your annotation to identify the main ideas of each paragraph or section of text. For example, the first paragraph gives us information about Aristotle. The second and third paragraphs give us more information about Aristotle's beliefs. The fourth paragraph tells us what happened to Aristotle's work during the Dark Ages. The fifth paragraph introduces the idea of the seventeenth-century Scientific Revolution and explains how people responded to it. The sixth paragraph describes some of the effects of the Scientific Revolution. You can summarize all six paragraphs in five sentences, based on the information you highlighted and the annotations you wrote.

Read the following summary of paragraphs 1–4. Then complete it by summarizing paragraphs 5 and 6.

Aristotle was a Greek who attempted to organize all the knowledge of the world that was known in his time, the fourth century B.C. Aristotle believed that everything in the heavens was perfect and unchangeable, whereas everything on the Earth was just the opposite, imperfect and changeable. Aristotle's work was not studied by Europeans during the Dark Ages, but it eventually became known and became a part of Christian beliefs.

_____

_____

_____

INTRODUCING THE MAIN READING

Activate Your Knowledge

Work with a partner or in a group. Answer the following questions.

1. How did people describe the universe *before* the Scientific Revolution? For example, what was thought to be in the center of the universe?

   _____

   _____

   _____

2. What were some of the problems with the Aristotelian description of the universe?

   _____

   _____

   _____

Reading and Study Skill Strategies

SCANNING AND SKIMMING

A Before you work with the Main Reading on pages 134–136, go through it and write down the headings on the lines below. Work with a partner or in a small group.

The Seventeenth-Century Scientific Revolution

_____

_____

_____

_____

B Read the following questions, then skim through the section of the Main Reading under the appropriate heading to find the answers. Read quickly. Compare your answers with a classmate's.

1. What was an advantage of Aristotle's understanding of heavenly revolutions?

_____

_____

2. What was one of the problems with Aristotle's description of the universe?

_____

_____

C Based on the title, headings, and your brief skimming, what do you think you are going to read about in the Main Reading?

1. In a few sentences, write your predictions.

_____

_____

_____

2. Write one or two questions that you expect to have answered in the Main Reading.

_____

_____

3. Go to page _iii_ of the Contents. Read the brief summary of this passage, then decide whether to make any changes to your predictions.

4. Compare your predictions and questions with a classmate's. Keep in mind that you may not agree.

MAIN READING

The following passage is from Civilization in the West, Volume B, Fourth Edition. *As you read, highlight the important ideas and the vocabulary used to express those ideas. Monitor your comprehension by completing the* Before You Continue Reading *statements. Annotate the text.*

The Seventeenth-Century Scientific Revolution

1   The two essential characteristics of the new science were that it was materialistic and mathematical. Its materialism was contained in the realization that the universe is composed of matter in motion. That meant that the stars and planets were not made of some perfect ethereal (abstract) substance but of the same matter that was found on earth. They were thus subject to the same rules of motion as were earthly objects. The mathematics of the new science was contained in the realization that calculation had to replace common sense as the basis for understanding the universe. Mathematics itself was transformed with the invention of logarithms, analytic geometry, and calculus. More importantly, scientific experimentation took the form of measuring repeatable phenomena. When Galileo attempted to develop a theory of acceleration, he rolled a brass ball down an inclined plane and recorded the time and distance of its descent 100 times before he was satisfied with his results.

THE EUROPEAN CONTRIBUTION

2   The new science was also a European movement. The spirit of scientific inquiry flourished everywhere. The main contributors to astronomy were a Pole, a Dane, a German, and an Italian. The founder of medical chemistry was a Swiss; the best anatomist was Belgian. England contributed most of all—the founders of modern chemistry, biology, and physics. By and large, the scientists operated outside the traditional seats of learning at the universities. Although most were university trained and not a few taught the traditional Aristotelian subjects, theirs was not an academic movement. Rather, it was a public one made possible by the printing press. Once published, findings became building blocks for scientists throughout the Continent and from one generation to the next. Many discoveries were made in the search for practical solutions to ordinary problems, and what was learned fueled advances in technology and the natural sciences. The new science gave seventeenth-century Europeans a sense that they might finally master the forces of nature.

BEFORE YOU CONTINUE READING

1. The topic of these two paragraphs is _____,
   and the main idea is _____
   _____ .

HEAVENLY REVOLUTIONS

3   There was much to be said for Aristotle's understanding of the world, for his cosmology. For one thing, it was harmonious. It incorporated a view of the physical world that coincided with a view of the spiritual and moral one. The heavens were unchangeable, and therefore they were better than the earth. The sun, moon, and planets were all faultless spheres, unblemished and immune from decay. Their motion was circular because the circle was the perfect form of motion. The earth was at the center of the universe because it was the heaviest planet and because it was at the center of the Great Chain of Being, between the underworld of spirits and the upper world of gods. The second advantage to the Aristotelian world view was that it was easily incorporated into Christianity. Aristotle's description of the heavens as being composed of a closed system of crystalline rings that held the sun, moon, and planets in their circular orbits around the earth left room for God and the angels to reside just beyond the last ring.

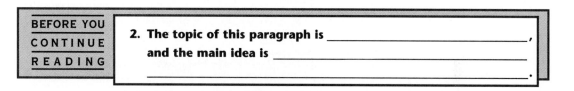

BEFORE YOU CONTINUE READING

**2. The topic of this paragraph is _____,
and the main idea is _____
_____ .**

PROBLEMS WITH ARISTOTLE'S UNIVERSE

4   There were, of course, problems with Aristotle's explanation of the universe as it was preserved in the work of Ptolemy, the greatest of the Greek astronomers. For one thing, if the sun revolved in a perfect circle around the earth, then why were the seasons not perfectly equal? If the planets all revolved around the earth in circles, then why did they look nearer or farther, brighter or darker at different times of year? To solve those problems, a lot of ingenious hypotheses were advanced. Perhaps the sun revolved around the earth in an eccentric circle, that is, a circle not centered on the earth. That would account for the differing lengths of seasons. Perhaps the planets revolved in circles that rested on a circle around the earth. Then, when the planet revolved within the larger circle, it would seem nearer and brighter, and when it revolved outside it, it would seem farther away and darker. That was the theory of *epicycles*. Yet to account for the observable movement of all the known planets, there had to be 55 epicycles. As ingeniously complex as they were, the modifications of Aristotle's views made by the theories of eccentric circles and epicycles had one great virtue: they accurately predicted the movements of the planets. Although they were completely hypothetical, they answered the most troubling questions about the Aristotelian system.

BEFORE YOU CONTINUE READING

**3. The topic of this paragraph is _____,
and the main idea is _____
_____ .**

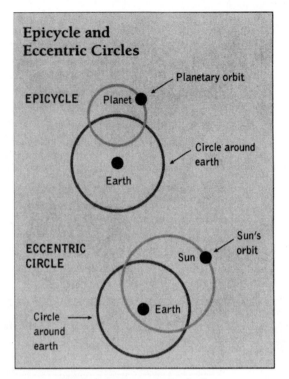

Fig. 5.4 Epicycle and eccentric circles

NICOLAUS COPERNICUS

5   In the 1490s, Nicolaus Copernicus (1473–1543) came to the Polish University of Krakow, which had one of the leading mathematical faculties in Europe. There they taught the latest astronomical theories and vigorously debated the existence of eccentric circles and epicycles. Copernicus came to Krakow for a liberal arts education before pursuing a degree in Church law. He became fascinated by astronomy and puzzled by the debate over planetary motion. Copernicus believed, like Aristotle, that the simplest explanations were the best. If the sun was at the center of the universe and the earth simply another planet in orbit, then many of the most elaborate explanations of planetary motion were unnecessary. "At rest, in the middle of everything is the Sun," Copernicus wrote in *On the Revolutions of the Heavenly Spheres* (1543). "For in this most beautiful temple who would place this lamp in another or better position than that from which it can light up the whole thing at the same time?" Because Copernicus accepted most of the rest of the traditional Aristotelian explanation, especially the belief that the planets moved in circles, his sun-centered universe was only slightly better at predicting the position of the planets than the traditional earth-centered one, but Copernicus's idea stimulated other astronomers to make new calculations.

■ ■ ■

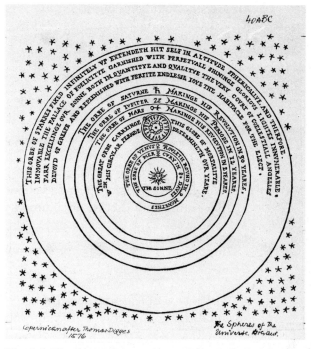

Fig. 5.5 *The Copernican universe (sixteenth century)*

Checking Comprehension

TEXT ANALYSIS

Very often writers introduce paragraphs with a sentence that outlines the paragraph. For example, in paragraph 1, the writer states that the new science had *two essential characteristics* and then tells the reader what they are: *materialistic* and *mathematical*. The reader can expect the author to explain these two features in the rest of the paragraph.

A **Reread paragraph 1. Use the chart below to organize the information in the paragraph.**

THE NEW SCIENCE		
Characteristic	**Realization**	**Explanation**

B **Answer the following questions in complete sentences.**

1. What was the difference between learning through common sense and learning through mathematics, experimentation, and deduction?

_____

2. **a.** Using common sense, what made people believe that the Earth stood still?

_____

_____

   b. Recall the types of learning you studied in Unit 1. Which type of learning does the use of common sense represent? Explain your answer.

_____

_____

3. Which type of learning does the use of mathematics, experimentation, and deduction represent? Explain your answer.

_____

_____

4. In what way did Copernicus revise Aristotle's explanations of planetary motion?

_____

_____

5. What was one of the results of Copernicus's work?

_____

_____

C Complete the following chart with information from the Main Reading.

TOPIC	WHAT ARISTOTLE HAD TAUGHT	THE PROBLEMS WITH ARISTOTLE'S BELIEFS
the nature of the universe		
the center of the universe		
the difference between the Earth and the rest of the universe		

D Review your annotations on pages 134–136. If you have any questions that have not been answered, discuss them now in your class.

SENTENCE FOCUS

In academic writing, authors vary their style to avoid repeating common ways of explaining and defining ideas. This may include the use of less common expressions or expressions with unusual negatives (e.g., *I wasn't alone on the train* means *there were other people on the train*).

Reread the paragraph excerpt. Pay attention to the italicized words. Then match the sentence to the sentence that has the same meaning.

PARAGRAPH 2

¹*By and large*, the scientists operated outside the traditional seats of learning at the universities. ²Although most were university trained and *not a few* taught the traditional Aristotelian subjects, theirs was *not* an academic movement. ³Rather, it was a public one made possible by the printing press. ⁴Once published, findings became building blocks for scientists throughout the Continent and from one generation to the next.

1. Sentence 1
   a. In general, the scientists did not work for the universities.
   b. Most of the scientists lived far from the universities.

2. Sentence 2
   a. Although most were university trained and almost none of them taught the traditional subjects, their subjects were not academic.
   b. Although most were university trained and many taught the traditional Aristotelean subjects, their movement was not an academic movement.

VOCABULARY IN CONTEXT

Reread the paragraphs indicated from the Main Reading to figure out the meaning of the italicized words. Then write or circle the correct answer.

Paragraph 1: *composed of* and *matter*

1. In this context, a synonym for *composed of* is _____.

2. In this context, a synonym for *matter* is _____.

Paragraph 3: *faultless*

In this context, *faultless* means ___.
  a. round
  b. perfect
  c. heavenly

Paragraph 4: *advanced* and *account for*

1. *Advanced* means ___.
  a. proposed
  b. questioned
  c. proved

2. *Account for* means ___.
  a. add up
  b. solve
  c. explain

USING THE DICTIONARY

Read the following excerpt and dictionary entries. Select the most appropriate entry for the italicized word based on the context. Then circle the correct choice to complete the sentences. If you choose an entry that includes subentries (for example 1a, 1b, 1c), indicate the letter as well as the number.

EXCERPT ONE

If the sun revolved in a perfect circle around the earth, then why were the seasons not perfectly equal? Perhaps the sun revolved around the earth in an *eccentric* circle, that is, a circle not centered on the earth. That would account for the differing lengths of seasons.

ec·cen·tric \ik-'sen-trik, ek-\ *adj* [ME, fr. ML *eccentricus*, fr. Gk *ekkentros*, fr. *ex* out of + *kentron* center] (ca. 1630) **1 a :** deviating from an established or usual pattern or style **b :** deviating from conventional or accepted usage or conduct esp. in odd or whimsical ways **2 a :** deviating from a circular path; *esp* : ELLIPTICAL 1 ⟨an ~ orbit⟩ **b :** located elsewhere than at the geometrical center; *also* : having the axis or support so located ⟨an ~ wheel⟩ *syn* see STRANGE — ec·cen·tri·cal·ly \-tri-k(ə-)lē\ *adv*

1. Given the context, the most appropriate definition for *eccentric* is number ___.

2. Which one of the following illustrations shows eccentric circles?

   a.

   b.

   c.

EXCERPT TWO

More importantly, scientific experimentation took the form of measuring repeatable phenomena. When Galileo attempted to develop a theory of *acceleration*, he rolled a brass ball down an inclined plane and recorded the time and distance of its descent 100 times before he was satisfied with his results.

ac·cel·er·ate \-lə-,rāt\ *vb* **-at·ed; -at·ing** [L *acceleratus*, pp. of *accelerare*, fr. *ad-* + *celer* swift — more at HOLD] *vt* (ca. 1530) **1 :** to bring about at an earlier time **2 :** to cause to move faster; *also :* to cause to undergo acceleration **3 a :** to hasten the progress or development of **b :** INCREASE (~ food production) **4 a :** to enable (a student) to complete a course in less than usual time **b :** to speed up (as a course of study) ~ *vi* **1 a :** to move faster : gain speed **b :** GROW, INCREASE (inflation was *accelerating*) **2 :** to follow an accelerated educational program — **ac·cel·er·at·ing·ly** \-,rā-tiŋ-lē\ *adv*
ac·cel·er·a·tion \ik-,se-lə-'rā-shən, (,)ak-\ *n* (1531) **1 :** the act or process of accelerating : the state of being accelerated **2 :** the rate of change of velocity with respect to time; *broadly :* change of velocity

1. Given the context, the most appropriate definition of *acceleration* is number ___.

2. Galileo rolled balls down an inclined plane in order to record ___.
   a. how far the balls traveled in a specific period of time
   b. how much the balls increased in speed as they traveled a specific distance

3. Through his experiments with the balls, Galileo discovered that ___.
   a. the balls traveled a specific distance at a steady speed
   b. the balls traveled increasingly faster as they rolled

WRITE A SUMMARY

Reread the Main Reading and write a summary. Write one sentence for paragraph 1 that captures the main idea. Write one sentence for paragraphs 2 and 3, and write one sentence for paragraph 4. Remember to give the important information, but not details. Refer to the summary of the Introductory Reading on page 132 as a guide.

_____

_____

_____

_____

LEARN AND USE WORD FORMS

A Study the word forms in the chart below. If you are not sure about the meaning of a word, reread the text, highlight the words and any of their forms, and try to understand them from context.

VERB	NOUN	ADJECTIVE	ADVERB
astonish	astonishment	astonishing/astonished	astonishingly
contradict	contradiction	contradictory	
contribute	contribution contributor	contributing/contributed	
dominate	domination dominance	dominating/dominated	
experiment	experiment experimentation	experimental	experimentally
modify	modification	modifying/modified	
observe	observation	observant observable	
predict	prediction	predictable	predictably
revolve	revolution	revolving	
hypothesize	hypothesis	hypothetical	hypothetically
systematize	system	systematic	systematically

B Read the sentences. Choose the appropriate word from the following sets and complete each sentence. Be sure to use the correct tense of verbs in either the affirmative or the negative and the singular or plural of nouns. Use each word only once.

contradict	dominate	predict
contribute	observe	

1. Copernicus probably never _____ the effect his sun-centered view of the universe would have on future scientists.

2. Although Copernicus lived in the sixteenth century, he was an important _____ to the new scientific ideas that emerged during the seventeenth-century Scientific Revolution.

3. At first, people did not accept the fact that the Earth revolves around the sun or that the Earth rotates, because such concepts _____ what they observed and felt.

4. Galileo was able to disprove many of Aristotle's beliefs. However, he had to publicly deny what he believed because at the time, the Church's doctrines _____ European culture.

5. As part of their experiments, seventeenth-century scientists performed many experiments and made many careful _____ of the world around them.

astonish	hypothesize	revolve
experiment	modify	systematize

6. Aristotle's _____ for classifying knowledge dominated the way people viewed the world for many centuries.

7. Galileo's discoveries were eventually accepted, and as a result, scientists greatly _____ their view of the universe.

8. Unlike Aristotle, Galileo conducted experiments in order to test all his _____.

9. Many people were truly _____ by the discovery of moons orbiting Jupiter.

10. Although Copernicus wrote that the sun _____ around the Earth, he did not get into trouble because he published his writing outside of Italy.

11. Aristotle used thinking, observation, and logic to understand and describe the world around him. _____ was not part of Aristotle's scientific methodology.

FOLLOW-UP ASSIGNMENTS

Before you begin any of the assignments, review the content-specific vocabulary and academic vocabulary below, and look over the vocabulary in the word form chart on page 142. If you are still unsure what any words or terms mean, go back through the chapter and review. As you complete the follow-up assignments, be sure to incorporate the appropriate vocabulary.

Content-Specific Vocabulary

Aristotle	experimentation	revolve
astronomy	Galileo	the Scientific
the Church	hypothesis	Revolution
the Dark Ages	Nicolaus	systematize
eccentric	Copernicus	

Academic Vocabulary

academic	aim	observation
acceleration	contradiction	perplexing
advancement	doctrine	scholarship

Writing Activities

1. Why was it so difficult for people in the seventeenth century to accept the new science? Write three paragraphs. In the first paragraph, describe why seventeenth-century people held the beliefs they did. In the second paragraph, write about the challenges to those beliefs. In the third paragraph, outline what was necessary for people to change their minds and accept the new knowledge proposed by seventeenth-century scientists.

2. What culture change processes were at work during the Scientific Revolution in the seventeenth century? Write three paragraphs. In the first paragraph, describe the culture change processes. In the second paragraph, discuss how these changes were a consequence of the scientific discoveries and inventions of the seventeenth century. In the third paragraph, explain whether these culture changes were rapid or slow, and give your reasons.

3. In paragraph 2 of the Main Reading, the author states that "the new science gave seventeenth-century Europeans a sense that they might finally master the forces of nature." What human need were these Europeans attempting to fulfill? How might a sense of mastering the forces of nature change their religious expression? Write three paragraphs. In the first paragraph, outline the human need that these people were attempting to address. In the second paragraph, describe the ways in which these people attempted to master the forces of nature. In the third paragraph, explain how their work might have changed their religious expression.

Extension Activities

1. What events led to the European Dark Ages? What was life like in Europe during the Dark Ages? Research this topic and prepare a report to present to your class.

2. How did Aristotle's works become diffused into European culture at the end of the Middle Ages (the Dark Ages)? Research this topic and prepare a report to present to your class.

3. The Church initially rejected Aristotle's works but ultimately accepted them and incorporated them into Church doctrine. Research the reasons for the Church's change in doctrine, and prepare a report to present to your class.

4. Conduct research on the Internet. Go online. Use a search engine such as Google, AltaVista, Yahoo, About, or Dogpile. Investigate a topic related to the information you read about in Chapter 5. Choose a topic that especially interests you. You may wish to follow up on one of the questions you wrote on page 122 or page 133. Use key words such as *Aristotle, Nicolaus Copernicus*, and *Scientific Revolution*. Prepare an oral report, a written report, or a poster, and present your findings to the class.

SCIENCE AND A NEW WORLD VIEW

Skills Goals

- *Review skills from Chapters 1–5.*
- *Understand language from primary sources, translations, or archaic texts.*
- *Analyze the author's use of questions in readings.*

Content-Specific Goals

- *Learn about the work of Galileo Galilei, Johannes Kepler, and Sir Isaac Newton.*
- *Learn how ways of understanding the world changed in seventeenth-century Europe.*
- *Understand the conflict between Galileo and the Church.*

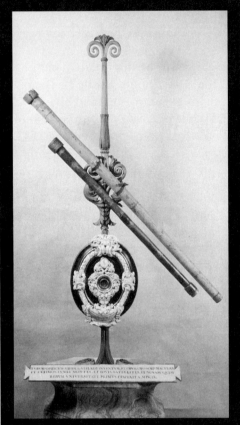

Fig. 6.0a Telescope and lens of Galileo Galilei (1564–1642)

Fig. 6.0b Saturn through a telescope (as Galileo may have observed it)

Chapter Readings

Galileo Galilei's Astronomical Observations

The New Science and the New Scientists

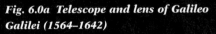

INTRODUCING THE READING

Activate Your Knowledge

Work in pairs or small groups.

A Imagine that you live in the seventeenth century. All your life, you have only looked up at the sky using your eyes. You have never used a telescope or binoculars and have never seen photographs of the sun, moon, or planets. Examine the pictures of the moon and the sun below, and describe them as you see them.

Fig. 6.1 View of the moon from Earth with the unaided eye

Fig. 6.2 View of the sun from Earth without the aid of a telephoto lens, binoculars, or telescope

B Now you have had an opportunity to view the sun and the moon through a telescope. Examine the photographs below and describe them.

Fig. 6.3 View of the moon with the aid of a telescope

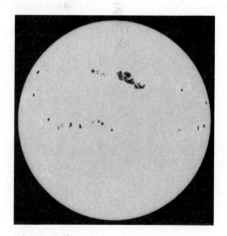

Fig. 6.4 The sun's sunspots

C Which of Aristotle's beliefs do the detailed photos disprove?

Reading and Study Skill Strategies

PREVIEW KEY VOCABULARY

Read the content-specific vocabulary below and determine how well you know each one. Use a scale of 1 to 4, where:

1 = I have never seen or heard this vocabulary before.
2 = I have seen or heard this vocabulary before, but I do not know what it means.
3 = I recognize the vocabulary, but I cannot define it accurately or use it with confidence.
4 = I can give an accurate definition or explanation of this vocabulary, and I can use it appropriately in a sentence.

___ celestial	___ orbit
___ elliptical	___ Scientific Revolution
___ heliocentric	___ telescope
___ hemisphere	___ terrestrial
___ heresy	___ theory of gravity
___ Inquisition	___ theory of inertia
___ laws of motion	

Do not try to learn the unfamiliar items before you begin reading. You will learn them as you work with the chapter.

SCANNING AND SKIMMING

A Before you work with the Introductory Reading on pages 149–151, go through it and write down the headings on the lines below.

Galileo Galilei's Astronomical Observations

_____

_____

B Read the following questions, then skim through the sections of the Introductory Reading under the appropriate headings to find the answers. Read quickly. Compare your answers with a classmate's.

1. What was the first celestial object Galileo observed through his telescope?

_____

2. What did Galileo observe about the moon that conflicted with previously held beliefs about heavenly bodies?

_____

C **Based on the title, headings, and your brief skimming, what do you think you are going to read about in the Introductory Reading?**

1. In a few sentences, write your predictions.

   _____

   _____

   _____

2. Write one or two questions that you expect to have answered in the Introductory Reading.

   _____

   _____

3. Go to page *iv* of the Contents. Read the brief summary of this passage, then decide whether to make any changes to your predictions.

4. Compare your predictions and questions with a classmate's. Keep in mind that you may not agree.

INTRODUCTORY READING

The Introductory Reading is from Civilization in the West, Volume B, **Fourth Edition.** *The passage includes an excerpt from* The Starry Messenger, *which Galileo wrote in 1610. Highlight the important ideas and details. As you read, monitor your comprehension by completing the* Before You Continue Reading *statement. Annotate the text.*

Galileo Galilei's Astronomical Observations

1   No single individual is as much associated with the Scientific Revolution as Galileo Galilei. He made formative contributions to mathematics, physics, and astronomy, but he also served as a lightning rod for the dissemination of the newest ideas. He popularized the work of Copernicus. Among his many accomplishments, Galileo was the first to use a telescope to make scientific observations. In 1610, in his publication *The Starry Messenger*, Galileo wrote about the telescope.

THE TELESCOPE

2   *About ten months ago a report reached my ears that a certain Fleming had constructed a spyglass by means of which visible objects, though very distant from the eye of the observer, were distinctly seen as if nearby. Of this truly remarkable effect several experiences were related, to which some persons gave credence while others denied them. A few days*

later the report was confirmed to me in a letter from a noble Frenchman at Paris, Jacques Badovere, which caused me to apply myself wholeheartedly to inquire into the means by which I might arrive at the invention of a similar instrument. This I did shortly afterwards, my basis being the theory of refraction. First I prepared a tube of lead, at the ends of which I fitted two glass lenses, both plane on one side while on the other side one was spherically convex and the other concave. Then placing my eye near the concave lens I perceived objects satisfactorily large and near, for they appeared three times closer and nine times larger than when seen with the naked eye alone. Next I constructed another one, more accurate which represented objects as enlarged more than sixty times. Finally, sparing neither labor nor expense, I succeeded in constructing for myself so excellent an instrument that objects seen by means of it appeared nearly one thousand times larger and over thirty times closer than when regarded with our natural vision.

Fig. 6.5 Galileo Galilei (1564–1642)

3   *It would be superfluous to enumerate the number and importance of the advantages of such an instrument at sea as well as on land. But forsaking terrestrial observations, I turned to celestial ones, and first I saw the moon from as near at hand as if it were scarcely two terrestrial radii.*

BEFORE YOU CONTINUE READING

The topic of this section by Galileo is _____,

and the main idea is _____

_____.

OBSERVATIONS OF THE MOON'S SURFACE

4   *. . . . Let us speak first of that surface of the moon which faces us. For greater clarity I distinguish two parts of this surface, a lighter and a darker; the lighter part seems to surround and to pervade the whole hemisphere, while the darker part discolors the moon's surface like a kind of cloud, and makes it appear covered with spots. . . . From observation of these spots repeated many times I have been led to the opinion and conviction that the surface of the moon is not smooth, uniform, and precisely spherical as a great number of philosophers believe it (and the other heavenly bodies) to be, but is uneven, rough, and full of cavities and prominences, being not unlike the face of the earth, relieved by chains of mountains and deep valleys.*

■ ■ ■

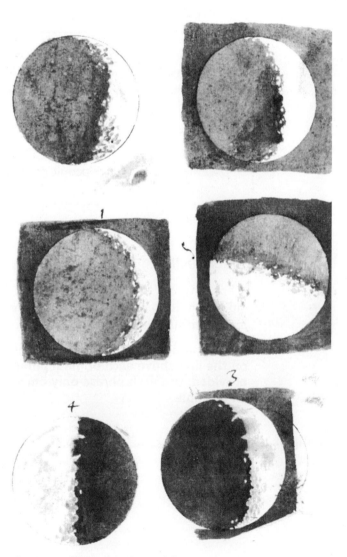

Fig. 6.6 Galileo's drawings of the moon

Checking Comprehension

TEXT ANALYSIS

Sometimes text is sequenced from the general to the specific. This is the case with Galileo's description of the moon. In such cases, the description may be organized in a flow chart.

A Reread paragraph 4. Create a flow chart for Galileo's description of the moon, from the general description to the details. Include the comparisons Galileo uses to help his readers imagine what he has seen.

B Answer the following questions in complete sentences.

1. Was Galileo the first person to construct a telescope? Explain.

   _____

   _____

2. Before Galileo observed the surface of the moon with a telescope, what did people believe about the appearance of the moon's surface?

   _____

   _____

3. What did Galileo observe about the moon's surface? How did these observations challenge people's beliefs?

   _____

   _____

SENTENCE FOCUS

When you read from a primary source, which may be translated and/or very old, you need to remember that the words and the structure of the sentences may seem strange.

Reread paragraph 2. Write the modern phrasing for the original phrase on the line above each original phrase. Select a phrase from the list provided. Use each phrase only once. The first three have been done as an example.

clearly saw things look big and close	look close	that made
far away	make	try very hard
find out how	reports were told	which some people believed
I heard		

PARAGRAPH 2

About ten months ago _____*I heard*_____ that a certain Fleming
1. (a report reached my ears)

had constructed a spyglass _____*that made*_____ visible objects,
2. (by means of which)

though very _____*far away*_____, _____
3. (distant from the eye of the observer)   4. (were distinctly seen as if nearby)

Of this truly remarkable effect several _____,
5. (experiences were related)

_____ while others denied them. A few days later
6. (to which some persons gave credence)

the report was confirmed to me in a letter from a noble Frenchman at Paris,

Jacques Badovere, which caused me to _____ to
7. (apply myself wholeheartedly)

_____ I might _____
8. (inquire into the means by which)   9. (arrive at the invention of)

a similar instrument. This I did shortly afterwards, my basis being the theory

of refraction. First I prepared a tube of lead, at the ends of which I fitted two

glass lenses, both plane on one side while on the other side one was

spherically convex and the other concave. Then placing my eye near the

concave lens I _____, for they appeared three
10. (perceived objects satisfactorily large and near)

times closer and nine times larger than when seen with the naked eye alone.

Learning Vocabulary

VOCABULARY IN CONTEXT

Reread the paragraphs indicated from the Introductory Reading to figure
out the meaning of the italicized words. Then write or circle the correct
answer.

Paragraph 2: *spyglass* and *deny*

1. Galileo's description of a *spyglass* is description of a _____.

2. From the context, we can understand that *deny* means ___.
   a. disagree with
   b. agree with

Paragraph 3: *forsaking*, *terrestrial*, and *celestial*

1. From the context, we can understand that *forsake* means
   a. count; number
   b. leave; abandon
   c. study; examine

2. Galileo's *celestial* observations were of objects such as _____,

   but his *terrestrial* observations were _____.

USING THE DICTIONARY

Read the following excerpts and dictionary entries. Select the most appropriate entry for the context, and choose the best answer to complete the sentence that follows. If you choose an entry that includes subentries (for example *1a, 1b, 1c*), indicate the letter as well as the number.

EXCERPT ONE

It would be *superfluous* to enumerate the number and importance of the advantages of such an instrument at sea as well as on land.

> **su•per•flu•ous** \su̇-'pər-flü-əs\ *adj* [ME, fr. L *superfluus*, lit., running over, fr. *superfluere* to overflow, fr. *super-* + *fluere* to flow — more at FLUID] (15c)
> **1 a :** exceeding what is sufficient or necessary : EXTRA   **b :** not needed : UNNECESSARY
> **2** *obs* : marked by wastefulness : EXTRAVAGANT — **su•per•flu•ous•ly**
> *adv* — **su•per•flu•ous•ness** *n*

1. In this context, the most appropriate definition for *superfluous* is number ___.

2. Galileo felt that it was *superfluous* to list the importance of the advantages of the telescope because ___.
   a. it was not necessary; his readers could easily make a list by themselves
   b. he did not have the space to write them
   c. he thought his readers would think he was wasting time

EXCERPT TWO

The surface of the moon is not smooth, uniform, and precisely spherical as a great number of philosophers believe it (and the other heavenly bodies) to be, but is uneven, rough, and full of cavities and *prominences*, being not unlike the face of the earth, relieved by chains of mountains and deep valleys.

> **prom•i•nence** \'prä-mə-nən(t)s, 'präm-nən(t)s\ *n* (1598) **1 :** something prominent : PROJECTION (a rocky ~) **2 :** the quality, state, or fact of being prominent or conspicuous **3 :** a mass of gas resembling a cloud that arises from the chromosphere of the sun

1. In this context, the most appropriate definition for *prominence* is number ___.
2. The *prominences* that Galileo observed on the moon's surface are ___.
   a. large rocks or mountains
   b. masses of gas resembling clouds
   c. conspicuous objects

WRITE A SUMMARY

Reread the Introductory Reading and write a summary. Write one sentence for paragraph 1 that captures the main idea. Write one sentence for paragraphs 2 and 3, and write a sentence for paragraph 4. Use your own words. Remember to give the main idea, but not details. Refer to the summary of the Introductory Reading on pages 131–132 as a guide.

_____

_____

_____

_____

_____

INTRODUCING THE MAIN READING

Activate Your Knowledge

A Work with a partner or in a group. Read the following excerpt from the Main Reading, about Sir Isaac Newton.

> The greatest of all English scientists was the mathematician and physicist Sir Isaac Newton (1642–1727). He made stunning contributions to the sciences of optics, physics, astronomy, and mathematics, and his magnum opus, *Mathematical Principles of Natural Philosophy* (1687), is one of a handful of the most important scientific works ever composed. Most important, Newton solved the single most perplexing problem: If the world was composed of matter in motion, what was motion?

B Now read Sir Isaac Newton's three laws of motion.

```
                    ┌─────────────────────────────────────┐
                    │   Newton's Three Laws of Motion      │
                    └─────────────────────────────────────┘
```

1
Objects at rest or in uniform linear motion remain in such a state unless acted upon by an external force.

2
Changes in motion are proportional to force.

3
For every action there is an equal and opposite reaction.

C Match the following situations with one of Newton's laws of motion.

1. ___ You are on a moving bus. You pour yourself a cup of coffee from your thermos. The coffee pours into the cup in the same way it would if the bus were sitting at the bus stop.

2. ___ A person holds a rifle to his shoulder and fires. As the bullet leaves the rifle, the rifle recoils (springs back) against his shoulder.

3. ___ A ball is on the ground, not moving. When you kick it hard, it moves quickly.

4. ___ As a bird spreads its wings and pushes down, it moves upward in the air.

5. ___ You are on a moving bus. You pour yourself a cup of coffee from your thermos. As you are pouring your coffee, the bus stops suddenly at a red light. The coffee spills outside the cup.

6. ___ A ball is on the ground, not moving. When you hit it gently, it moves slowly.

D Get together as a class. Compare your responses.

Reading and Study Skill Strategies

SCANNING AND SKIMMING

A Before you work with the Main Reading on pages 158–161, go through the first passage and write down the headings on the lines below.

The New Science and the New Scientists

_____

_____

_____

_____

B Read the following questions, then skim through the sections of the Main Reading under the appropriate headings to find the answers. Read quickly. Compare your answers with a classmate's.

1. What was Tycho Brahe's discovery?

_____

2. What was Johannes Kepler's discovery?

_____

3. What perplexing problem did Sir Isaac Newton solve?

_____

C Before you work with the Main Reading on pages 162–164, go through the second passage and write down the headings on the lines below.

What Happened to Galileo?

_____

_____

_____

D Work with a partner or in a group.

1. Recall Chapter 5. Whose scientific beliefs were part of official Church doctrine?

_____

2. Skim paragraph 12. What was the main difference between the beliefs accepted by the Church and Galileo's beliefs, based on his observations?

_____

3. Skim paragraphs 14 and 15. Was Galileo more interested in advocating a new view of the universe or in destroying Church doctrine? Explain.

_____

E Based on the title, headings, and your brief skimming, what do you think you are going to read about in the two passages of the Main Reading?

1. In a few sentences, write your predictions.

    _____

    _____

    _____

2. Write one or two questions that you expect to have answered in the Main Reading.

    _____

    _____

3. Go to page *iv* of the Contents. Read the brief summary of this passage, then decide whether to make any changes to your predictions.

4. Compare your predictions and questions with a classmate's. Keep in mind that you may not agree.

MAIN READING

The following passages are from Civilization in the West, Volume B, Fourth Edition. *Highlight the important ideas and details. As you read, monitor your comprehension by completing the* Before You Continue Reading *statements. Annotate the text.*

The New Science and the New Scientists

1   In Chapter 5, we read about Copernicus and his description of a sun-centered (i.e., heliocentric) universe. Although he placed the sun in the center of the universe, with the Earth and planets revolving around it, he maintained that they all orbited the sun in perfectly circular orbits. He also did not challenge other Aristotelian teachings. This challenge was left for others to make, based on their observations, mathematical calculations, and logical deductions. These people included Tycho Brahe, Johannes Kepler, Galileo Galilei, and Isaac Newton.

TYCHO BRAHE AND JOHANNES KEPLER

2   Under the patronage of the king of Denmark, Tycho Brahe (1546–1601) built a large observatory to study planetary motion. In 1572, Brahe discovered a nova, a brightly burning star that was previously unknown. The discovery challenged the idea of an immutable, or unchanging, universe composed of crystalline rings. In 1577, the appearance of a comet cutting through the supposedly impenetrable rings punched another hole into the old cosmology.

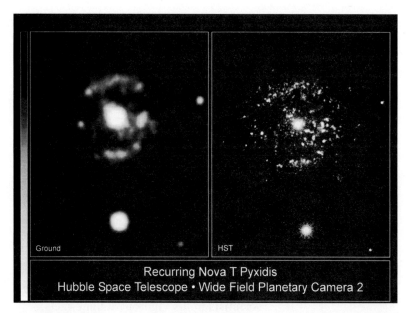

Recurring Nova T Pyxidis
Hubble Space Telescope • Wide Field Planetary Camera 2

Fig. 6.7 A nova

3   Brahe's own views were a hybrid of old and new. He believed that all planets but the earth revolved around the sun and that the sun and the planets revolved around a fixed earth. To demonstrate his theory, Brahe and his students compiled the largest and most accurate mathematical tables of planetary motion yet known. From this research, Brahe's pupil Johannes Kepler (1571–1630), one of the great mathematicians of the age, formulated laws of planetary motion. Kepler discovered that planets orbited the sun in an elliptical rather than a circular path, which accounted for their movements nearer and farther from the earth. More importantly, he demonstrated that there was a precise mathematical relationship between the speed with which a planet revolved and its distance from the sun. Kepler's findings supported the view that the galaxy was heliocentric and that the heavens, like the earth, were made of matter that was subject to physical laws.

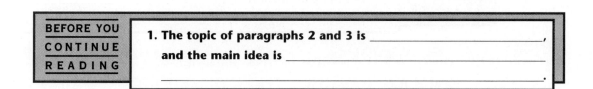

BEFORE YOU CONTINUE READING

1. The topic of paragraphs 2 and 3 is _____,
   and the main idea is _____
   _____.

GALILEO GALILEI

4   What Kepler demonstrated mathematically, the Italian astronomer Galileo Galilei (1564–1642) confirmed by observation. Creating a telescope by using magnifying lenses and a long tube, Galileo saw parts of the heavens that had never been dreamed of before. In 1610, he discovered four moons of Jupiter, proving conclusively that all heavenly bodies did not revolve around the earth. He observed the landscape of the earth's

moon and described it as full of mountains, valleys, and rivers. It was of the same imperfect form as the earth itself. He even found spots on the sun, which suggested that it, too, was composed of ordinary matter. Through the telescope, Galileo gazed upon an unimaginable universe. "The Galaxy is nothing else but a mass of innumerable stars," he wrote. Galileo's greatest scientific discoveries had to do with motion—he was the first to posit a law of inertia—but his greatest contribution to the new science

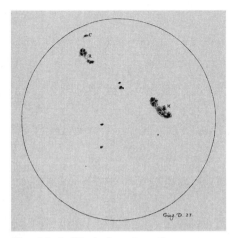

Fig. 6.8 Galileo's drawing of sunspots

was his popularization of the Copernican theory. He took the debate over the structure of the universe to the public, popularizing the discoveries of scientists in his vigorous Italian tracts.

5   As news of his experiments and discoveries spread, Galileo became famous throughout the Continent, and his support for heliocentrism became a celebrated cause. In 1616, the Roman Catholic church cautioned him against promoting his views. In 1633, a year after publishing his *A Dialogue Between the Two Great Systems of the World*, Galileo was tried by the Inquisition for heresy and forced specifically to recant the idea that the earth moves. He spent the rest of his life under house arrest. Galileo insisted that there was nothing in the new science that was anti-Christian. He rejected the view that his discoveries refuted the Bible, arguing that the words of the Bible were often difficult to interpret and that nature was another way in which God revealed himself. In fact, Galileo feared that the Church's opposition to what he deemed as scientific truth could only bring the Church into disrepute.

BEFORE YOU CONTINUE READING

2. The topic of paragraphs 4 and 5 is _____,
   and the main idea is _____
   _____.

SIR ISAAC NEWTON

6   The greatest of all English scientists was the mathematician and physicist Sir Isaac Newton (1642–1727). He made stunning contributions to the sciences of optics, physics, astronomy, and mathematics, and his magnum opus, *Mathematical Principles of Natural Philosophy* (1687), is one of a handful of the most important scientific works ever composed. Most important, Newton solved the single most perplexing problem: If the world was composed of matter in motion, what was motion?

Fig. 6.9 Sir Isaac Newton (1642–1727)

7   Newton came from a moderately prosperous background and was trained at a local grammar school before entering Cambridge University. There was little in his background or education to suggest his unique talents, and in fact his most important discoveries were not appreciated until years after he had made them. Newton was the first to understand the composition of light, the first to develop a calculus, and the first to build a reflecting telescope. Newton became a professor at Cambridge, but he spent much of his time alone.

NEWTON'S THREE LAWS OF MOTION

8   Although Galileo had developed a *theory of inertia*, the idea that a body at rest stays at rest, most materialists believed that motion was the result of the interaction of objects and that it could be calculated mathematically. From his experiments, Newton formulated the concept of force and his famous laws of motion: (1) that objects at rest or in uniform linear motion remain in such a state unless acted upon by an external force; (2) that changes in motion are proportional to force; (3) that for every action there is an equal and opposite reaction. From the laws of motion, Newton advanced one step further. If the world was no more than matter in motion and if all motion was subject to the same laws, then the movement of the planets could be explained in the same way as the movement of an apple falling from a tree. There was a mathematical relationship between attraction and repulsion—a universal gravitation, as Newton called it—that governed the movement of all objects. Newton's theory of gravity joined together Kepler's astronomy and Galileo's physics. The mathematical, materialistic world of the new science was now complete.

BEFORE YOU
CONTINUE
READING

3. The topic of paragraphs 6–8 is _____,

and the main idea is _____

_____.

What Happened to Galileo?

9   Galileo publicized his findings in the *Starry Messenger*. He also popularized Copernicus' work, which included the "new" concept that the Earth, not the sun, is at the center of the solar system. His work conflicted with the beliefs of the Church, which took action against him, and eventually put him on trial. The reading that follows describes what took place.

GALILEO'S EARLY WORK

10   For eight years he had held his peace. Since 1616 he had bided his time, waiting for a change in the attitudes of the Catholic authorities—or, as he believed, waiting for reason to prevail. For a time he had even abandoned his astronomical investigations for the supposedly safer fields of motion and physics. Even there, Aristotle had been wrong. No matter what he touched, his reasons showed him that the conclusions of Aristotle, the conclusions adopted and supported by the Roman Catholic church, were wrong. Now finally, with the accession of Pope Urban VIII, old Cardinal Barbarini, who was himself a mathematician, Galileo felt confident that he could resume his writing and publishing.

11   Galileo's rebellion began early, when he decided to study mathematics rather than medicine. Galileo was fascinated with the manipulation of numbers, and by the age of 25 was teaching at the University of Pisa. There he began to conduct experiments to measure rates of motion. Galileo was soon in trouble with his colleagues and was forced to leave Pisa for Padua.

12   It was in Padua that his real difficulties began. After seeing a small prototype made in Holland, Galileo developed a telescope that could magnify objects to 30 times their size, which made it possible to see clearly the stars and planets that had been only dimly perceptible before. In 1610, Galileo had looked at the moon and discovered that its properties were similar to those of the earth. He had seen four moons of Jupiter, the first conclusive proof that there were heavenly bodies that did not revolve around the earth. Even before he had gazed at the stars, Galileo was persuaded that Copernicus must be right in arguing that the earth revolved around the sun. Now he believed he had irrefutable proof: the proof of his own eyes.

13   From the publication of *The Starry Messenger* in 1610, Galileo became the most active and best known advocate of the Copernican universe. In 1616, he was called to Rome and warned about his opinions. Belief in the theories of Copernicus was heresy, he was told. If Galileo held or maintained them, he would incur a heavy penalty. The Church accepted unequivocally the Ptolemaic explanations of the structure of the universe and could cite innumerable passages in the Bible to support them. It was willful and stubborn to oppose official doctrine, doctrine that had been frequently and fully examined. At first it seemed that Galileo would be

silenced, but the erudite Cardinal Bellarmine, to whom the case had been assigned, wanted only to caution him. Galileo might still examine the Copernican hypotheses, he might still discuss them with his learned colleagues, as long as he did not hold or maintain them to be true.

BEFORE YOU CONTINUE READING

4. The topic of paragraphs 9–13 is _____,

and the main idea is _____

_____.

GALILEO'S CONFLICT WITH THE CHURCH

14   For eight years Galileo kept his peace. When he decided to write again, it was in the belief that things were changing. He created a dialogue between a Ptolemaist and a Copernican. Let the one challenge the other on the most basic points, just as if they were in formal academic dispute. How did each explain the most difficult things that there were to explain, the existence of spots on the sun or the movement of the tides? Especially the tides. . . . If the earth stood still and the sun moved, why were there tides in the seas that moved with such regularity that they could be predicted?

15   Galileo was no heretic. He had no desire to challenge the Church. He would not print his tract anonymously in a Protestant country. Rather, he would create a true dialogue, one with which not even the most narrow-minded censor of the Roman church could find fault. He submitted his book to the official censor in Rome for approval, then to the official censor in Florence. The censors struck out passages, changed some words and deleted others. They demanded a new preface, even a new title: *A Dialogue Between the Two Great Systems of the World*. Finally, in 1632, the book went to press and was an immediate success.

16   Indeed, it was a success that could not be ignored. The Jesuits, who regarded learning and education as their special mission, demanded that action be taken against Galileo. Their teachings had been held up to ridicule; their official astronomers had been challenged; their doctrines had been repudiated. There was much at stake. Galileo's book had not been the vigorous academic dispute that he promised, and it had not concluded with the triumph of Church doctrine over the speculations of Copernicus. No, it had been advocacy. Anyone could see where the author's true sympathies lay. The character chosen to speak the part of Aristotle was not named Simplicio for nothing. Although this was the name of an ancient Aristotelian, it was also a perfect description of the arguments that the speaker advanced. Especially in the matter of the tides, Galileo had reduced the Aristotelian position to nonsense. The Jesuits brought their case directly to the pope and won an investigation, an investigation that they knew would end with Galileo's condemnation.

BEFORE YOU CONTINUE READING

5. The topic of paragraphs 14–16 is _____,

and the main idea is _____

_____.

GALILEO'S TRIAL

17   Although initially Pope Urban VIII was reluctant to prosecute the 70-year-old astronomer, "the light of Italy," ultimately he had no choice. The great war to stamp out heresy was going badly for the Church. The pope needed the support of the Jesuits in Vienna and in Madrid much more than he needed the support of a scientist who had seen the moons of Jupiter. Nevertheless, when the case was turned over to the Inquisition, it proved weak in law. Galileo had only to present the book itself to show that he had received the official sanction of not one, but two censors of the Roman Catholic church. If there was still anything in his book that offended, could the fault be his alone?

18   The argument stymied the prosecutors, who were forced to find evidence where none existed. Resurrecting the agreement between Galileo and Bellarmine, they attempted to make it say that Galileo was under an absolute ban from even discussing the Copernican theories. Either Galileo would agree to recant his views, admit his errors, and beg the forgiveness of the Church or he would be tried and burned as a heretic. But though he could be forced to recant his view that the earth orbits the sun, Galileo could not be forced to change his mind. After his recantation, Galileo was sentenced to live out his days under house arrest. Five years after his death in 1642, his greatest scientific work, *The Two New Sciences*, was smuggled out of Italy and printed anonymously in Holland.

■ ■ ■

Fig. 6.10 Galileo Galilei standing trial before the Inquisition (1633)

Checking Comprehension

TEXT ANALYSIS

When important figures in history are introduced in a text, you will often find similar key pieces of information about each person.

A **Reread paragraphs 2 and 3. Then examine the diagram about Johannes Kepler.**

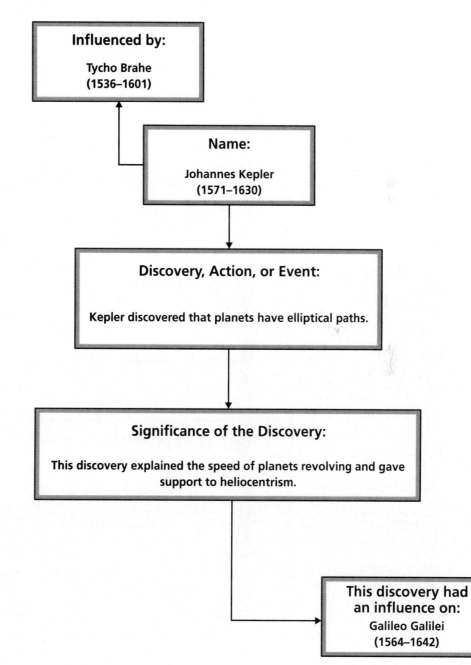

Influenced by:

Tycho Brahe
(1536–1601)

Name:

Johannes Kepler
(1571–1630)

Discovery, Action, or Event:

Kepler discovered that planets have elliptical paths.

Significance of the Discovery:

This discovery explained the speed of planets revolving and gave support to heliocentrism.

This discovery had an influence on:

Galileo Galilei
(1564–1642)

B Now analyze paragraphs 2–8. Complete the diagram about Sir Isaac Newton.

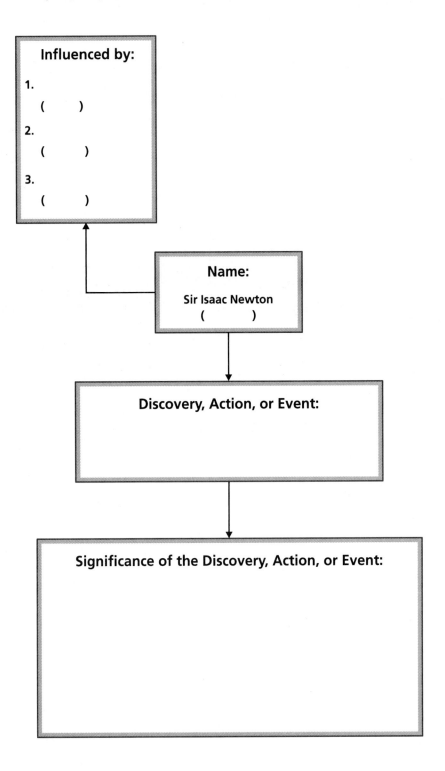

Influenced by:

1.
    (   )
2.
    (   )
3.
    (   )

Name:

Sir Isaac Newton
(   )

Discovery, Action, or Event:

Significance of the Discovery, Action, or Event:

C Answer the following questions in complete sentences.

1. What was Copernicus's major contribution to the new science?

_____

_____

2. In 1610, Galileo discovered four moons of Jupiter. In what way was his discovery conclusive (irrefutable) proof that all heavenly bodies did not revolve around the Earth?

_____

_____

3. What was the nature of Galileo's conflict with the Church?

_____

_____

D Review your annotations on pages 158–164. If you have any questions that have not been answered, discuss them now in your class.

SENTENCE FOCUS

You will notice that some academic texts also include questions in the writing. Authors have several reasons for doing so. Questions:

- stimulate the reader's curiosity

- vary the style of writing

- help the reader understand a problem or side of an argument or controversy

- make a transition to the next section or paragraph.

Reread paragraphs 6, 14, and 17, and the title of the second passage. List the reasons for the author's questions.

PARAGRAPH 6 QUESTION
Most important, Newton solved the single most perplexing problem: If the world was composed of matter in motion, what was motion?

Reason for question: _____

TITLE OF SECOND PASSAGE
What Happened to Galileo?

Reason for question: _____

PARAGRAPH 14 QUESTIONS
How did each explain the most difficult things that there were to explain, the existence of spots on the sun or the movement of the tides? Especially the tides. . . . If the earth stood still and the sun moved, why were there tides in the seas that moved with such regularity that they could be predicted?

Reason for questions: _____

PARAGRAPH 17 QUESTION

If there was still anything in his book that offended, could the fault be his alone?

Reason for question: _____

Learning Vocabulary

VOCABULARY IN CONTEXT

Reread the paragraphs indicated from the Main Reading to figure out the meaning of the italicized words. Then write or circle the correct answer.

Paragraph 1: *orbited*

In this sentence, the synonym for *orbit* is _____.

Paragraph 2: *nova, immutable,* and *impenetrable*

1. A *nova* is _____.

2. In this context, the synonym for *immutable* is _____.

3. From this context, we can understand that *impenetrable* means ___.
   a. round
   b. sharp
   c. impassable

Paragraph 3: *elliptical*

Which of the following shapes is *elliptical*?

a.

b.

c.

Paragraph 6: *magnum opus*

From this context, we can understand that the Latin term *magnum opus* refers to ___.
   a. the title of a book
   b. a scientific experiment
   c. a very significant work

Paragraph 10: *bided his time*

From this context, we can understand that when a person *bides his time,* he ___.
   a. holds his attitudes
   b. believes in time
   c. waits

USING THE DICTIONARY

Read the following excerpt and dictionary entries. Then answer the questions that follow.

EXCERPT

As news of his experiments and discoveries spread, Galileo became famous throughout the Continent, and his support for heliocentrism became a celebrated cause. In 1616, the Roman Catholic church cautioned him against promoting his views. In 1633, a year after publishing his *A Dialogue Between the Two Great Systems of the World*, Galileo was tried by the *Inquisition* for *heresy* and forced specifically to *recant* the idea that the earth moves. He spent the rest of his life under house arrest.

---

her•e•sy \'her-ə-sē, 'he-rə-\ *n, pl* **-sies** [ME *heresie*, fr. AF, fr. LL *haeresis*, fr. LGk *hairesis*, fr. Gk, action of taking, choice, sect, fr. *hairein* to take] (13c) **1 a :** adherence to a religious opinion contrary to church dogma **b :** denial of a revealed truth by a baptized member of the Roman Catholic Church **c :** an opinion or doctrine contrary to church dogma **2 a :** dissent or deviation from a dominant theory, opinion, or practice **b :** an opinion, doctrine, or practice contrary to the truth or to generally accepted beliefs or standards
her•e•tic \'her-ə-,tik, 'he-rə-\ *n* (14c) **1 :** a dissenter from established religious dogma; *esp* : a baptized member of the Roman Catholic Church who disavows a revealed truth **2 :** one who dissents from an accepted belief or doctrine : NONCONFORMIST

---

in•qui•si•tion \,in-kwə-'zi-shən, ,iŋ-\ *n* [ME *inquisicioun*, fr. AF *inquisition*, fr. L *inquisition-, inquisitio*, fr. *inquirere*] (14c) **1 :** the act of inquiring : EXAMINATION **2 :** a judicial or official inquiry or examination usu. before a jury; *also* : the finding of the jury **3 a** *cap* : a former Roman Catholic tribunal for the discovery and punishment of heresy **b :** an investigation conducted with little regard for individual rights **c :** a severe questioning — **in•qui•si•tion•al** \-'zi-sh (ə-) nᵊl\ *adj*

---

re•cant \ri-'kant\ *vb* [L *recantare*, fr. *re-* + *cantare* to sing — more at CHANT] *vt* (1535) **1 :** to withdraw or repudiate (a statement or belief) formally and publicly : RENOUNCE **2 :** REVOKE ∼ *vi* : to make an open confession of error *syn* see ABJURE — **re•can•ta•tion** \,rē-,kan-'tā-shən\ *n*

What was Galileo's crime? Who charged Galileo with this crime? Why? What did he have to do in order to save his own life? Write a paragraph in which you respond to these questions. In your paragraph, demonstrate your understanding of the words and definitions above.

_____

_____

_____

_____

_____

WRITE A SUMMARY

Reread the Main Reading and write a summary. Write one sentence for paragraph 1 that captures the main idea. Write one sentence for paragraphs 2 and 3, and write a sentence for paragraph 4. Remember to give the main idea, but not details. Refer to the summary of the Introductory Reading on page 155 as a guide.

LEARN AND USE WORD FORMS

A Study the word forms in the chart below. If you are not sure about the meaning of a word, reread the text, highlight the words and any of their forms, and try to understand them from context.

Verb	Noun	Adjective	Adverb
compile	compilation	compiled	
formulate	formulation	formulated	
interpret	interpretation		
react	reaction	reactive	
reject	rejection	rejected	
reveal	revelation	revealed revelatory	
challenge	challenge	challenging	
debate	debate	debatable debated	
orbit	orbit	orbiting	
support	support	supportive supporting/supported	supportively

B Read the sentences below. Choose the appropriate word from the following sets and complete each sentence. Be sure to use the correct tense of verbs in either the affirmative or the negative and the singular or plural of nouns. Use each word only once.

challenge	formulate	orbit	reject	support

1. Sir Isaac Newton _____ three laws of motion in order to account for the motion of all objects, from a falling apple to the movement of planets.

2. Galileo believed he had very strong evidence in support of Copernicus's sun-centered view of the universe. In spite of his evidence, the Church _____ his conclusions, for example, that the sun and moon were imperfect and that Jupiter had moons.

3. Galileo _____ the Church's beliefs. He insisted that his discoveries did not refute the words of the Bible.

4. Many scientists, both in Italy and in other countries, were very _____ of Galileo. Some tried to help him, but in the end, he remained under house arrest for the rest of his life.

5. When Johannes Kepler discovered that the _____ of planets was elliptical, he made a major contribution to scientific knowledge.

compile	debate	interpret	react	reveal

6. Newton understood that every action has an equal and opposite _____.

7. Galileo carefully _____ all his observations in his notebooks, many of which are preserved in the Vatican Library in Rome.

8. Galileo believed that God _____ himself through the order he imposed on the universe. The Church held that God showed himself through the Bible.

9. The decisions of the Church were not _____. Everyone had to accept them without comment. Outside Italy, however, the Church's influence was not quite as strong.

10. The Church held that _____ the Bible was its domain, and that people must accept its explanations.

FOLLOW-UP ASSIGNMENTS

Before you begin any of the assignments, review the content-specific vocabulary and academic vocabulary below, and look over the vocabulary in the word form chart on page 170. If you are still unsure what any words or terms mean, go back through the chapter and review. As you complete the follow-up assignments, be sure to incorporate the appropriate vocabulary.

Content-Specific Vocabulary

celestial	Inquisition	telescope
elliptical	laws of motion	terrestrial
heliocentric	orbit	theory of gravity
hemisphere	Scientific	theory of inertia
heresy	Revolution	

Academic Vocabulary

credence	immutable	observation
debate	impenetrable	prominence
deny	instrument	recant
dissemination	interpret	superfluous
enumeration		

Writing Activities

1. Newton's concept of force and laws of motion are well known. Review his work in the Main Reading on page 161. Write three paragraphs. In the first paragraph, explain Newton's first law of motion, and give an example. In the second paragraph, explain Newton's second law of motion, and give an example. In the third paragraph, explain Newton's third law of motion, and give an example.

2. Which were the most important discoveries or inventions of the Scientific Revolution? Write three paragraphs. In the first paragraph, describe the discoveries or inventions you have chosen. In the second paragraph, explain why they were important. In the third paragraph, explain why they have significance even today.

3. In this chapter you learned how important discoveries help lead to other important discoveries. Write three paragraphs. In the first paragraph, briefly outline the discoveries described in this chapter. In the second paragraph, trace how each discovery paved the way for the next discovery. In the third paragraph, describe how such a process of discovery has taken place in our own time.

Extension Activities

1. Study Galileo's drawings of the moon below. Use the vocabulary listed below to describe the surface of the moon. Use any one of the six drawings.

cavities	light part	uneven
chain(s) of mountains	mountain peak(s)	valleys
dark part	prominence(s)	

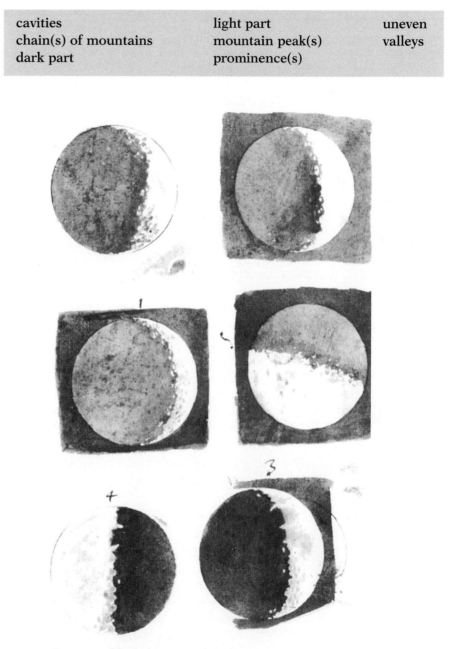

Fig. 6.11 Galileo's drawings of the moon

2. Galileo made a number of discoveries, including the four largest moons of Jupiter. He illustrated his observations in his writings. Research one of Galileo's other achievements. Prepare an oral report, a written report, or a poster, and present your findings to the class.

3. Conduct research on the Internet. Go online. Use a search engine such as Google, AltaVista, Yahoo, About, or Dogpile. Investigate a topic related to the information you read about in Chapter 6. Choose a topic that especially interests you. You may wish to follow up on one of the questions you wrote on page 149 or page 158. Use key words such as *Copernicus, Tycho Brahe, Johannes Kepler, Galileo Galilei, Sir Isaac Newton, laws of motion, Scientific Revolution*, and *planetary motion*. Prepare an oral report, a written report, or a poster, and present your findings to the class.

HOW DO CULTURE AND HISTORY INFLUENCE ART?

The Parthenon (450 B.C.), Athens, Greece. The temple shows fluted columns and a sculpted frieze above the columns.

The Arch of Titus (81 A.D.) Rome, Italy. The structure shows a rounded arch and an inscription.

THE RISE OF
THE WESTERN ARTIST

Skills Goals

- *Review skills from Chapters 1–6.*
- *Recognize and understand the passive voice.*

Content-Specific Goals

- *Learn the changing attitudes toward artists in classical Greece and in classical Rome, in medieval Europe, and in seventeenth-century Europe.*
- *Understand the influence of classical Greek and classical Roman art and architecture on European art and architecture.*
- *Understand the development of perspective in European art.*
- *Learn about Renaissance art in Italy and in Flanders.*

Fig. 7.0 Bronze statue of Hercules and Antaeus by Pallaiuolo (ca. 1470)

Chapter Readings

Art and Artists in History

The Early Renaissance in Italy and Flanders

INTRODUCING THE READING

Activate Your Knowledge

Work alone or in a small group. Answer the following questions.

Fig. 7.1 The tomb of Leonardo Bruni by Rossellino (ca. 1445)

1. The bronze statue of *Hercules and Antaeus* on page 176 shows two figures from Greek mythology in a struggle to the death. Hercules (wearing his characteristic lion's skin) is lifting Antaeus off the ground, depriving him of contact with Mother Earth, his mother and the source of his strength. Their struggle is evident in their faces, in their posture, and in the overall effect of the piece.

   The statue was made by a fifteenth-century artist who was hired to create it by a wealthy Italian family. Why do you think the subject of mortal struggle might have interested Italians at that time?

2. Examine the two photographs of classical Greek and classical Roman architecture on page 175. Then examine the photograph on the left. In what ways did the fifteenth-century artist copy classical styles when creating Bruni's tomb? In what ways does the tomb reflect fifteenth-century Italian culture?

Reading and Study Skill Strategies

Read the content-specific vocabulary below and determine how well you know each one. Use a scale of 1 to 4, where:

1 = I have never seen or heard this vocabulary before.
2 = I have seen or heard this vocabulary before, but I do not know what it means.
3 = I recognize the vocabulary, but I cannot define it accurately or use it with confidence.
4 = I can give an accurate definition or explanation of this vocabulary, and I can use it appropriately in a sentence.

___ aesthetic	___ mercantile class
___ antiquity	___ merchant society
___ artist	___ Middle Ages
___ guild	___ perspective
___ humanism	___ Renaissance
___ liberal arts	___ vanishing-point perspective
___ medieval	

Do not try to learn the unfamiliar items before you begin reading. You will learn them as you work with the chapter.

SCANNING AND SKIMMING

A Before you work with the Introductory Reading on pages 180–182, go through it and write down the headings on the lines below.

Art and Artists in History

_____

_____

_____

_____

B Read the following questions. Then skim through the sections of the reading under the appropriate headings to find the answers. Read quickly. Compare your answers with a classmate's.

1. How were artists regarded in ancient Greece and Rome?

_____

2. How were artists regarded during the Middle Ages?

_____

3. How were artists regarded during the Renaissance?

_____

C Based on the title, headings, and your brief skimming, what do you think you are going to read about in the Introductory Reading?

1. In a few sentences, write your predictions.

_____

_____

_____

2. Write one or two questions that you expect to have answered in the Introductory Reading.

_____

_____

3. Go to page *iv* of the Contents. Read the brief summary of this passage, then decide whether to make any changes to your predictions.

4. Compare your predictions and questions with a classmate's. Keep in mind that you may not agree.

RECOGNIZE AND UNDERSTAND THE PASSIVE VOICE

When you read academic texts, you will often encounter sentences in the passive voice. The passive voice consists of the verb *be* in any tense and the past participle of a verb. Most passive voice sentences do not clearly identify the *agent* (who or what is performing the action). A writer will use the passive voice when the agent is not known or not important, or to emphasize the action rather than the agent of the action. Here are several examples from the Introductory Reading:

- The word art is *derived* from the Latin *ars*, meaning either "manual skills" or "professional activity." (The agent is not known.)

- The term art *has* historically *been used* very broadly. (The agent is not important.)

- As early as the classical world of ancient Greece and Rome, the making of art *was* generally *viewed* as a manual profession taught in workshops. (The writer is focusing on the way art was *viewed*.)

Read the paragraph below. Highlight the passive voice. Then answer the questions.

> ¹Virtually all cultures, ancient or modern, have nurtured specialists who design and/or embellish everday items or materials used in ritual. ²Whether Hopi, African, Mesoamerican, European, or Asian, these men and women were highly skilled workers. ³Sometimes those who were considered best at such expression were recognized as "artists" and were elevated in their society to a high level of regard; in some cultures they were encouraged to sign their works. ⁴Although not all these creators are recognized as artists, the visual arts—grand or modest, public or private, religious or secular—are a regular feature of human culture, and those who create these works are fundamental to most societies. ⁵Individuals in some cultures, for example fifth-century China and fifteenth-century Italy, began to write down their aesthetic aspirations and deeply held values as expressed in the visual arts.

1. Who was recognized and elevated?
   a. ancient specialists
   b. the best-skilled workers
   c. ancient men and women

2. Who recognized and elevated them?
   a. men and women
   b. the leaders of rituals
   c. society

3. Who encouraged them to sign their work?
   a. men and women
   b. the leaders of rituals
   c. society

INTRODUCTORY READING

The following reading is from Art Past, Art Present. *As you read, highlight the important ideas and the vocabulary used to express those ideas. Monitor your comprehension by completing the* Before You Continue Reading *statements. Annotate the text.*

Art and Artists in History

1   Virtually all cultures, ancient or modern, have nurtured specialists who design and/or embellish everday items or materials used in ritual. Whether Hopi, African, Mesoamerican, European, or Asian, these men and women were highly skilled workers. Sometimes those who were considered best at such expression were recognized as "artists" and were elevated in their society to a high level of regard; in some cultures they were encouraged to sign their works. Although not all these creators are recognized as artists, the visual arts—grand or modest, public or private, religious or secular—are a regular feature of human culture, and those who create these works are fundamental to most societies. Individuals in some cultures, for example fifth-century China and fifteenth-century Italy, began to write down their aesthetic aspirations and deeply held values as expressed in the visual arts.

2   Throughout most of Western history, definitions of art were different from our modern view. The word *art* is derived from the Latin *ars*, meaning either "manual skills" or "professional activity." The term has historically been used broadly, encompassing what we now think of as the sciences, as well as many practical handicrafts and occupations. An artist, for example, might practice the art of painting, while a physician practices the art of medicine.

BEFORE YOU CONTINUE READING

1. The topic of paragraphs 1 and 2 is _____,

and the main idea is _____

_____.

ARTISTS IN ANCIENT GREECE AND ROME

3   As early as the classical world of ancient Greece and Rome, the making of art was generally viewed as a manual profession which was taught in workshops, and it was not related to the more esteemed liberal arts—mathematics, grammar, philosophy, and logic—which were distinguished by intellectual, speculative thinking.

ARTISTS IN THE MIDDLE AGES

4   During the Middle Ages in the West, from about 500 to 1500 C.E., art continued to be identified as a manual profession. Artists formed **guilds**—legal organizations rather like trade unions. While guilds assured professional standards, they also reinforced the distinction that was then drawn between manual arts—including the production of works of art—and the so-called liberal arts.

BEFORE YOU CONTINUE READING

2. The topic of paragraphs 3 and 4 is _____,

and the main idea is _____

_____.

ARTISTS IN THE RENAISSANCE

5   The traditional classification of the Western visual arts as manual, or mechanical, arts was transformed in the fourteenth and fifteenth centuries. Both artists and writers began to emphasize the scientific and intellectual aspects of art, often incorporating the liberal arts into the education of artists. It was argued that mathematics, for example, was necessary for the study of proportion, and that geometry figured in the calculation of perspective. The artist was beginning to be seen as an educated professional versed in both the practice and the theory of art. This attitude that the artist had to be a skilled and educated individual was accompanied by a new social status: artists became the companions of intellectuals, princes, popes, and emperors.

THE IDEA OF A RENAISSANCE

6   Naturalistic representations of human figures were introduced to Western art in the Hellenistic and ancient Roman periods, a period often referred to as antiquity. These attitudes toward the figure in art, reintroduced in fifteenth-century Italy, helped to establish the foundation for the cultural epoch known as the *Renaissance*, French for "rebirth" (circa 1400–1620 C.E.). The reasons behind the appeal of antiquity in this period are not easy to simplify, but the richness and splendor of antique monuments, even in ruins, had had an impact throughout the Middle Ages, and as society and economic life blossomed at the end of the medieval period, such monuments provided appropriate models for new construction. The new self-confidence expressed in politics, business, and learning in the fifteenth century found important models and inspiration not only in ancient texts but also in ancient sculpture, especially the Greek emphasis on the dignity and beauty of the human figure and the Roman ability to capture the individual in portraiture.

7   For Italian Renaissance artists, the models of classical antiquity provided an impetus for artistic transformation, but it would be a mistake to view these artists as merely copying ancient works of art. They adapted the classical aesthetic to the attitudes of their own times, creating works of art distinctly different from those of antiquity. This "rebirth" of the antique encompassed not only works of art, but also the recovery of ancient texts and classical literary style. Much of the artistic activity of western Europe during the fifteenth century was centered in Florence, Italy and in Flanders, an area roughly equivalent to present-day Belgium. Consequently, discussion of Renaissance art in this chapter will focus on these two geographical areas.

■ ■ ■

Checking Comprehension

TEXT ANALYSIS

Writers sometimes organize text in sections that involve comparisons among the sections, as in the Introductory Reading, where perceptions about artists are compared in three different periods. The writer often concludes a passage by making a connection to information that was presented earlier in the text. In this case, a concept map with appropriate links helps us organize this information and understand it more clearly.

A Reread the Introductory Reading and complete the diagram below. Part of the diagram has been completed.

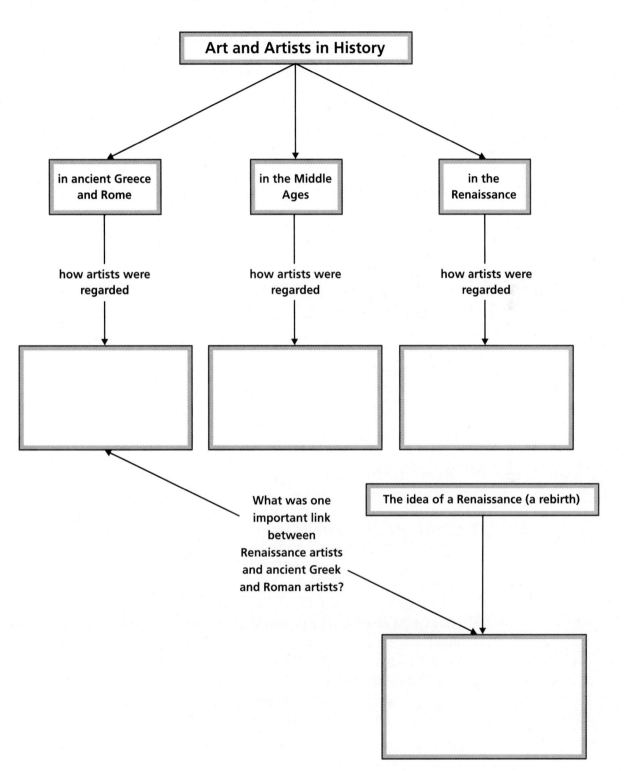

Art and Artists in History

in ancient Greece and Rome

in the Middle Ages

in the Renaissance

how artists were regarded

how artists were regarded

how artists were regarded

What was one important link between Renaissance artists and ancient Greek and Roman artists?

The idea of a Renaissance (a rebirth)

B **Answer the following questions in complete sentences.**

1. What were the main differences between the manual arts and the liberal arts?

   _____

   _____

2. What are **guilds**? Why did artists form guilds?

   _____

   _____

3. In what ways were artists seen differently in the Renaissance as compared to the Middle Ages?

   _____

   _____

4. What were some reasons for the change in the status of artists?

   _____

   _____

5. Why is the Renaissance considered a "rebirth"?

   _____

   _____

SENTENCE FOCUS

You learned on page 179 that writers use the passive voice when the agent is not known or not important, or to emphasize the action rather than the agent of the action. Another reason for using the passive voice is to avoid repetition of the same subject, or agent. For example, in paragraph 3, an appropriate agent for *was viewed, was taught*, and *were distinguished* is the same—*people*. In the active voice, the paragraph might be written as follows:

As early as the classical world of ancient Greece and Rome, *people* viewed the making of art as a manual profession that *people* taught in workshops, and it was not related to the more esteemed liberal arts—mathematics, grammar, philosophy, and logic—which *people* distinguished by intellectual, speculative thinking.

Reread paragraph 5. Highlight the passive voice. Then circle the correct answer to the following questions.

1. Who transformed the traditional classification of the Western visual arts?
   a. classical artists
   b. people in the fourteenth and fifteenth centuries
   c. Renaissance artists

2. Who argued that mathematics was necessary for the study of proportion?
  a. Renaissance artists
  b. mathematicians
  c. educated people

3. Who began to see the artist as an educated professional?
  a. mathematicians
  b. scientists
  c. people in the fourteenth and fifteenth centuries

Learning Vocabulary

VOCABULARY IN CONTEXT

Reread the paragraphs indicated from the Introductory Reading to figure out the meaning of the italicized words. Then circle the correct choice to complete the sentences.

Paragraph 1: *secular*

From the context, we can understand that *secular* refers to something ___.
  a. religious in nature
  b. nonreligious in nature

Paragraph 5: *transformed*

From this context, we can understand that *transformed* means ___.
  a. changed in a major way
  b. changed in a minor way

Paragraph 6: *antiquity*, *epoch*, and *Middle Ages*

1. From this context, we can understand that *antiquity* refers to ___.
  a. the ancient Greek and Roman periods
  b. the medieval European period
  c. the early Renaissance period

2. From this context, we can understand that an *epoch* is ___.
  a. a cultural rebirth
  b. an artistic style
  c. a period of time

3. From this context, it is clear that *Middle Ages* and *medieval period* ___.
  a. refer to different epochs
  b. refer to the same epoch

Paragraph 7: *impetus*

From this context, we can understand that *impetus* means ___.
  a. stimulation
  b. original
  c. antiquity

USING THE DICTIONARY

Read the following excerpt and dictionary entries. Then circle the correct choice to complete the sentence.

EXCERPT

Individuals in some cultures, for example fifth-century China and fifteenth-century Italy, began to write down their *aesthetic aspirations* and deeply held values as expressed in the visual arts.

> **aesthetic** *also* **esthetic** *n* (1822) **1 :** *pl but sing or pl in constr* : a branch of philosophy dealing with the nature of beauty, art, and taste and with the creation and appreciation of beauty **2 :** a particular theory or conception of beauty or art **:** a particular taste for or approach to what is pleasing to the senses and esp. sight ⟨modernist ~s⟩ ⟨staging new ballets which reflected the ~ of the new nation —Mary Clarke & Clement Crisp⟩ **3** *pl* **:** a pleasing appearance or effect **:** BEAUTY ⟨appreciated the ~s of the gemstones⟩

> **as•pi•ra•tion** \,as-pə-'rā-shən\ *n* (14c) **1 a :** audible breath that accompanies or comprises a speech sound **b :** the pronunciation or addition of an aspiration; *also* : the symbol of an aspiration **2 :** a drawing of something in, out, up, or through by or as if by suction: as **a :** the act of breathing and esp. of breathing in **b :** the withdrawal of fluid or tissue from the body **c :** the taking of foreign matter into the lungs with the respiratory current **3 a :** a strong desire to achieve something high or great **b :** an object of such desire *syn* see AMBITION—**as•pi•ra•tion•al** \-'rā-sh(ə-)nə l\ *adj*

Individuals in some cultures, for example fifth-century China and fifteenth-century Italy, began to write down their ___ and deeply held values as expressed in the visual arts.

  a. desires for the achievement of artistic beauty
  b. rules for what artistic beauty looks like
  c. plans for beautiful artistic creations

WRITE A SUMMARY

In five or six sentences, write a summary of the Introductory Reading. Refer to the statements you wrote in the Before You Continue Reading sections. Remember to use your own words.

_____

_____

_____

_____

_____

_____

INTRODUCING THE MAIN READING

Activate Your Knowledge

Work alone or with a partner. Answer the following questions.

1. Examine the two paintings below. Describe the similarities and differences between them.

   _____

   _____

   _____

Fig. 7.2 Charlemagne attacks a city (from a medieval manuscript)

Fig. 7.3 Christ Giving the Keys to Saint Peter by Perugino (1482)

2. During the Middle Ages (500–1400 CE), much art was religious in nature, and artists were frequently unknown because they did not sign their work. By the fifteenth century, many people employed artists to paint their individual portraits, and the artists signed their work. What changes might have taken place in society and culture to transform these views about art and artists?

_____

_____

Fig. 7.4 **Madonna and Child** *by a follower of Berlighiero (ca. 1230)*

Fig. 7.5 **Portrait of Federigo Da Montefeltro by Piero della Francesca (1474)**

Reading and Study Skill Strategies

SCANNING AND SKIMMING

A Before you work with the Main Reading on pages 190–195, go through it and write down the headings and subheadings in the outline below.

The Early Renaissance in Italy and Flanders

I. _____

II. _____

    A. _____

    B. _____

    C. _____

III. _____

_____

B **Based on the title, headings, subheadings, and your brief skimming, what do you think you are going to read about in the Main Reading?**

1. In a few sentences, write your predictions.

   _____

   _____

   _____

2. Write one or two questions that you expect to have answered in the Main Reading.

   _____

   _____

3. Go to page *iv* of the Contents. Read the brief summary of this passage, then decide whether to make any changes to your predictions.

4. Compare your predictions and questions with a classmate's. Keep in mind that you may not agree

Fig. 7.6 A map of Renaissance Europe

MAIN READING

The following reading is also from Art Past, Art Present. *As you read, highlight the important ideas and the vocabulary used to express those ideas. Monitor your comprehension by completing the* Before You Continue Reading *statements. Annotate the text.*

The Early Renaissance in Italy and Flanders

1   The origins, development, and flowering of the Renaissance as it developed from the Middle Ages cannot be understood outside its historical context. The economic changes that took place in Europe, including the rise of a wealthy merchant class, influenced the philosophical and artistic changes of this period.

2   As mentioned in the Introductory Reading, much of the artistic activity of western Europe during the fifteenth century was centered in Flanders and in Florence, which at the time was an independent republic. Scholar Leonardo Bruni praised Florence as "The new Athens on the Arno." He likened the civic values of his time to those fostered in democratic Athens and in Rome during the Republic. In actuality, Florence was led by an oligarchy of commercial interests. The Florentine government was eventually dominated by the Medici family whose wealth was derived from banking and commerce. Beginning with Cosimo de' Medici, the family maintained power for a long period of time.

> **BEFORE YOU CONTINUE READING**
>
> **1. The topic of paragraphs 1 and 2 is** _____ ,
> **and the main idea is** _____ .
> _____ .

ITALIAN RENAISSANCE HUMANISM

3   The Renaissance concept of humanism had a profound philosophical foundation. The title *humanist* was originally applied to a teacher of humanistic studies, a curriculum that included rhetoric, grammar, poetry, history, and moral philosophy; at the base of many of these disciplines was the study of ancient texts on these topics in Latin and eventually, in Greek as well. Already in the fourteenth century, scholars and writers had been inspired by the ideas they found in ancient Greek and Roman texts, which formed their new intellectual and scientific interest in understanding the world. The praise for the deeds of great figures from antiquity that the humanists found in the Greek and Roman texts supported the notions of pride and fame that were becoming important in a society whose major figures were successful businessmen and bankers. Humanist values are visually exemplified on the Tomb of Leonardo

Fig. 7.7 The tomb of Leonardo Bruni

Bruni, the Florentine diplomat and champion of humanist education. An effigy (image) of the deceased Bruni rests atop a bier supported by two eagles, standards of ancient Rome. Crowned with laurel, the ancient symbol of honor and victory, and with his hands embracing the book he wrote, *History of the Florentine People*, Bruni lies eternally in state.

BEFORE YOU CONTINUE READING

2. The topic of paragraph 3 is _____,
and the main idea is _____
_____.

THE FIFTEENTH-CENTURY ARTIST IN EUROPE

4   The dignity of the individual and the new self-consciousness promoted by the humanists had an important influence on attitudes about artists. In contrast to the prevalent medieval attitude that the artist was a humble craftsperson serving God, some Renaissance artists were viewed as trained intellectuals, versed in the classics and geometry. Artists became famous; in 1481, for example, an author named Cristoforo Landino made a list of Italian and Flemish artists and praised them for their skill and innovations. He even suggested that Donatello could be "counted among" the ancient masters—the highest praise possible at the time. Artists began to sign their works with more frequency, and one artist, Lorenzo Ghiberti, wrote his autobiography. The modern ideal of the artist as a genius has its origins in these developments in the fifteenth century.

Changing Patterns of Patronage in Europe

5   During the fifteenth century, artists and workshops received a variety of secular and religious commissions. Rulers continued to employ works of art for the traditional purposes of exalting and consolidating their power, but now their imagery more often had an ancient basis and/or was inspired by models from antiquity. A relatively new development is patronage by city governments in the Italian communes and patronage by the mercantile class in Flanders and Italy; based on the writing of the humanists, patronage was now viewed as an important activity of the responsible and enlightened citizen. While devotional images were produced in increasing numbers to adorn the rooms of the expanding middle class, new types of art—portraits, mythological subjects, and secular decorations—were commissioned by individuals to adorn their private palaces, town houses, or country villas.

6   In Florence, Cosimo de' Medici was generous in his support of libraries. He took an avid interest in the art of Donatello. Cosimo's grandson Lorenzo the Magnificent collected antique works of art and encouraged commissions for Florentine artists; he was also a good friend and supporter of the young Michelangelo. Such involvement with the arts was not solely altruistic, for support of humanist scholarship and the arts demonstrated benevolence and was useful in forming public opinion and securing fame.

The Significance of Perspective

7   The study of perspective, the rendering of figures or objects in illusionary space, was an important innovation in Renaissance art. Perspective had been a conscious development in ancient Greek painting, and many examples of Roman art attest to the accomplished use of perspective in antiquity. During the Middle Ages, however, pictorial reproduction of the physical world became less significant within a culture that emphasized spiritual and otherworldly values. Perspective gradually became valued in the later Middle Ages, but a coherent system allowing artists to determine the relative diminution of size of figures and objects was lacking.

8   That problem was solved by Filippo Brunelleschi (1377–1446), the Early Renaissance architect. Around 1415, Brunelleschi demonstrated a **scientific perspective** (also called **linear** and **vanishing-point perspective**) system in two lost paintings. Scientific perspective is based on the assumption that parallel lines receding from us seem to converge at a point on the horizon. This is the basis for the meeting of these lines at the vanishing point. Scientific perspective also assumes that the diminution in size of objects is in direct proportion to their distance from us and that space is, therefore, quantifiably measurable. Brunelleschi's new perspective system was incorporated in works by other artists, including Masaccio in *The Trinity with the Virgin Mary, Saint John, and Two Donors* and Perugino in *Christ Giving the Keys to Saint Peter*. In this work, the diagonal lines created by the recession of architectural elements parallel to each other converge at a vanishing point. The convergence of these diagonal lines helps determine the accurate diminution of figures and

Fig. 7.8 Christ Giving the Keys to Saint Peter *by Perugino (1482)*

Fig. 7.9 *Perugino's* **Christ Giving the Keys to Saint Peter,** *with perspective lines*

architecture. Additionally, scientific perspective is combined with **atmospheric perspective** for a unified effect that encompasses vast spaces, correctly proportioned figures, and the subtle qualities of the sky and distant landscape as they appear to the eye.

Masaccio's Great Work

9   The triangle, symbol of the Trinity, becomes the unifying compositional form in *The Trinity with the Virgin Mary, Saint John, and Two Donors*, which Masaccio was commissioned to paint. With the head of God the Father forming the apex, or peak, and the donors comprising the base, the triangular composition, popular in the Early Renaissance, is visually clear and easy to read. This clarity is supported by the illusionary space created by the use of scientific perspective. To the viewer positioned in front of the painting, the effect is of an actual chapel with real figures. The architectural forms are closely related to the Renaissance architecture being developed by Filippo Brunelleschi at the time. He

Fig. 7.10 The Trinity with the Virgin Mary, Saint John, and Two Donors *by Masaccio (ca. 1425–1428)*

may well have assisted Masaccio with this aspect of painting. The clarity of the composition is combined with boldly three-dimensional figures. Masaccio created a coherent illusionary space that distinguishes Renaissance painting.

BEFORE YOU CONTINUE READING

4. The topic of paragraphs 7–9 is _____,

and the main idea is _____

_____.

THE RENAISSANCE IN FLANDERS

10   In Flanders, a prosperous new merchant society based on the wool trade and banking was established during the fourteenth and fifteenth centuries. The flourishing city of Bruges (Brussels) was the most important center, and the presence of foreign bankers, such as the Medici from Florence, made it the banking capital of northern Europe. As in Italy, trade guilds controlled manufacturing, as well as the production of works of art.

11   Flanders was distinguished by a rich and diverse culture, which included a revolutionary school of composers that dominated European musical developments throughout the century. Northern intellectuals, however, were not very interested in the revival of the forms and subject matter of ancient Greece and Rome that were so important to the Italians.

Flemish Painting: The Limbourg Brothers

12   The puff of frosty breath from the mouth of the figure hurrying across the farmyard and the smoke curling form the chimney are the kinds of subtle details that characterize the comprehensive realism developing in Flemish painting at the beginning of the fifteenth century. The traditional calendar page for February showed people sitting by a fire, but the Limbourg brothers' representation encompasses a modest farm, complete with dovecote, beehives, and sheepfold, set within a vast snowy landscape with a distant village. Several figures reveal the peasants' restricted winter activities. The sky is no longer merely a flat blue background, but offers atmospheric midwinter effects that reveal the Limbourgs' study of natural phenomena.

13   The *Très Riches Heures du Duc de Berry* marks a final phase in the development of manuscript painting in the North. This sumptuous manuscript, with 130 illustrations, includes devotions for different periods of the day in a format that is called a Book of Hours, thus the book's name. The heightened interest in representing naturalistic lighting effects, panoramic landscapes, and precise details explains why this manuscript has been so admired and its compositions so often copied by later artists.

■ ■ ■

Fig. 7.11 **Très Riches Heures du Duc de Berry** *by the Limbourg Brothers (1416)*

Checking Comprehension

TEXT ANALYSIS

When authors write about the arts (literature, music, dance, or visual arts), they must connect important elements of the work to ideas and definitions of artistic or historical trends and innovations.

A Reread paragraph 9. Then examine Masaccio's *The Trinity with the Virgin Mary, Saint John, and Two Donors* on the next page. Identify the elements in the painting. Note their significance according to the reading. Part of the exercise has been completed for you, as a guide.

THE TRINITY WITH THE VIRGIN MARY, SAINT JOHN, AND TWO DONORS	
Elements of the Painting	**Significance of the Elements**
three-dimensional figures: ___ donors ___ God the Father ___ St. John ___ Virgin Mary	• •
___ illusionary space	
_b_ triangle	The triangle symbolizes the Trinity. It is the unifying compositional form in the painting.

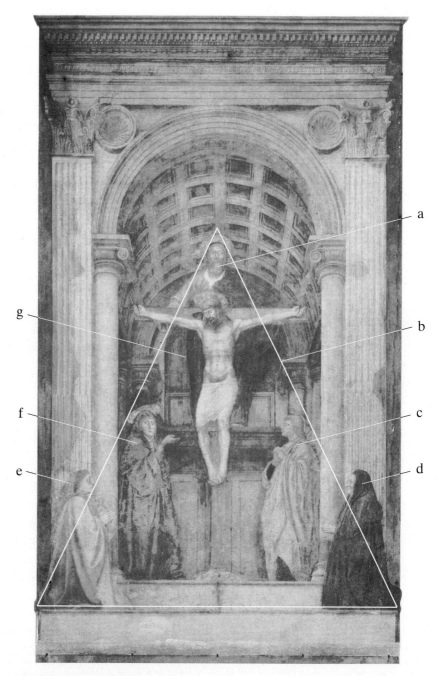

Fig. 7.12 Masaccio's **The Trinity**

B **Answer the following questions in complete sentences.**

1. How did humanist attitudes about the self change attitudes about artists?

_____

_____

2. How did the rise of a wealthy middle class change the nature of art?

_____

_____

3. What were the most important innovations in Renaissance art?

_____

_____

4. What were a few differences between Flemish art and Italian art during the Renaissance?

_____

_____

SENTENCE FOCUS

When you write about a topic, you need to use your own words. One way of doing so is to convert the writer's passive voice into the active voice.

A **Reread paragraph 2. Then read the summary of this paragraph, with the passive voice converted to the active voice.**

Much of the artistic activity of western Europe during the fifteenth century _was centered_ in Flanders and in Florence, which at the time was an independent republic. Scholar Leonardo Bruni praised Florence as "The new Athens on the Arno." He likened the civic values of his time to those fostered in democratic Athens and in Rome during the Republic. In actuality, Florence _was led_ by an oligarchy of commercial interests. The Florentine government _was_ eventually _dominated_ by the Medici family whose wealth _was derived_ from banking and commerce. Beginning with Cosimo de' Medici, the family maintained power for a long period of time.

In fifteenth-century western Europe, most artists worked in Flanders and Florence. Leonardo Bruni called Florence "The new Athens on the Arno" because he believed that the city's values were very similar to the values people had in Athens and Rome in antiquity. This was not really true, however. The Medici family, who became rich from business and banking, controlled the Florentine government for a long time.

B **Now reread paragraph 3. Using a separate piece of paper, write a summary of the paragraph. Use your own words, and convert the passive voice into the active voice.**

Learning Vocabulary

VOCABULARY IN CONTEXT

Reread the paragraphs indicated from the Main Reading to figure out the meaning of the italicized words. Then circle the correct choice to complete the sentences.

Paragraph 4: *dignity*

From this context we can understand that *dignity* refers to an individual's ___.
   a. intelligence
   b. artistry
   c. worth

Paragraph 5: *inspired*

From this context we can understand that *inspired* means ___.
   a. copied
   b. stimulated
   c. changed

Paragraph 6: *commission*

From this context we can understand that when an artist received a *commission*, he ___.
   a. was asked to create a work of art for which he would be paid
   b. was ordered to create a work of art as part of his service to God
   c. was commanded to create a work of art for the government

USING THE DICTIONARY

Read the following excerpts and dictionary entries. Select the most appropriate entry for the italicized word, based on the context. Then circle the correct choice to complete the sentences. If you choose an entry that includes subentries (for example *1a, 1b, 1c*), indicate the letter as well as the number.

EXCERPT ONE

A relatively new development is *patronage* by city governments in the Italian communes and patronage by the mercantile class in Flanders and Italy; based on the writing of the humanists, *patronage* was now viewed as an important activity of the responsible and enlightened citizen.

> **pa•tron** \'pā-trən, *for 6 also* pa-'trō"\ *n* [ME. fr. AF, fr. ML & L; ML *patronus* patron saint, patron of a benefice, pattern, fr. L, defender, fr. *patr-, pater*] (14c) **1 a :** a person chosen, named, or honored as a special guardian, protector, or supporter **b :** a wealthy or influential supporter of an artist or writer **c :** a social or financial sponsor of a social function (as a ball or concert) **2 :** one that uses wealth or influence to help an individual, an institution, or a cause **3 :** one who buys the goods or uses the services offered esp. by an establishment **4 :** the holder of the right of presentation to an English ecclesiastical benefice **5 :** a master in ancient times who freed his slave but retained some rights over him **6** [F. fr. MF] **:** the proprietor of an establishment (as an inn) esp. in France **7 :** the chief male officer in some fraternal lodges having both men and women members — **pa•tron•al** \'pā-trə-nᵊl: *Brit* pə-'trō-nᵊl, pa-\ *adj*

> **pa•tron•age** \\'pa-trə-nij, 'pā-\\ *n* (14c) **1 :** ADVOWSON **2 :** the support or influence of a patron **3 :** kindness done with an air of superiority **4 :** business or activity provided by patrons (the new branch library is expected to have a heavy ～) **5 a :** the power to make appointments to government jobs esp. for political advantage **b :** the distribution of jobs on the basis of patronage **c :** jobs distributed by patronage

1. In this context, the most appropriate definition for *patronage* is number ___.

2. A patron of the arts could be ___.
   a. a government
   b. a businessman
   c. an individual
   d. all of the above

EXCERPT TWO

In Masaccio's *The Trinity*, illusionary space is created by the use of scientific *perspective*. To the viewer positioned in front of the painting, the effect is of an actual chapel with real figures.

> **perspective** *n* [MF, prob. modif. of OIt *prospettiva*, fr. *prospetto* view, prospect, fr. L *prospectus*—more at PROSPECT] (1563) **1 a :** the technique or process of representing on a plane or curved surface the spatial relation of objects as they might appear to the eye; *specif* : representation in a drawing or painting of parallel lines as converging in order to give the illusion of depth and distance **b :** a picture in perspective **2 a :** the interrelation in which a subject or its parts are mentally viewed (places the issues in proper ～); *also* : POINT OF VIEW **b :** the capacity to view things in their true relations or relative importance (urge you to maintain your ～ and to view your own task in a larger framework—W.J. Cohen) **3 a :** a visible scene; *esp* : one giving a distinctive impression of distance : VISTA **b :** a mental view or prospect (to gain a broader ～ on the international scene—*Current Biog.*) **4 :** the appearance to the eye of objects in respect to their relative distance and positions— **per•spec•tiv•al** \\pər-'spek-ti-vəl, ˌpər-(ˌ)spek-'tī-vəl\\ *adj*

1. In this context, the most appropriate definition for *perspective* is number ___.

2. In Masaccio's *The Trinity*, scientific perspective ___.
   a. enables the artist to create a visible scene
   b. gives a mental view of a subject and its parts
   c. gives the illusion of depth and distance

WRITE A SUMMARY

In five or six sentences, write a summary of the Main Reading. Refer to the statements you wrote in the Before You Continue Reading sections. Remember to use your own words.

_____

_____

_____

_____

_____

LEARN AND USE WORD FORMS

A Study the word forms in the chart below. If you are not sure about the meaning of a word, reread the text, highlight the words and any of their forms, and try to understand them from context.

VERB	NOUN	ADJECTIVE	ADVERB
compose	composition composer	compositional	
demonstrate	demonstration	demonstrative	demonstratively
incorporate	incorporation	incorporating/ incorporated	
inspire	inspiration	inspiring/inspired inspirational	
recede	recession	receding/receded	
represent	representation	representative	representatively
reproduce	reproduction	reproduced	
commission	commission	commissioned	
model	model	modeling/modeled	
support	support supporter	supportive	supportively

B Read the sentences below. Choose the appropriate word from the following sets and complete each sentence. Be sure to use the correct tense of verbs in either the affirmative or the negative and the singular or plural of nouns. Use each word only once.

commission	model	represent
demonstrate	recede	

1. In a realistic painting, people and objects must become proportionately smaller as they gradually _____ into the background.

2. Many artists in the past, and in the present, work on _____. Sometimes they are hired to do a painting for an individual, for a government office, or for a business.

3. During both the Middle Ages and the Renaissance, artistic works often consisted of _____ of religious events in the Old and New Testaments. However, in the Renaissance, these events were depicted more realistically.

4. Renaissance artists studied Greek and Roman paintings, sculpture, and architecture, but did not copy them exactly. Instead, they _____ their work on the classical styles and incorporated elements from their own culture at the same time.

5. When Brunelleschi _____ the concept of scientific perspective, he created a sensation and solved a major artistic problem.

compose	inspire	support
incorporate	reproduce	

6. Throughout the Middle Ages and the Renaissance, people found religious topics to be very _____. However, with regard to style, they were influenced by Greek and Roman artists.

7. Bruni's tomb is a clear example of the successful _____ of humanist ideals into the classical style.

8. Many wealthy people, including the Pope, were enthusiastic _____ of artists.

9. The fifteenth-century _____ of Greek and Roman themes had a beauty and appeal that are appreciated today.

10. To fully understand the _____ of a work of art, we need to know what influenced the artist.

FOLLOW-UP ASSIGNMENTS

Before you begin any of the assignments, review the content-specific vocabulary and academic vocabulary below, and look over the vocabulary in the word form chart on page 201. If you are still unsure what any words or terms mean, go back through the chapter and review. As you complete the follow-up assignments, be sure to incorporate the appropriate vocabulary.

Content-Specific Vocabulary

aesthetic	liberal arts	perspective
antiquity	medieval	Renaissance
artist	mercantile class	vanishing-point
guild	merchant society	perspective
humanism	Middle Ages	

Academic Vocabulary

blossom	diagonal lines	impetus
commerce	diminution	patronage
commission	elevate	revival
composition	illusionary	secular
converge		

Writing Activities

1. For Italian Renaissance artists, the models of classical antiquity provided an impetus for artistic transformation, but it would be a mistake to view these artists as merely copying ancient works of art. They adapted the classical aesthetic to the attitudes of their own times, creating works of art distinctly different from those of antiquity. This "rebirth" of the antique encompassed not only works of art but also the recovery of ancient texts and classical literary style. Write three paragraphs. In the first paragraph, describe some aspects of classical Greek and Roman art. In the second paragraph, describe a work of Italian Renaissance art that interests you. In the third paragraph, tell which aspects of this Renaissance art represent classical Greek and Roman influence.

2. Before the Renaissance, artists sometimes created scenes of everyday life, but they often revolved around religious and noble themes. During the Renaissance, however, scenes of everyday life became much more common. Additionally, the scenes were depicted in great detail, as you saw in the Limbourg brothers' *Très Riches Heures*. Write three paragraphs. In the first paragraph, explain why artists focused mainly on religious themes before the Renaissance. In the second paragraph, describe what might have led to this increased interest in depicting scenes from everyday life. In the third paragraph, give examples of art that represent this change and explain your reasons for your choices.

3. Review the Introductory Reading and the Main Reading. Then reexamine the artwork on pages 175, 176, 177, 187, 188, 193, and 195. Write three paragraphs. In the first paragraph, describe what Italian Renaissance people admired in classical Greek and Roman art. In the second paragraph, describe the artwork: what aspects of it reflect classical Greek and Roman culture, and what aspects of it reflect Italian Renaissance culture. In the third paragraph, describe the differing attitudes toward artists during these periods.

Extension Activities

1. In the Introductory Reading, the author states that much of the artistic activity of Western Europe during the fifteenth century was centered in Florence and in Flanders. Research the reasons for the dominance of Florentine and Flemish influence during this period. You might focus on the Florentine Medici family and their banking and commerce activities, and on the wool trade in Flanders as you begin your research. Present your findings to your class.

2. During the Renaissance, artists often depended on wealthy patrons, who commissioned works of art. Research present-day artists. Find out how they support themselves and their art. Present your findings to your class.

3. Research a Renaissance artist who interests you. Visit a local art museum if possible. Find out when this artist lived, the type of art this person created, who the artist's patron was, if any, and any other information you can learn. Prepare a presentation for your class. Include examples of the artist's work to show your classmates.

4. Conduct research on the Internet. Go online. Use a search engine such as Google, AltaVista, Yahoo, About, or Dogpile. Investigate a topic related to the information you read about in Chapter 7. Choose a topic that especially interests you. You may wish to follow up on one of the questions you wrote on page 179 or page 189. Use key words such as *Tres Riches Heures, perspective painting, Renaissance art, Flemish painting, Limbourg brothers, Leonardo Bruni, Lorenzo Ghiberti, Brunelleschi, Perugino,* and *Masaccio*. Prepare an oral report, a written report, or a poster, and present your findings to the class.

Chapter 8

THE FOUNDATIONS OF CHINESE ART

Skills Goals

- Review skills from Chapters 1–7.
- Understand use of prepositional phrases.
- Analyze writing about art.
- Understand author's use of "we."

Content-Specific Goals

- Understand the significance of calligraphy in Chinese art.
- Learn about Chinese aesthetic theory.
- Understand the concept of realism in Chinese landscape painting.

Fig. 8.0   Chinese calligraphy, Shanghai 1992

Chapter Readings

Art and Artists in China

Chinese Art: Landscape Painting

INTRODUCING THE READING

Activate Your Knowledge

Work alone or in a small group. Answer the following questions.

Fig. 8.1 *Topkapi Palace calligraphy*

Fig. 8.2 *Fifteenth-century manuscript lettering*

Fig. 8.3 **Grove of Trees, Pavilion, and Distant Peaks** *by Ni Zan, China (fourteenth century)*

1. What do these three illustrations have in common?

_____

2. Why do you think the people who created these illustrations included writing as part of their work?

_____

3. Do you consider these three pieces to be art? Why or why not?

_____

PREVIEW KEY VOCABULARY

Read the content-specific vocabulary below and determine how well you know each one. Use a scale of 1 to 4, where:

1 = I have never seen or heard this vocabulary before.

2 = I have seen or heard this vocabulary before, but I do not know what it means.

3 = I recognize the vocabulary, but I cannot define it accurately or use it with confidence.

4 = I can give an accurate definition or explanation of this vocabulary, and I can use it appropriately in a sentence.

___ aesthetic	___ landscape
___ calligraphy	___ media (*singular* medium)
___ Confucianism	___ monochrome
___ canon	___ realism
___ *dao*	___ Way of Nature

Do not try to learn the unfamiliar items before you begin reading. You will learn them as you work with the chapter.

SCANNING AND SKIMMING

A **Before you work with the Introductory Reading on pages 208–209, go through it and write down the headings on the lines below.**

Art and Artists in China

_____

_____

B **Read the following questions. Then skim through the sections of the reading under the appropriate headings to find the answers. Read quickly. Compare your answers with a classmate's.**

1. What was the highest aesthetic aim of the Chinese literati painters?

_____

2. Which one of the Six Canons of Painting do you think was most essential to achieving the aim of these painters?

_____

C **Based on the title, headings, and your brief skimming, what do you think you are going to read about in the Introductory Reading?**

1. In a few sentences, write your predictions.

   _____

   _____

   _____

2. Write one or two questions you expect to have answered in the Introductory Reading.

   _____

   _____

3. Go to page *iv* of the Contents. Read the brief summary of this passage, then decide whether to make any changes to your predictions.

4. Compare your predictions and questions with a classmate's. Keep in mind that you may not agree.

INTRODUCTORY READING

The following reading is from the Introduction to Art Past, Art Present. *As you read, highlight the important ideas and vocabulary used to express those ideas. Monitor your comprehension by completing the* Before You Continue Reading *statements. Annotate the text.*

Art and Artists in China

1   Among cultures outside the Western tradition, China nurtured the oldest continuous painting tradition in the world. Its historical isolation, imperial patronage, art academies (begun as early as the eighth century C.E.), and a bureaucratic elite of Confucian scholar-officials contributed to a unique tradition in the visual arts. Most Chinese artists were not only painters but also poets, calligraphers, government officials, antiquarians, scholars, collectors, connoisseurs, and mystics. Painters such as Ni Zan were part of the cultured elite who were the main participants in the Chinese classical tradition. Among the Chinese aristocracy, painting and **calligraphy** (artistic writing) were revered media for the preservation of social, political, and aesthetic values.

CHINESE AESTHETIC THEORY

2   Chinese painting is derived from the art of writing and is, therefore, a linear art. Its brushwork is imbued with calligraphic formulas. The highest aesthetic aim of the literati painters was to capture the spirit of what was depicted, rather than merely its appearance. For these literati painters, the creative process embodied the *dao*, or Way of Nature, with its holistic vision of organic and metaphysical properties. In many Chinese paintings, idea and technique are one; the act of painting and the picture itself both carry meaning. Interestingly, these literati artists did not create sculpture or architecture, which were the work of highly skilled artisans.

<table>
<tr><td>

BEFORE YOU

CONTINUE

READING
</td></tr>
</table>

The topic of paragraphs 1 and 2 is _____,
and the main idea is _____
_____.

THE SIX CANONS OF PAINTING

3   As mentioned earlier, among the Chinese aristocracy, painting and calligraphy were revered media for examination and for the preservation of social, political, and aesthetic values. The earliest-known treatise (essay) on aesthetics was written in the second quarter of the sixth century by a man named Xie He (c. 500–c. 535). Called the *Gu hua pin lu (Classified Record of Ancient Painters)*, it graded earlier painters into six classes. What made the treatise so influential was its Preface, known as the Six Canons of Painting, which were used to judge painters and paintings. Because its language is filled with abstract philosophic thinking and presents generalized and theoretical prescriptions for painting, the canons have been translated and interpreted many times. An approximate translation of the Six Canons is:

1. A painting must have spirit or breath of life (*qi yun*).
2. The brushwork must be structurally sound.
3. The painting must faithfully portray forms.
4. A painting must have fidelity of color.
5. A painting must also be a properly planned composition.
6. A painting must transmit knowledge of past painting traditions.

4   The first canon, animation through spirit consonance, emphasizes the need for painting to have *qi yun*. **Qi** was thought to be the cosmic spirit that vitalized all things; to capture its essence was fundamental for "good" painting. Canons 2–5 clearly concentrate on technical matters, and canon 6 emphasizes the transmission of and reverence for tradition. Each generation of artists established a sense of external and internal reality in painting that could be challenged and reconsidered during the following period. Xie He's treatise remained the backbone of aesthetic criticism until the modern period in China, when its imperial, elitist roots were challenged by new socialist policies.

5   The ideals of painting of the tenth century were written down by a man named Ching Hao, who lived in the tenth century. In his essay *Record of Brush Methods*, or *Essay on Landscape Painting*, Ching Hao recorded his thoughts through a narrator, an old man whom he pretended to meet while wandering in the mountains. This wise man told him the six essentials of painting: spirit, rhythm, thought, scenery, brush, and ink. This logical system, based on Xie He, first lays down the concept of painting and then its expression. It distinguishes further between resemblance, which reproduces the formal, outward aspects of what is depicted, and truth (or spirit), which involves knowing and representing inner reality. Correct balance between representing visible forms of nature and their deeper significance was the goal of these Chinese painters.

■ ■ ■

Checking Comprehension

TEXT ANALYSIS

A When a text presents multiple descriptions of historic figures, their works, and defining ideas, it is usually necessary to list and take notes on the important facts about them in order to understand and remember them for papers and exams. Use the chart below to distinguish defining points of the work of Xie He and Ching Hao.

	XIE HE	CHING HAO
Century		
Title of Work and Format		
Summary of Ideas		
Significance		

B Answer the following questions in complete sentences.

1. Why does Chinese art include artistic forms of writing?

_____

_____

2. What two concepts are combined in many Chinese paintings?

_____

_____

3. What were the three major points made in the Six Canons of Painting?

_____

_____

_____

SENTENCE FOCUS

Writers often begin sentences with prepositional phrases to emphasize the information in the phrase or to make the reference clearer to the reader.

Read the following pairs of sentences. Then circle the correct answer to the questions that follow.

PAIR ONE

• China nurtured the oldest continuous painting tradition in the world among cultures outside the Western tradition.

• Among cultures outside the Western tradition, China nurtured the oldest continuous painting tradition in the world.

What does the phrase *among cultures outside the Western tradition* refer to?
    a. China
    b. the world
    c. tradition

PAIR TWO

• Among the Chinese aristocracy, painting and **calligraphy** (artistic writing) were revered media for the preservation of social, political, and aesthetic values.

• Painting and **calligraphy** (artistic writing) were revered media for the preservation of social, political, and aesthetic values among the Chinese aristocracy.

What did the Chinese aristocracy wish to preserve?
    a. social values
    b. political values
    c. aesthetic values
    d. all of the above

PAIR THREE

• For these literati painters, the creative process embodied the *dao*, or Way of Nature, with its holistic vision of organic and metaphysical properties.

• The creative process embodied the *dao*, or Way of Nature, with its holistic vision of organic and metaphysical properties for these literati painters.

For the literati painters, what was essential to the creative process?
    a. metaphysical properties
    b. holistic visions
    c. the embodiment of the Way of Nature

Learning Vocabulary

VOCABULARY IN CONTEXT

Reread the paragraphs indicated from the Introductory Reading to figure out the meaning of the italicized words. Then circle the correct choice to complete the sentences.

Paragraph 1: *elite, calligraphy*, and *media*

1. In this context, the *elite* are ___.
   a. historians
   b. bureaucrats
   c. the aristocracy

2. From this context, we can understand that *calligraphy* is ___.
   a. a form of painting
   b. an artistic form of writing
   c. a meaningful way of painting

3. From this context, we can understand that artistic *media* are ___.
   a. different ways to express one's ideas
   b. different values that people have
   c. styles of writing

4. Which of the following are artistic *media*? Circle all that apply.
   a. calligraphy   d. newspapers
   b. government documents e. sculpture
   c. painting   f. photography

Paragraph 2: *dao*

According to the context, *dao* refers to ___.
   a. the Way of Nature
   b. literati painters
   c. the meaning of a painting

Paragraph 3: *aesthetic* and *revered* and **Paragraph 4:** *reverence*

1. We can understand from the context that *aesthetic* refers to ___.
   a. society
   b. politics
   c. beauty

2. From the two contexts, we can understand that *revere* means ___.
   a. honor
   b. understand
   c. like

USING THE DICTIONARY

Read the following excerpts and dictionary entries. Select the most appropriate entry for the italicized word, based on the context. Then circle the correct choice to complete the sentences. If you choose an entry that includes subentries (for example *1a, 1b, 1c*), indicate the letter as well as the number.

EXCERPT ONE

The earliest-known treatise (essay) on aesthetics was written in the second quarter of the sixth century by a man named Xie He (c. 500–c. 535). Called the *Gu hua pin lu (Classified Record of Ancient Painters)*, it graded earlier painters into six classes. What made the treatise so influential was its Preface, known as the *Six **Canons** of Painting*, which were used to judge painters and paintings.

> **can·on** \'ka-nən\ *n* [ME, fr. OE, fr. LL, fr. L, ruler, rule, model, standard, fr. Gk *kanōn*] (bef. 12c) **1 a :** a regulation or dogma decreed by a church council **b :** a provision of canon law **2** [ME, prob. fr. AF, fr. LL, fr. L, model] : the most solemn and unvarying part of the Mass including the consecration of the bread and wine **3** [ME, fr. LL, fr. L, standard] **a :** an authoritative list of books accepted as Holy Scripture **b :** the authentic works of a writer **c :** a sanctioned or accepted group or body of related works ⟨the ∼ of great literature⟩ **4 a :** an accepted principle or rule **b :** a criterion or standard of judgment **c :** a body of principles, rules, standards, or norms **5** [LGk *kanōn*, fr. Gk, model] **:** a contrapuntal musical composition in which each successively entering voice presents the initial theme usu. transformed in a strictly consistent way *syn* see LAW

1. In this context, the most appropriate definition for *canon* is number ___.

2. The Six Canons of Painting were ___.
   a. rules of painting decreed by religious people
   b. an authoritative set of books about painting
   c. a set of rules for evaluating artists and their paintings

EXCERPT TWO

Among cultures outside the Western tradition, China *nurtured* the oldest continuous painting tradition in the world. Its historical isolation, imperial patronage, art academies (begun as early as the eighth century C.E.), and a bureaucratic elite of Confucian scholar-officials contributed to a unique tradition in the visual arts.

> **nurture** *vt* **nur·tured; nur·tur·ing** \'nərch-riŋ, 'nər-chə-\ (15c) **1 :** to supply with nourishment **2 :** EDUCATE **3 :** to further the development of : FOSTER—**nur·tur·er** \'nər-chər- ər\ *n*

1. In this context, the most appropriate definition for *nurture* is number ___.

2. In what ways did China nurture the visual arts? Circle all that apply.
   a. historical isolation
   b. imperial patronage
   c. art academies
   d. Confucian scholar-officials

WRITE A SUMMARY

In five or six sentences, write a summary of the Introductory Reading. Refer to the statements you wrote in the Before You Continue Reading sections. Remember to use your own words.

_____

_____

_____

_____

_____

_____

INTRODUCING THE MAIN READING

Activate Your Knowledge

Work alone or with a partner. Compare the two paintings below. In what ways are they similar? In what ways are they different? How does culture influence an artist's work?

Fig. 8.4 **Très Riches Heures du Duc de Berry** *by the Limbourg Brothers*

Fig. 8.5 **Buddhist Temple in the Hills after Rain** *by Li Cheng, China (tenth century)*

Reading and Study Skill Strategies

SCANNING AND SKIMMING

A Before you work with the Main Reading on pages 216–220, go through it and write down the headings in the outline below.

Chinese Art: Landscape Painting

I. _____

II. _____

III. _____

IV. _____

B Read the following questions. Then skim through the sections of the reading under the appropriate headings to find the answers. Read quickly. Compare your answers with a classmate's.

1. Why is Li Cheng such an important Chinese artist?

_____

2. What is the primary aim of realism in Chinese landscape art?

_____

C Based on the title, headings, and your brief skimming, what do you think you are going to read about in the Main Reading?

1. In a few sentences, write your predictions.

_____

_____

_____

2. Write one or two questions that you expect to have answered in the Main Reading.

_____

_____

3. Go to page *v* of the Contents. Read the brief summary of this passage, then decide whether to make any changes to your predictions.

4. Compare your predictions and questions with a classmate's. Keep in mind that you may not agree.

MAIN READING

The following reading is from Art Past, Art Present. *As you read, highlight the important ideas and the vocabulary used to express those ideas. Monitor your comprehension by completing the* Before You Continue Reading *statements. Annotate the text.*

Chinese Art: Landscape Painting

1   In *Buddhist Temple in the Hills after Rain*, a landscape attributed to Li Cheng (active from about 940 to 967), the autumn skies are clearing, leaving only mist in the low valleys and above the mountain pathways. In the immediate foreground are a group of huts and two pavilions built over water. The buildings and figures are painted with such detail that we can distinguish peasants and courtiers at their meals in the rustic inn and scholars at the wine shops gazing off into the landscape from the pavilions. The temple that occupies the center of the painting is parallel to the peaks that dominate the distance. Such axially symmetrical monumental configurations of mountains and water came to be associated with the Chinese empire in the tenth century—grand, ordered, and powerful.

THE ARTIST LI CHENG (919–967)

2   Li Cheng as a person was thought to represent the ideal Chinese painter—an artist who claimed descent from the imperial clan of the Tang dynasty (618–907), was educated in the humanities through study of the *Classic Books* (ancient texts on history, philosophy, and literature), and was occupied with painting for his own delight without ambition for honors or advancement. A scholar and a gentleman, he enjoyed a quiet life devoted to the philosophic study of Nature as opposed to merely copying forms in the out-of-doors (nature). **Monochrome** ink paintings of landscape were the preferred type of art produced by Li Cheng and his colleagues.

3   Like many other landscape painters of the tenth century, Li Cheng had a preference for autumnal or wintry scenes full of bleak, stony crags, gnarled trees with leafless crab-claw-shaped branches, and looming distant

Fig. 8.6 **Buddhist Temple in the Hills after Rain** *by Li Cheng*

peaks. He shares with other landscapists of the period a preference for monochrome ink, laid on the silk in broad and jagged strokes, to describe the essential outlines of the rocks, trees, and buildings. These shapes are then broken up and modeled with washes of ink. On top of the washes are placed **cun**, small brush strokes dabbed on quickly to create the sense of texture. Such paintings were then mounted on a vertical hanging or horizontal hand scroll. Closely associated with calligraphy, the brush paintings of China were produced for and by the intelligentsia, who painted as an avocation.

BEFORE YOU CONTINUE READING

1. The topic of paragraphs 1–3 is _____,

and the main idea is _____

_____.

REALISM IN CHINESE ART

4   The Chinese doctrine of realism seen here aims for truth to natural appearance but not at the expense of a pictorial examination of how Nature operates. In Li Cheng's painting, the bent and twisted trees, for example, are organically constructed to expose their full skeletons—roots, trunk, branches, and even the dormant buds ready for spring awakening. This approach to realism also explains the attitude behind **shifting perspective** in Chinese painting. In *Buddhist Temple* we are invited to "enter" the picture on the lower left and to explore as we move through the landscape. We can wander across the bridge, look down at rooftops, up at pavilions and the temple, and across to the towering peaks, but we cannot take a panoramic view from a single position outside (or inside) the painting, and the artist does not intend

that we do so. Rather, little by little, nature is revealed as if we were actually walking in the out-of-doors. In this sense, the Chinese landscape painter combines the element of time in much the same way as it is experienced in music. Shifting perspective allows for a journey and for a powerful personal impact on the individual participant. These paintings were meant to be visual exercises that allowed for examination of both the structure of nature or the universe and the contemplation of minute details. The power of these paintings is to take us out of ourselves and to provide spiritual solace and refreshment.

5   Guo Xi, a pupil of Li Cheng, declared in an essay that "The virtuous man above all delights in landscapes." The virtuous (or Confucian) man

Fig. 8.7 **Early Spring** *by Kuo Hi (Guo Xi) (1072)*

during this period accepted his civil responsibilities to society and to the state, which tied him to an urban life as an official, but he could nourish his spirit by taking imaginary trips into nature through viewing a landscape painting such as Guo Xi's *Early Spring*. The poem in the upper right-hand corner of the painting reads:

> Leaves are twisted on the trees and the stream is melting,
> On the top are dwellings of the immortals.
> We do not need a willow tree to tell the season,
> The mountain is already misted with the coming of spring.

BEFORE YOU CONTINUE READING

2. The topic of paragraphs 4 and 5 is _____,
and the main idea is _____
_____.

LANDSCAPE PAINTING DURING THE TENTH–TWELFTH CENTURIES

6   There was important support for landscape painters during the Five Dynasties (907–960) and the Northern Song dynasty (960–1126). An important occurrence of the period was the initial printing of the *Classical Texts* in 952; for the first time, books became inexpensive and abundant. Scholars multiplied, and the knowledge of ancient literature was more widespread. The political consequences of the expansion of the literate class was manifest in the Song, the third centralized empire in Chinese history. The unification of the empire was the work of policy rather than conquest, a powerful submission of an aristocracy weary of disunion and aware of its own cultural identity. The traditional civil service examination system returned civilians to positions of prestige and power in government that had been lost under previous military dictatorships. The prevailing pacifist policies and a series of enlightened sovereigns who were tolerant, humane, artistic, and intellectual provided substantial and consistent patronage for the arts. The collection of the Song emperor Hui Zong (ruled 1100–1126), for example, was said to include 159 paintings by Li Cheng. The Song period produced the first important academy of painting in the Far East; among the early members were the landscapists.

7   The Song dynasty was an age of many-sided intellectual activity— poetry, history, and especially, philosophy. Characteristic of Song thought was the return to older Chinese sources, a conscious archaism and cultural introspection. The renaissance of classical literature branched off into the formation of a new system of philosophy called neo-Confucianism, which enveloped traditional moral and ethical teachings with Daoist thinking about nature and the cosmos, especially as presented in the *I-jing* (*Book of Changes*). No distinction was made between the law of nature and moral law. The world was thought to be inspired by the "Supreme Ultimate" (or what the Daoists called the *dao*, or the Way); the neo-Confucianists referred to this as *li* (law), a moral law that was identical to the ethical code

upon which human conduct should be modeled. These Song thinkers were also interested in correspondences in nature. The manifestation of *li* painting included faithfulness to nature as well as conventionalized symbols for representation of rocks, foliage, bark, water, and so forth. *Li* also governed the way a picture was put together.

8   Under pressure from the Jin Tartars on the northern borders of China, the Song court fled south in 1127. In 1135, a new capital was founded at Hangzhou, where the academy of painting was reestablished under imperial patronage and every effort was made to assemble an imperial art collection equal to that of the Northern Song emperors. The Southern Song rulers were even more concerned with internal affairs than their predecessors, and a new mode of painting evolved that focused on depiction of what was nearby and up close.

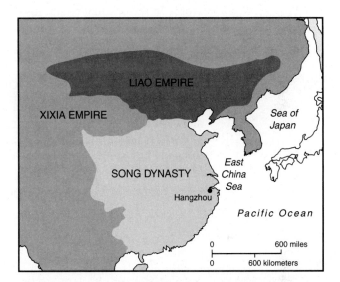

Fig. 8.8 Map of China in the tenth–twelfth centuries

BEFORE YOU CONTINUE READING

3. The topic of paragraphs 6–8 is _____,

and the main idea is _____

_____.

LATER LANDSCAPE PAINTERS

9   Later Southern Song landscape painters such as Xia Gui (active 1180–1230) concentrated on rivers, lakes, and mists of south China. Xia Gui developed a shorthand manner in which forms are suggested rather than depicted, as they had been in the earlier style of Li Cheng and Guo Xi. His softer and less literal expression is organized asymmetrically, in a style called a "one-corner" composition by the Chinese. There is more mist than ink, and the subjective expression omits large sections of the landscape to concentrate on closer components. Xia Gui evokes a mood; he does not describe a particular place. *Sailboat in the Rain* (see below) was commissioned by the imperial court. The inscription in the album leaf to the left of the painting is written by the Emperor Gaozong (1127–1162) of the Southern Song Dynasty, and is based on a poem written by Su Shi (1036–1101), a Northern Song poet. The Emperor changed some of the words in the original to suit his own mood:

> While sailing through endless rain,
> I enjoyed a good sleep.
> While boating all day long,
> We cut through the wind from the shore.

Xia Gui and other painters at court were associated with the politically weak and ineffectual court of the Southern Song in subsequent periods. For later Chinese critics, who commingled aesthetic and moral judgment, the South Song paintings were less highly valued than they were in Japan and the West.

■ ■ ■

Fig. 8.9 **Sailboat in Rainstorm** *by Xia Gui (ca. 1180)*
Sailboat in Rainstorm © 2004 Museum of Fine Arts, Boston

Checking Comprehension

You learned in Chapter 7 that when authors write about the arts (literature, music, dance, or visual arts), they must connect important elements of the work to ideas and definitions of artistic or historical trends and innovations.

A Reread the Main Reading. Then examine the paintings *Buddhist Temple in the Hills after Rain* by Li Cheng and *Early Spring* by Guo Xi. Identify the elements in the painting. Note their significance according to the reading.

PAINTING	ELEMENTS OF THE PAINTING	SIGNIFICANCE OF THE ELEMENTS
Buddhist Temple in the Hills after Rain		
Early Spring		

B Answer the following questions in complete sentences.

1. Why is the painter Li Cheng an important figure in the history of Chinese art?

   _____

   _____

   _____

2. How can tenth-century Chinese landscape art be characterized?

   _____

   _____

3. From the tenth through the twelfth centuries, in what ways were landscape artists supported?

   _____

   _____

   _____

4. Paragraph 7 mentions a "renaissance of classical literature." What does the author imply by the use of the word *renaissance*?

_____

_____

5. Paragraphs 5 and 7 make reference to *Confucianism*. From these references, what can we understand about Confucius's teachings?

_____

_____

SENTENCE FOCUS

In most writing, the pronouns *we* and *us* are used to refer to the speaker or writer, plus one or more known person(s). For example, "My friend and I went to the museum. *We* viewed the exhibit on Chinese art." In academic writing, an author might use *we* to mean "you" the reader, and "me," the writer. The writer's intention is to draw you, the reader, into the observations being made.

Reread paragraph 4 below. The words *we*, *us*, and *ourselves* have been replaced with a blank line. Identify possible nouns to replace these words. Write them in the spaces provided. The first one has been done as an example.

The Chinese doctrine of realism seen here aims for truth to natural appearance but not at the expense of a pictorial examination of how Nature operates. In Li Cheng's painting, the bent and twisted trees, for example, are organically constructed to expose their full skeletons—roots, trunk, branches, and even the dormant buds ready for spring awakening. This approach to realism also explains the attitude behind **shifting perspective** in Chinese painting. In *Buddhist Temple*, _____viewers_____ are invited to
(1)
"enter" the picture on the lower left and to explore as _____
(2)
move through the landscape. _____ can wander across the
(3)
bridge, look down at rooftops, up at pavilions and the temple, and across to the towering peaks, but _____ cannot take a panoramic view
(4)
from a single position outside (or inside) the painting, and the artist does not intend that _____ do so. Rather, little by little, nature is
(5)
revealed as if _____ were actually walking in the out-of-
(6)
doors. In this sense, the Chinese landscape painter combines the element of time in much the same way as it is experienced in music. Shifting

perspective allows for a journey and for a powerful personal impact on the individual participant. These paintings were meant to be visual exercises that allowed for examination of both the structure of nature or the universe and the contemplation of minute details. The power of these paintings is to take _____ out of _____ and to provide
(7)   (8)
spiritual solace and refreshment.

Learning Vocabulary

VOCABULARY IN CONTEXT

Reread the paragraphs indicated from the Main Reading to figure out the meaning of the italicized words. Then circle the correct choice to complete the sentences.

Paragraph 4: *realism*

From this context, we can understand that artistic *realism* refers to ___.
   a. painting in true color
   b. painting objects as we see them
   c. painting in great detail

Paragraph 8: *depiction* and **Paragraph 9:** *depicted*

From these two contexts, we can understand that a *depiction* is ___.
   a. a representation
   b. a painting
   c. an idea

USING THE DICTIONARY

Read the following excerpts and dictionary entries. Select the most appropriate entry for the italicized word, based on the context. Then circle the correct choice to complete the sentences.

EXCERPT ONE

Monochrome ink paintings of landscape were the preferred type of art produced by Li Cheng and his colleagues.

> **monochrome** *adj* (1849) **1 :** of, relating to, or made with a single color or hue **2 :** involving or producing visual images in a single color or in varying tones of a single color (as gray) ⟨~ film⟩ ⟨~ television monitor⟩

1. In this context, the most appropriate definition for *monochrome* is number ___.

2. Monochrome ink paintings were probably ___.
   a. very subtle
   b. very colorful
   c. very bright

EXCERPT TWO

Shifting perspective allows for a journey and for a powerful personal impact on the individual participant. These paintings were meant to be visual exercises that allowed for examination of both the structure of nature or the universe and the contemplation of *minute* details.

mi·nute \mī-'nüt, mə-,-'nyüt\ *adj* **mi·nut·er; -est** [L *minutus*] (ca. 1606) **1 :** very small : INFINITESIMAL **2 :** of small importance : TRIFLING **3 :** marked by close attention to details *syn* see SMALL, CIRCUMSTANTIAL— **mi·nute·ness** *n*

1. In this context, the most appropriate definition for *minute* is number ___.

2. In Chinese art of this period, the details were ___.
   a. very small
   b. of small importance
   c. paid attention to

WRITE A SUMMARY

In five or six sentences, write a summary of the Main Reading. Refer to the statements you wrote in the Before You Continue Reading sections. Remember to use your own words.

_____

_____

_____

_____

_____

_____

LEARN AND USE WORD FORMS

A Study the word forms in the chart below. If you are not sure about the meaning of a word, reread the text, highlight the words and any of their forms, and try to understand them from context.

Verb	Noun	Adjective	Adverb
commission	commission	commissioned	
compose	composition composer	composed	
depict	depiction	depicting/depicted	
influence	influence	influential	
model	model	modeling/modeled	
nurture	nurture	nurturing/nurtured	
prefer	preference	preferred preferential	
represent	representation	representing/represented representative	
reveal	revelation	revealing/revealed	
revere	reverence	reverential	
support	support supporter	supportive	supportively

B Read the sentences below. Choose the appropriate word from the following sets and complete each sentence. Be sure to use the correct tense of verbs in either the affirmative or the negative and the singular or plural of nouns. Use each word only once.

compose	influence	nurture	represent	reveal

1. Li Cheng was a very _____ artist of the tenth century. Many other artists modeled their work after his paintings.

2. When we examine the _____ of *Buddhist Temple*, we realize that the artist has arranged the painting to lead our eyes in a specific direction.

3. Although realism was a goal of Chinese landscape painting, the artist often _____ objects that could not ordinarily be seen, for example, the roots of trees.

4. Chinese culture _____ artists. Imperial patronage of the arts played an important role in this support.

5. Artists often painted objects such as trees, flowers, and animals, which were less realistic but more _____ of trees, flowers, or animals as a whole.

commission	model	revere
depict	prefer	support

6. The Chinese people's _____ for tradition has existed for many centuries. To this day they continue to honor it.

7. Chinese artists' _____ of landscapes differ significantly from those of Western artists.

8. Popular and well-respected artists received hundreds of _____ during their lifetime.

9. Tenth-century Chinese artists' _____ for creating monochrome ink paintings often resulted in subtle but dramatic compositions.

10. In the past, artists sometimes _____ their own work after that of established artists. Artists sometimes follow this practice today as well.

11. Artists have relied on the _____ of patrons for many centuries.

FOLLOW-UP ASSIGNMENTS

Before you begin any of the assignments, review the content-specific vocabulary and academic vocabulary below, and look over the vocabulary in the word form chart on page 225. If you are still unsure what any words or terms mean, go back through the chapter and review. As you complete the follow-up assignments, be sure to incorporate the appropriate vocabulary.

Content-Specific Vocabulary

aesthetic	*dao*	monochrome
calligraphy	landscape	realism
canon	media (*singular*	Way of Nature
Confucianism	medium)	

Academic Vocabulary

commission	minute	patronage
composition	nurture	reverence
depict		

Writing Activities

1. Review the Six Canons of Painting in the Introductory Reading. What might have been canons of painting for Italian Renaissance artists? Write three paragraphs. In the first paragraph, summarize the six canons and explain why they were important to Chinese landscape artists, given their historical and cultural context. In the second paragraph, describe canons of painting that Italian Renaissance artists may have had. In the third paragraph, explain why these canons might have been important to these artists, given their historical and cultural context.

2. The concept of perspective was important in both Italian Renaissance art and Chinese landscape art. Write three paragraphs. In the first paragraph, describe the Renaissance concept of perspective. In the second paragraph, describe the Chinese landscape concept of perspective. In the third paragraph, discuss the similarities and differences between them.

3. Chapter 7 describes European Renaissance art, particularly Italian art. Chapter 8 describes Chinese landscape painting. Review the descriptions of both types of art and what the artists intended to show. Write three paragraphs. In the first paragraph, describe the goals of the Renaissance artists, especially with regard to the use of perspective. In the second paragraph, describe the aims of Chinese landscape painters. In the third paragraph, outline the differences between these two artistic styles, and explain the differences in terms of their historical and cultural context.

Extension Activities

1. Research a Chinese artist who interests you. Visit a local art museum if possible. Find out when this artist lived, the type of art this person created, and any other information you can learn. Prepare a presentation for your class. Include examples of the artist's work to show your classmates.

2. Research Byzantine art. Compare it to the Chinese art you studied in this chapter. What are the major differences? Do you see any similarities? Prepare a presentation for your class. Include examples of the artist's work to show your classmates.

3. Research the use of calligraphy in medieval manuscripts or some other medium that interests you. Prepare a presentation for your class. Include examples of the artist's work to show your classmates.

4. Conduct research on the Internet. Go online. Use a search engine such as Google, AltaVista, Yahoo, About, or Dogpile. Investigate a topic related to the information you read about in Chapter 8. Choose a topic that especially interests you. You may wish to follow up on one of the questions you wrote on page 208 or page 215. Use key words such as *Confucius (K'ung-fu-tzuor Kongfuzi), Chinese landscape painting, Song Dynasty, Li Cheng, Xia Gui*, and *Chinese calligraphy*. Prepare an oral report, a written report, or a poster, and present your findings to the class.

HOW DO WE EXPLAIN OUR SIMILARITIES AND DIFFERENCES?

Bayei village in Northern Botswana, Africa

Trulli house, Alberobello, Puglia, Italy

Skills Goals

- Review skills from Chapters 1–8.
- Understand the use of dashes.
- Recognize clues about text organization.
- Critique information in textbooks.

Content-Specific Goals

- Learn the nature of cross-cultural psychology.
- Understand the concepts of psychological diversity and psychological universals.
- Learn about cross-cultural approaches to studying human behavior.

Fig. 9.0 Indian wedding in South Africa

Chapter Readings

The Nature of Cross-Cultural Psychology

Cross-Cultural Approaches to Studying Human Behavior

INTRODUCING THE READING

Activate Your Knowledge

Work in pairs or small groups. Answer the following questions.

1. In Unit 2, you read about culture from an anthropological perspective. According to anthropologists, what are the main characteristics of cultural behavior? (You may want to review Chapter 3.)

_____

_____

2. The members of a cultural group share a number of characteristics and behaviors. Does this commonality mean that the individuals who belong to that group think alike? Explain your reasons for your answer.

_____

_____

PREVIEW KEY VOCABULARY

Read the content-specific vocabulary below and determine how well you know each one. Use a scale of 1 to 4, where:

1 = I have never seen or heard this vocabulary before.

2 = I have seen or heard this vocabulary before, but I do not know what it means.

3 = I recognize the vocabulary, but I cannot define it accurately or use it with confidence.

4 = I can give an accurate definition or explanation of this vocabulary, and I can use it appropriately in a sentence.

___ access to resources	___ psychological diversity
___ cross-cultural psychology	___ psychological universals
___ culture	___ Social Darwinisim
___ ecocultural approach	___ sociobiological approach
___ ecological environment	___ sociology
___ explicit characteristics	___ sociopolitical context
___ implicit characteristics	___ tradition
___ integrative approach	

Do not try to learn the unfamiliar items before you begin reading. You will learn them as you work with the chapter.

Reading and Study Skill Strategies

SCANNING AND SKIMMING

A Before you work with the Introductory Reading on pages 233–236, go through it and write down the headings on the lines below.

The Nature of Cross-Cultural Psychology

_____

_____

_____

B Skim through the sections of the reading under the appropriate headings to find the definitions of the following words. Read quickly. Compare your answers with a classmate's.

cross-cultural psychology: _____

psychological universals: _____

culture: _____

explicit characteristics: _____

implicit characteristics: _____

C Based on the title, headings, and your brief skimming, what do you think you are going to read about in the Introductory Reading?

1. In a few sentences, write your predictions.

_____

_____

_____

2. Write one or two questions that you expect to have answered in the Introductory Reading.

_____

_____

3. Go to page *v* of the Contents. Read the brief summary of this passage, then decide whether to make any changes to your predictions.

4. Compare your predictions and questions with a classmate's. Keep in mind that you may not agree.

INTRODUCTORY READING

The following reading is from Introduction to Cross-Cultural Psychology: Critical Thinking and Contemporary Applications. *As you read, highlight the important ideas and the vocabulary used to express those ideas. Monitor your comprehension by completing the* Before You Continue Reading *statements. Annotate the text.*

The Nature of Cross-Cultural Psychology

1   Before reaching adulthood, most of us do not choose a place to live or a language to speak. Growing up in cities, towns, and villages, no matter where—near a snowy Oslo or in a humid Kinshasa—people learn how to take action, feel, and understand events around them according to the wishes of their parents, societal requirements, and the traditions of their ancestors. The way people learn to relate to the world through feelings and ideas affects what these individuals do. Their actions, in turn, have a bearing on their thoughts, needs, and emotions.

2   Conditions in which people live vary from place to place. Human actions and mental sets—formed and developed in various environments—may also fluctuate from group to group. These kinds of differences—and of course, similarities—are studied by cross-cultural psychology. **Cross-cultural psychology** is the critical and comparative study of cultural effects on human psychology. Please notice two important elements of the definition. This is a *comparative* field. Any study in cross-cultural psychology draws its conclusions from at least two samples that represent at least two cultural groups. Because cross-cultural psychology is all about comparisons, and the act of comparison requires a particular set of critical skills, this study is inseparable from *critical thinking.*

3   Cross-cultural psychology examines psychological diversity and the underlying reasons for such diversity. In particular, cross-cultural psychology studies—again, from a comparative perspective—the linkages between cultural norms and behavior and the ways in which particular human activities are influenced by different, sometimes dissimilar social and cultural forces. Cross-cultural psychology studies cross-cultural interactions. For instance, during several centuries (eighth–fifteenth), southern and central Spain was under Arab control. How did Islam and Arab culture in general influence the culture and subsequent behavior, tradition, and values of predominantly Christian Spaniards? Can we find any traces of Arab influence in individual behavior in Spain and Hispanic cultures today? Is it possible to measure such traces at all?

Fig. 9.1 The Interior of Santa Maria la Blanca, Toledo, Spain (twelfth century)

BEFORE YOU CONTINUE READING

1. The topic of paragraphs 1–3 is _____,

   and the main idea is _____

   _____.

THE CONCEPT OF PSYCHOLOGICAL UNIVERSALS

4   Cross-cultural psychology cares not only about differences between cultural groups. It also establishes *psychological universals*, that is, phenomena common for people in several, many, or perhaps all cultures. The structure of human personality—relatively enduring patterns of thinking, feeling, and acting—is, perhaps, one of such universals. For example, it was found that the same composition of personality is common in people in various countries (such as Germany, Portugal, Israel, China, Korea, and Japan). These universal traits include neuroticism, extroversion, openness to experience, agreeableness, and conscientiousness.

5   Cross-cultural psychological examination is not just a single observation made by a researcher, psychotherapist, or social worker. Listening to an anecdote or witnessing a vivid event cannot substitute for systematic comparisons of behavior and experience measured under different cultural conditions.

BEFORE YOU CONTINUE READING

2. The topic of paragraphs 4 and 5 is _____,

   and the main idea is _____

   _____.

BASIC DEFINITIONS: CULTURE

6   There are perhaps hundreds of definitions of culture. Some of them are elegant and brief, like one proposed by Herskovits (1948), who considered culture as the human-made part of the environment. Other definitions are more specific and state that culture is a wide range of settings in which human behavior occurs. Culture is manifested through particular behaviors and values—typically transmitted from generation to generation—and held by individuals of a society. Culture may function as a moderator of the relationship between experience and social behavior. Culture may also be a label for a set of contextual variables (political, social, historical, ecological, etc.) that is thought by the researcher to be theoretically linked to individual behavior. In brief, most existing definitions of culture focus on ideas, values, practices, norms, roles, and self-definitions.

7   For the purpose of this chapter, we define **culture** as a set of attitudes, behaviors, and symbols shared by a large group of people and usually communicated from one generation to the next. *Attitudes* include beliefs (political, ideological, religious, moral, etc.), values, general knowledge (empirical and theoretical), opinions, superstitions, and stereotypes. *Behaviors* include a wide variety of norms, roles, customs, traditions, habits, practices, and fashions. *Symbols* represent things or ideas, the meaning of which is bestowed on them by people. A symbol may have the form of a material object, a color, a sound, a slogan, a building, or anything else. People attach specific meaning to specific symbols and pass them to the next generation, thus producing cultural symbols. For example, a piece of land may mean little for a group of people living a few miles away. The same land, nevertheless, may be a symbol of unity and glory for the people living on this land.

Fig. 9.2 Traditional Japanese bride and groom

BEFORE YOU CONTINUE READING

3. The topic of paragraphs 6 and 7 is _____ ,
and the main idea is _____
_____ .

CHARACTERISTICS OF CULTURES

8   Cultures can be described as having both *explicit* and *implicit characteristics*. Explicit characteristics of culture are the set of observable acts regularly found in this culture. These are overt customs, observable practices, and typical behavioral responses, such as saying "hello" to a stranger. Implicit characteristics refer to the organizing principles that are inferred to lie behind these regularities on the basis of

consistent patterns of explicit culture. For example, grammar that controls speech, rules of address, hidden norms of bargaining, or particular behavioral expectations in a standard situation may be viewed as examples of implicit culture. In studying cultures, it must be kept in mind that no two cultures are either entirely similar or entirely different. Within the same cultural cluster there can be significant variations and dissimilarities. For instance, any capitalist society is diverse and stratified. However, some Western countries are more stratified than others, and others achieve relative equality among their citizens.

■ ■ ■

Checking Comprehension

TEXT ANALYSIS

A In the earlier units, you created charts, outlines, diagrams, and flow charts to organize the information presented in the readings. Reread paragraphs 7 and 8. On a separate piece of paper, use one of the formats you have learned to organize the information in these two paragraphs.

B Answer the following questions in complete sentences.

1. What are the main concepts in cross-cultural psychology?

   _____

   _____

2. What are some psychological universals that cross-cultural psychologists have identified?

   _____

   _____

3. Reread the author's definition of *culture*. Which of the three components of culture—attitudes, behavior, and symbols—are implicit? explicit? both? Give examples to support your response.

   _____

   _____

   _____

   _____

SENTENCE FOCUS

Sometimes sentences may be difficult to understand because of the use of dashes. Some authors use dashes as a way of adding information to a sentence. The information between the dashes might be an explanation, a definition, an example, an opinion, emphasis, or any extra information the author wishes to insert.

Reread the paragraph excerpts. Pay attention to the information between the dashes. Then answer the questions that follow.

PARAGRAPH 1

Before reaching adulthood, most of us do not choose a place to live or a language to speak. Growing up in cities, towns, and villages, no matter where—near a snowy Oslo or in a humid Kinshasa—people learn how to take action, feel, and understand events around them according to the wishes of their parents, societal requirements, and the traditions of their ancestors.

Why does the author mentions *snowy Oslo* and *humid Kinshasa*?
    a. To show examples of harsh climates in the world
    b. To show examples of important world capitals
    c. To show examples of societies that are geographically distant from one another

PARAGRAPH 2

Conditions in which people live vary from place to place. Human actions and mental sets—formed and developed in various environments—may also fluctuate from group to group. These kinds of differences—and of course, similarities—are studied by cross-cultural psychology.

What information does the author give about human actions and mental sets? Check all that apply.
    a. ___ They are formed and developed in various environments.
    b. ___ They may fluctuate from group to group.
    c. ___ They are always different in different cultures.
    d. ___ They are studied by cross-cultural psychologists.
    e. ___ They are always the same within a culture.

PARAGRAPH 3

Cross-cultural psychology examines psychological diversity and the underlying reasons for such diversity. In particular, cross-cultural psychology studies—again, from a comparative perspective—the linkages between cultural norms and behavior and the ways in which particular human activities are influenced by different, sometimes dissimilar social and cultural forces.

Why does the author write *again, from a comparative perspective* between dashes?
    a. He is giving an example of cross-cultural psychology.
    b. He is providing a definition of psychological diversity.
    c. He is reminding the reader of something written earlier.

PARAGRAPH 4

Cross-cultural psychology cares not only about differences between cultural groups. It also establishes *psychological universals*, that is, phenomena common for people in several, many, or perhaps all cultures. The structure of human personality—relatively enduring patterns of thinking, feeling, and acting—is, perhaps, one of such universals.

What is the purpose of the phrase *relatively enduring patterns of thinking, feeling, and acting*?

    a. This phrase gives an example of a personality characteristic.

    b. This phrase explains the meaning of *the structure of human personality*.

    c. This phrase provides emphasis for the concept of psychological universals.

Learning Vocabulary

VOCABULARY IN CONTEXT

Reread the paragraphs indicated from the Introductory Reading to figure out the meaning of the italicized words. Then write or circle the correct choice to complete the sentences.

Paragraph 1: *have a bearing on*

The phrase *have a bearing on* means ___.

    a. carry weight with

    b. influence

    c. press down on

Paragraph 2: *fluctuate*

In this paragraph, a synonym of *fluctuate* is _____.

Paragraph 3: *diversity*

In this paragraph, the synonyms of *diversity* are ___.

    a. examination; study

    b. influence; force

    c. difference; dissimilarity

Paragraph 8: *overt*

In this paragraph, a synonym of *overt* is _____.

USING THE DICTIONARY

Read the following excerpts and dictionary entries. Select the most appropriate entry for the context. Then choose the best answer to complete the sentence that follows. If you choose an entry that includes subentries (for example *1a, 1b, 1c*), indicate the letter as well as the number. For Excerpt Two, complete the sentence that follows by using the most appropriate definition. Make sure your sentence is grammatically correct.

EXCERPT ONE

During several centuries (eighth–fifteenth) southern and central Spain was under Arab control. How did Islam and Arab culture in general influence the culture and subsequent behavior, tradition, and values of predominantly Christian Spaniards? Can we find any *traces* of Arab influence in individual behavior in Spain and Hispanic cultures today? Is it possible to measure such *traces* at all?

> **trace** \'trās\ *n* [ME, fr. AF, fr. *tracer* to trace] (14c) **1** *archaic* : a course or path that one follows **2 a :** a mark or line left by something that has passed, *also* : FOOTPRINT **b :** a path, trail, or road made by the passage of animals, people, or vehicles **3 a :** a sign or evidence of some past thing : VESTIGE **b :** ENGRAM **4 :** something (as a line) traced or drawn: as **a :** the marking made by a recording instrument (as a seismograph or kymograph) **b :** the ground plan of a military installation or position either on a map or on the ground **5 a :** the intersection of a line or plane with a plane **b :** the usu. bright line or spot that moves across the screen of a cathode-ray tube; *also* : the path taken by such a line or spot **6 a :** a minute and often barely detectable amount or indication (a ~ of a smile) **b :** an amount of a chemical constituent not always quantitatively determinable because of minuteness — **trace•less** \-ləs\ *adj*
> *syn* TRACE, VESTIGE, TRACK mean a perceptible sign made by something that has passed. TRACE may suggest any line, mark, or discernible effect (a snowfield pockmarked with the *traces* of caribou). VESTIGE applies to a tangible reminder such as a fragment or remnant of what is past and gone (boulders that are *vestiges* of the last ice age). TRACK implies a continuous line that can be followed (the fossilized *tracks* of dinosaurs).

1. In this context, the most appropriate definition of the word *trace* is ___.

2. An example of a *trace* of Arab influence on Spain and on Hispanic culture would be ___.
   a. an Arabic style of architecture in an office building
   b. an Arabic-language newspaper on the newsstand
   c. a mosque for the Islamic people of a Spanish city

Culture is a wide range of settings in which human behavior occurs. Culture is *manifested* through particular behaviors that are held by individuals of a society.

---

¹man•i•fest \'ma-nə-,fest\ *adj* [ME, fr. AF or L; AF *manifeste*, fr. L *manifestus* caught in the act, flagrant, obvious, perh. fr. *manus* + -*festus* (akin to L in*festus* hostile)] (14c) **1 :** readily perceived by the senses and esp. by the sight **2 :** easily understood or recognized by the mind **:** OBVIOUS *syn see* EVIDENT — **man•i•fest•ly** *adv*
²manifest *vt* (14c) : to make evident or certain by showing or displaying *syn see* SHOW — **man•i•fest•er** *n*

Read the two dictionary entries for the word *manifest*. From the entries, we can understand that culture is _____ through the behaviors of people in a society.

WRITE A SUMMARY

In five or six sentences, write a summary of the Introductory Reading. Refer to the statements you wrote in the Before You Continue Reading sections. Remember to use your own words.

_____

_____

_____

_____

_____

_____

INTRODUCING THE MAIN READING

Activate Your Knowledge

A Work with a partner or in a small group. How might people interpret the same event depending on their perspective? For example, imagine people who experience a natural disaster such as an earthquake or a volcanic eruption. How might each of the following people think about and react to such an event?

PERSON	PERSPECTIVE	REACTION
Biologists		
Geologists		
The people who live where the disaster took place		
Anthropologists		

B Put the groups' charts on the board. Work as a class. Discuss the groups' responses. Be prepared to explain your group's work.

Reading and Study Skill Strategies

SCANNING AND SKIMMING

A Before you work with the Main Reading on pages 242–246, go through it and write down the headings on the lines below.

Cross-Cultural Approaches to Studying Human Behavior

_____

_____

_____

_____

B Skim through the sections of the reading under the appropriate headings to find the definitions of the following words. Read quickly. Compare your answers with a classmate's.

sociobiology: _____

sociological approach: _____

ecocultural approach: _____

integrative approach: _____

C **Based on the title, headings, and your brief skimming, what do you think you are going to read about in the Main Reading?**

1. In a few sentences, write your predictions.

_____

_____

_____

2. Write one or two questions you expect to have answered in the Main Reading.

_____

_____

3. Go to page *v* of the Contents. Read the brief summary of this passage, then decide whether to make any changes to your predictions.

4. Compare your predictions and questions with a classmate's. Keep in mind that you may not agree.

MAIN READING

The following reading is from Introduction to Cross-Cultural Psychology: Critical Thinking and Contemporary Applications. *As you read, highlight the important ideas and the vocabulary used to express those ideas. Monitor your comprehension by completing the* Before You Continue Reading *statements. Annotate the text.*

Cross-Cultural Approaches to Studying Human Behavior

1   Cross-cultural psychologists use a variety of models in their approach to studying human behavior. Some cross-cultural psychologists focus on a particular factor that influences human behavior, while others use a more integrative model which incorporates several approaches.

SOCIOBIOLOGICAL APPROACH

2   *Sociobiology* is a theoretical model that explores the ways in which biological factors affect human behavior and thus lay a natural foundation for human culture. This theoretical paradigm claims that general biological laws of behavior are perfectly suited as a fundamental explanation of human behavior. Culture is just a form of existence that provides for fundamental human needs and subsequent goals. According to this approach, the prime goal of human beings is survival. To endure, humans need food and resources. People look for mates, conceive, give birth, and then protect their offspring until children mature. Humans of all cultures, like animals, try to avoid unnecessary pain and eliminate anything that threatens their well-being.

3   One of sociobiology's strongholds is Social Darwinism. According to the natural selection principle, described by Charles Darwin, some organisms—due to various, primarily biological, reasons—are more likely to

survive than others. Typically, healthy, strong, and adaptive individuals have better chances of survival than weak, unhealthy, and slow-adapting human beings. According to the "survival of the fittest" principle, if members of a particular group are better fit to live in an environment than members of other groups, the first group has more of a chance to survive and, consequently, develops a social infrastructure. Therefore, its members have a chance to live in improved social conditions that will make people more competitive. Natural selection also removes practices, norms, and beliefs that have outlived their usefulness. Competition steadily develops society by favoring its best-fit

Fig. 9.3 Charles Darwin (1869)

members. Survivors pass on their advantageous genes to their offspring. Over generations, genetic patterns that promote survival—such as aggressiveness, initiative, curiosity, or obedience—become dominant and then form foundations for a culture. All in all, proponents of this approach offer natural and evolutionary explanations for a diverse array of human behaviors, including cooperation, aggression, intelligence, morality, prejudice, sexual preference, and infidelity.

BEFORE YOU CONTINUE READING

1. The topic of paragraphs 2 and 3 is _____,
   and the main idea is _____
   _____.

SOCIOLOGICAL APPROACH

4   This is a general view of human behavior that focuses on broad social structures that influence society as a whole, and subsequently its individuals. Several prominent sociological theories have had a profound impact on scientific and comparative understanding of human behavior in cultural contexts. On the whole, these theories imply that society exists objectively, apart from our individual experience. There are particular social forces that shape the behavior of large social groups, and human beings develop and adjust their individual responses in accordance to the demands and pressures of larger social groups and institutions. Thus culture is both a product of human activity and its major forming factor.

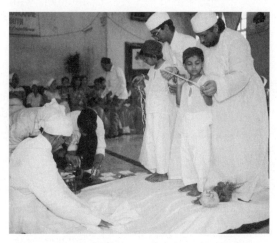

Fig. 9.4 Parsi children performing the Navjote Ritual, a "rite-of-passage" for acceptance into the Parsi community

5   In societies with simple technologies, strong tradition becomes a powerful moral regulator demanding conformity from the society's members. Sharing the same collective conscience, members of such societies penalize those who are different. Everyone is expected to act and think in the same way. This coercive "solidarity" provides people with a powerful sense of belonging. In modern, wealthy societies, on the other hand, discarded traditions break psychological ties among the individuals—like pieces in a broken vase. A huge variety of specializations in the society should make people bond back together. They are interested in relying on one another, but this confidence is based on specialization and diversity and not on tradition or survival needs.

6   The views of another prominent social scientist, Max Weber, are represented in the symbolic-interactionist approach to understanding society and the individual within it. According to Weber (1922), preindustrial societies develop traditions. Passing traditions on from generation to generation, these societies evaluate particular actions of individuals as either appropriate or inappropriate. Capitalist societies, on the contrary, endorse rationality. Rationality is a deliberate assessment of the most efficient ways of accomplishing a particular goal. Reason defeats emotions, calculation replaces intuition, and scientific analysis eliminates speculation.

BEFORE YOU CONTINUE READING

2. The topic of paragraphs 4–6 is _____,
and the main idea is _____
_____.

ECOCULTURAL APPROACH

7   According to this crossdisciplinary comprehensive approach, the individual cannot be separated from his or her environmental context. People constantly exchange messages with the environment, thus transforming it and themselves. In other words, these interactions are reciprocal. The individual is seen not as a passive and static entity influenced by the environment, but as a dynamic human being who interacts with and changes the environment. For example, parents educate their children and at the same time their children educate them.

8   According to Urie Bronfenbrenner, cross-cultural psychologists ought to do their investigation beyond the direct experience of the individual in laboratory conditions. The specialist should pay serious attention to the variety of settings in which the individual develops and understand the culture in its entirety. Bronfenbrenner divides the ecological environment into four interdependent categories: Microsystem, Mesosystem, Exosystem, and Macrosystem. The Microsystem involves immediate family members, schoolteachers, friends, and others who can have face-to-face interaction with the individual. The Mesosystem comprises the linkages between two or more environmental settings. For example, a child may attend a religious school on Sundays, and the teacher from this school and the child's parents may work together, improving the child's understanding of religion. The Exosystem includes the media, extended family, legal and social organizations, and other influencing agents who may have an indirect impact on the individual. Finally, the Macrosystem consists of customs and beliefs most valued in a particular society.

9   According to the ecocultural approach, human environment is a part of a larger cultural system. Both the environment and the individual are seen as open and interchanging systems. Each individual's development takes place within a particular "developmental niche" that can be viewed as a combination of various settings. First there are physical and social settings in which the individual lives: the people, the available products, and services. Second, there are collections of customary practices that convey messages to and from the individual. Finally, there are caretakers' beliefs and expectations about children and their rearing. These three types of settings mediate the individual's development within the larger culture.

BEFORE YOU CONTINUE READING

3. The topic of paragraphs 7 and 8 is _____ ,
and the main idea is _____
_____ .

THE INTEGRATIVE APPROACH

10   To combine and critically apply these—and possibly other approaches to cross-cultural psychology—let us introduce two general concepts: **activity** and **availability of resources**. For the cross-cultural psychologist, human behavior is not only a "result" or "product" of cultural influences. People are also free, active, and rational individuals who are capable of exercising their own will. **Activity** is a process of the individual's goal-directed interaction with the environment. Human motivation, emotion, thought, and reactions cannot be separated from human activity, which is (1) determined by individual, socioeconomic, environmental, political, and cultural conditions and also (2) changes in these conditions. In fact, human psychology develops within human activity and manifests through it. Imagine, for example, a child who grows up in a zone of an ethnic conflict and for whom survival becomes a primary activity. He or she develops emotions, motivation, and cognitive processes quite different from those children who grew up in safe conditions. At the same time, because this child can also engage in activities similar for children in most environments—like playing, learning arithmetic, thinking about the future, helping parents, to name a few—the child will be likely to share many common psychological characteristics with his or her counterparts around the world. Cultures may be similar and different in terms of the most common activities of their members.

11   Presence of and access to resources essential for the individual's well-being largely determine type, scope, and direction of human activities. There are societies with plenty of resources available and there are regions in which resources are extremely scarce. Geographic location, climate, natural disasters, or absence of such may determine what resources are available to individuals.

12   Quality of environment and access to resources may become crucial factors determining many cultural characteristics. They may directly or indirectly affect human activities and individual psychological developments. Poverty, for instance, is clearly linked to a shorter life span and poorer health. The poor tend to live in more harmful environments and are more likely to be exposed to diseases and other risks than those who are not poor. Malnutrition in childhood, particularly during the first year of life, childhood infections, and exposure to accidents and injuries

all make chronic and sometimes disabling diseases more likely in adult life, causing substantial changes in individual activities. Overall, would a condition such as poverty affect the way people make decisions, see themselves, others, and their environment?

Fig. 9.5 Women from a village in Senegal, Africa, drawing water from a well

13   Presence of resources does not mean equal availability to all members of that society. **Access to resources** is another important factor that unifies and separates people and cultures from one another. People's access to resources affects many aspects of culture and individual behavior. Geographic isolation, inequality within a country or region, and the extent of such inequality may influence people's activities and their well-being. Most psychological studies that examine ethnic and cultural minorities point at inequality and oppression as major causes of psychological differences between minorities and mainstream cultural groups. As an example, oppression is often defined as an unequal distribution of resources that causes a sense of psychological inferiority among the oppressed.

14   However, not only material resources and access to them determine major characteristics of culture and culture-linked behavior. Ideas and practices that implement these ideas are inseparable from individual psychology. As we mentioned earlier, Weber revolutionized scientific views on the role of ideas in human life. Take, for example, the role that people assign to their families and ancestors. Since ancient times in Chinese society, contrary to European countries, the family—not the individual—has been regarded as the basic social unit. The human being, therefore, is valued primarily as part of a larger community and not as a self-contained individual.

■ ■ ■

Checking Comprehension

TEXT ANALYSIS

You learned in earlier chapters that text often contains key words that help the reader organize ideas. For example, paragraph 1 tells you that cross-cultural psychologists use a variety of models in their approach to studying human behavior. The phrase *variety of models* alerts the reader that several approaches are going to be discussed. The headings in the Main Reading give you the names of each approach. Now you can organize the information in a way that will help you understand and remember it.

A Use the chart below to organize the information in the text with regard to the four theories presented in this chapter.

CROSS-CULTURAL APPROACHES TO STUDYING HUMAN BEHAVIOR		
Approach	**Key Concepts**	**Proponents of This Approach**
Sociobiological approach explores the ways in which biological factors affect human behavior and lay a natural foundation for human culture		

Sometimes you want to create graphic representations of text to help you understand it better. For example, paragraph 8 describes Urie Bronfenbrenner's ecological systems theory.

B Work with a partner or in a small group. On a separate piece of paper, create a diagram which illustrates the four interdependent categories in Bronfenbrenner's theory. Be sure to indicate the interactions between the four categories.

C Put the groups' diagrams on the board. Work as a class. Create a class diagram of Bronfenbrenner's ecological systems theory.

D **Answer the following questions in complete sentences.**

1. How do proponents of the sociobiological approach explain human behavior?

   _____

   _____

   _____

2. According to the sociological approach, what role do traditions play in some societies?

   _____

   _____

   _____

3. According to the ecocultural approach, what settings mediate the development of the individuals within a culture?

   _____

   _____

   _____

4. How does a theoretical model, or theoretical approach, help people study a particular subject? Give an example.

   _____

   _____

   _____

SENTENCE FOCUS

When reading academic texts, you need to be able to critique the author. Read the following statements about the theories and approaches presented in the Main Reading. Then read the list of critiques on the next page. Think critically about the information being presented and match it to the appropriate statement. One has been done as an example.

STATEMENTS

___f___ 1. According to Social Darwinism, competition steadily develops society by favoring its best-fit members. Survivors pass on their advantageous genes to their offspring.

_____ 2. Proponents of the sociobiological approach offer natural and evolutionary explanations for a diverse array of human behaviors, including cooperating, aggression, intelligence, morality, prejudice, sexual preference, and infidelity.

_____ 3. On the whole, theories that support the sociological approach imply that society exists objectively, apart from our individual experience.

_____ **4.** Capitalist societies endorse rationality. Rationality is a deliberate assessment of the most efficient ways of accomplishing a particular goal. Reason defeats emotions, calculation replaces intuition, and scientific analysis eliminates speculation.

_____ **5.** According to the ecocultural approach, physical and social settings, collections of customary practices, and caretakers' beliefs and expectations about children and their rearing mediate the individual's development within the larger culture.

_____ **6.** Oppression is often defined as an unequal distribution of resources that causes a sense of psychological inferiority among the oppressed.

CRITIQUES

a. This idea is too general. Not everyone who has unequal access to resources feels inferior to those who do have access.

b. This approach implies that individuals can never influence the society in which they live, but in Chapter 4 we saw how individuals such as Sequoyah, Galileo, and Newton had a major influence on their cultures.

c. To a large degree, this approach seems true, but there is also the individual's response to all these factors. Individuals may be in conflict with, or even reject, the beliefs, customs, and environment in which they live.

d. This approach doesn't seem to address the fact that many times people do not cooperate even when doing so will help them, or the fact that intelligence has not been proven to be hereditary.

e. This is a very general statement. Many people in such societies do not make decisions by objectively evaluating the best way to do or decide something. How can the author explain why people overeat, or drive inefficient cars?

f. The problem with this theory is that in many societies, the ill, injured, and less fit are often cared for, survive, and have children.

Learning Vocabulary

VOCABULARY IN CONTEXT

Reread the paragraphs indicated from the Main Reading to figure out the meaning of the italicized words. Then write or circle the correct choice to complete the sentences.

Paragraph 2: *thus* and *endure*

1. From the context, we can understand that *thus* means ___.
   a. however
   b. in this way
   c. afterward

2. In this paragraph, a synonym for *endure* is _____.

Paragraph 3: *proponents*

From the context, we can understand that *proponents* ___.
  a. support a particular theory
  b. oppose a particular theory
  c. study a particular theory

Paragraph 6: *rationality*

In this context, a synonym for *rationality* is _____.

Paragraph 7: *reciprocal*

From the context, we can understand that in a *reciprocal* relationship, people ___.
  a. do something for another person who pays them
  b. do something for each other of equal value
  c. always do the same thing for each other

USING THE DICTIONARY

Read the following excerpts and dictionary entries. Select the most appropriate entry for the context, and choose the best answer to complete the sentence that follows or answer the question that follows.

EXCERPT ONE

Sociobiology is a theoretical model that explores the ways in which biological factors affect human behavior and thus lay a natural foundation for human culture. This theoretical *paradigm* claims that general biological laws of behavior are perfectly suited as a fundamental explanation of human behavior.

par•a•digm \'per-ə-,dīm, 'pa-rə *also* -,dim\ *n* [LL *paradigma,* fr. Gk *paradeigma,* fr. *paradeiknynai* to show side by side, fr. *para-* + *deiknynai* to show — more at DICTION] (15c) **1 :** EXAMPLE, PATTERN; *esp* : an outstandingly clear or typical example or archetype **2 :** an example of a conjugation or declension showing a word in all its inflectional forms **3 :** a philosophical and theoretical framework of a scientific school or discipline within which theories, laws, and generalizations and the experiments performed in support of them are formulated — **par•a•dig•mat•ic** \,per-ə-dig-'ma-tik, ,pa-rə- \ *adj* — **par•a•dig•mat•i•cal•ly** \-ti-k(ə-)lē\ *adv*

1. In this context, the most appropriate definition for *paradigm* is number ___.

2. According to these sentences, sociobiology is ___.
  a. a framework for systematically studying human behavior from a biological perspective
  b. an example of a word that illustrates how human beings behave
  c. a philosophical perspective on the biological laws that human beings obey

Excerpt Two

In societies with simple technologies, strong tradition becomes a powerful moral regulator demanding conformity from the society's members. Sharing the same collective conscience, members of such societies penalize those who are different. Everyone is expected to act and think in the same way. This *coercive* "solidarity" provides people with a powerful sense of belonging.

> **co•erce** \kō-'ərs\ *vt* **co•erced; co•erc•ing** [ME *cohercen,* fr. AF **cohercer* L *coercēre,* fr. co- + *arcēre* to shut up, enclose — more at ARK] (15c) **1 :** to restrain or dominate by force ⟨religion in the past has tried to ∼ the irreligious — W. R. Inge⟩ **2 :** to compel to an act or choice ⟨was *coerced* into agreeing⟩ **3 :** to achieve by force or threat ⟨∼ compliance⟩ *syn* see FORCE — **co•erc•ible** \-'ər-sə-bəl\ *adj*
> **co•er•cion** \-'ə r-zhən, -shən\ *n* (15c) : the act, process, or power of coercing
> **co•er•cive** \-'ə r-siv\ *adj* (ca. 1600) : serving or intended to coerce ⟨∼ power⟩ ⟨∼ measures⟩—**co•er•cive•ly** *adv* — **co•er•cive•ness** *n*

When people are coerced, do they act willingly or unwillingly? Do people experience any advantages by acting and thinking in ways their society expects of them? Write a paragraph in which you respond to these questions. In your paragraph, demonstrate your understanding of the concept of coercion.

_____

_____

_____

_____

_____

WRITE A SUMMARY

In five or six sentences, write a summary of the Main Reading. Refer to the statements you wrote in the Before You Continue Reading sections. Remember to use your own words.

_____

_____

_____

_____

_____

_____

LEARN AND USE WORD FORMS

A Study the word forms in the chart below. If you are not sure about the meaning of a word, reread the text, highlight the words and any of their forms, and try to understand them from context.

VERB	NOUN	ADJECTIVE	ADVERB
adapt	adaptation	adaptive	
compare	comparison	comparative	comparatively
fluctuate	fluctuation	fluctuating	
interact	interaction	interactive	interactively
observe	observation	observable observed/observing	
represent	representation	representative	
vary	variation/ variety/variable	varied/varying	
diversify	diversity	diverse	
rationalize	rationality	rational	rationally
symbolize	symbol	symbolic	symbolically
theorize	theory	theoretical	theoretically

B Read the sentences below. Choose the appropriate word from the following sets and complete each sentence. Be sure to use the correct tense of verbs in either the affirmative or the negative and the singular or plural of nouns. Use each word only once.

adapt	observe	represent
compare	rationalize	vary

1. Traditions among cultural groups can be quite _____, depending on social, environmental, ecological, and other factors.

2. Cultures with simple technologies usually _____ their actions. They rely instead on traditions to guide their actions.

3. Cross-cultural psychologists always make _____ between two or more cultural groups. They do not study a single culture in isolation.

4. A symbol is a concrete or abstract _____ of a thing or an idea.

5. Organisms that _____ to changing environmental conditions have a better chance of survival than those that cannot adjust.

6. Explicit characteristics are _____, for example, the way people greet each other, how people dress, or how they celebrate holidays.

diversify	interact	theorize
fluctuate	symbolize	

7. Most disciplines use _____ frameworks or models to help them conduct research in their subject areas.

8. Cultures that _____ with each other, whether peacefully or not, invariably influence each other.

9. In many cultures, a handshake is a _____ gesture. Its original meaning has been lost over time.

10. When anthropologists or cross-cultural psychologists study past cultures, they learn that those cultures _____ over time, just as cultures today vary.

11. In the twenty-first century, many cultures are much more _____ than they may have been in the past.

FOLLOW-UP ASSIGNMENTS

Before you begin any of the assignments, review the content-specific vocabulary and academic vocabulary below, and look over the vocabulary in the word form chart on page 252. If you are still unsure what any words or terms mean, go back through the chapter and review. As you complete the assignments, be sure to incorporate the appropriate vocabulary.

Content-Specific Vocabulary

access to resources	implicit	Social Darwinisim
cross-cultural	characteristics	sociobiological
psychology	integrative approach	approach
culture	psychological	sociology
ecocultural approach	diversity	sociopolitical
ecological	psychological	context
environment	universals	
explicit		
characteristics		

Academic Vocabulary

availability	endure	paradigm
coercive	fluctuate	rationality
culture	interact	symbol
diversity	manifest	trace
dominant	overt	tradition

Writing Activities

1. Paragraph 4 in the Introductory Reading discusses psychological universals and points out that the structure of human personality is one such universal. Select two or three of the universals mentioned in paragraph 4 and consider them in light of two cultures you are familiar with. Write three paragraphs. In the first paragraph, describe the two cultures you have chosen. In the second paragraph, discuss one of the psychological universals you have chosen and outline how they are the same in both cultures. In the third paragraph, do the same with the second psychological universal you have selected.

2. In Chapters 3 and 4, you researched several cultural groups. Choose two of those cultural groups. Compare the two groups from the point of view of a cross-cultural psychologist. Choose one approach: sociobiological, sociological, ecocultural, or integrative. In the first paragraph, describe the first culture. In the second paragraph, describe the second culture. In the third paragraph, compare the two cultures.

3. Paragraphs 10–13 in the Main Reading discuss *activity* and *availability of resources* as important concepts in the integrative approach. Choose two cultural groups you are familiar with. Compare the two groups, taking into consideration their availability of resources. Write three paragraphs. In the first paragraph, describe the first culture. In the second paragraph, describe the second culture. In the third paragraph, compare the two cultures with regard to their availability of resources and the effect this has had on each culture.

Extension Activities

1. Paragraph 14 in the Main Reading mentions the role that people assign to their families and ancestors. Choose two cultures to research. Investigate the roles that family and ancestors have in each of the cultures, and compare them. Prepare an oral report, a written report, or a poster, and present your findings to the class.

2. Research two cultures that interest you. Do not choose any of the cultural groups that you have already learned about in previous chapters. Take one of the approaches outlined in this chapter, i.e., sociobiological, sociological, ecocultural, or integrative. Investigate some aspects of these cultures, for example, their attitudes, explicit characteristics, implicit characteristics, or symbols. Prepare an oral report, a written report, or a poster, and present your findings to the class.

3. Paragraph 3 in the Introductory Reading mentions that the areas of southern and central Spain were under Arab control for several centuries and asks what influence Islam and Arab culture may have had on the Christian Spaniards of that time and later times. Research this subject. Find out when Spain was under Arab control and what the cultural and behavior influences were. Prepare an oral report, a written report, or a poster, and present your findings to the class.

4. Conduct research on the Internet. Go online. Use a search engine such as Google, AltaVista, Yahoo, About, or Dogpile. Investigate a topic related to the information you read about in Chapter 9. Choose a topic that especially interests you. You may wish to follow up on one of the questions you wrote on page 232 or page 242. Use key words such as *cross-cultural psychology, sociobiological approach, ecocultural approach, ecological environment, integrative approach, psychological diversity, psychological universals, Social Darwinisim, Urie Bronfenbrenner, Max Weber,* and the names of two cultures that interest you, for comparison. Prepare an oral report, a written report, or a poster, and present your findings to the class.

CHAPTER
10

THEORIES OF HUMAN MOTIVATION

Fig. 10.0 Elementary school children raising their hands to answer a question

Chapter Readings

Motivation and Behavior

Universal Mechanisms of Human Motivation

INTRODUCING THE READING

Activate Your Knowledge

A Read the following situations. As you read, consider why the people in these situations acted as they did. In a similar situation, would you have behaved the same or differently? Why?

1. Daniel Crocker was a 38-year-old professional who lived peacefully in suburban Virginia with his wife and two children. One day he quit his job, consulted his minister and family, and boarded a plane to Kansas, where he willingly confessed to strangling a woman 19 years earlier.

2. Clementina Geraci, three months pregnant, made the decision of her life when doctors told her that her breast cancer had spread. She could fight the cancer aggressively and have an abortion, or she could take less hazardous cancer drugs and carry the baby to term but risk her own life. She gave birth to her son, Dylan. Four months after his birth, she died.

3. Continuous harassment, abuse, insults, and, finally, a 16-year imprisonment did not break Nelson (Rolihlahla) Mandela. Over the years, his beliefs grew stronger, and his motivation and faith became an extraordinary symbol of black resistance against racism in South Africa. He became South Africa's first black president.

4. During World War II, Soviet dictator Joseph Stalin refused a German offer to exchange his son—a Red Army officer and prisoner of war—for a German general captured earlier by the Soviet troops. Stalin allegedly said that one wouldn't exchange a captured soldier for a general. Stalin's son was later killed by the Nazis.

Brief descriptions of people's actions can reveal a lot about human behavior. However, they usually say very little about what motivated people to take extraordinary steps. What causes their determination, stamina, and will power? Where do people find resources to pursue their goals—religion? instincts? rational calculations? individual desires? collective goals? To survive, we all need to breathe, eat, and avoid unnecessary pain and discomfort. But where do other needs come from? Do we learn about greed, aggression, and success? Does culture have any influence on our needs?

B Before you begin the next section, take a few moments to think about the questions posed above. Think about one of the situations described. Write what you think the answers might be to these questions for that particular person's behavior.

_____

_____

_____

_____

_____

PREVIEW KEY VOCABULARY

Read the content-specific vocabulary below and determine how well you know each one. Use a scale of 1 to 4, where:

1 = I have never seen or heard this vocabulary before.

2 = I have seen or heard this vocabulary before, but I do not know what it means.

3 = I recognize the vocabulary, but I cannot define it accurately or use it with confidence.

4 = I can give an accurate definition or explanation of this vocabulary, and I can use it appropriately in a sentence.

___ Abraham Maslow

___ achievement motivation

___ collectivist-success motivation

___ extrinsic motivation

___ hierarchy of needs

___ humanistic theories

___ individualist-success motivation

___ industrial society

___ instincts

___ intrinsic motivation

___ natural selection

___ preindustrial society

___ self-actualization

___ sociobiological approach

___ sociological approach

Do not try to learn the unfamiliar items before you begin reading. You will learn them as you work with the chapter.

SCANNING AND SKIMMING

A **Before you work with the Introductory Reading on pages 259–262, go through it and write down the headings and subheadings on the lines below.**

Motivation and Behavior

_____

_____

_____

B **Read the following questions. Then skim through the sections of the reading under the appropriate headings to find the answers. Read quickly. Compare your answers with a classmate's.**

1. What is the working definition of **motivation** in this chapter?

_____

2. What aspect of evolution is addressed by sociobiologists?

_____

3. What two types of society are described by social scientists?

_____

C **Based on the title, headings, and your brief skimming, what do you think you are going to read about in the Introductory Reading?**

1. In a few sentences, write your predictions.

_____

_____

_____

2. Write one or two questions that you expect to have answered in the Introductory Reading.

_____

_____

3. Go to page _v_ of the Contents. Read the brief summary of this passage, then decide whether to make any changes to your predictions.

4. Compare your predictions and questions with a classmate's. Keep in mind that you may not agree.

INTRODUCTORY READING

The following reading is from Introduction to Cross-Cultural Psychology: Critical Thinking and Contemporary Applications. _As you read, highlight the important ideas and the vocabulary used to express those ideas. Monitor your comprehension by completing the_ Before You Continue Reading _statements. Annotate the text._

Motivation and Behavior

1   **Motivation** is a condition—usually an internal one—that initiates, activates, or maintains the individual's goal-directed behavior. The nature of human motivation is a subject of discussions and continuous attempts to find a universal theory that would explain it. Sociobiologists, for example, generally believe that biological factors best explain social behavior. Some sociological theories claim the nature of human motivation is social or economic. Classical psychologists have also contributed to the theory of motivation by determining major psychological mechanisms that underlie basic human needs. Let us briefly examine several well-established theories of motivation. A critical examination of these approaches provides cross-cultural psychologists with valuable ideas that can be used to analyze specific kinds of human motivation.

1. The topic of paragraph 1 is _____,
   and the main idea is _____
   _____.

SOCIOBIOLOGY: A GLANCE INTO EVOLUTION

2   The origin of human motivation is biological, according to sociobiology. Human beings make rational decisions, develop arts and sciences, and build up modern technologies. Still, despite obvious cultural and economic achievements, people remain a part of the larger biological universe. Above all, people need to survive.

Fig. 10.1 Australian Aborigine hunting in a swamp

The *natural selection* principle, first described by Charles Darwin in the nineteenth century, becomes a key interpreter of human behavior in sociobiology. Due to genetic variations, some organisms are more likely to survive than others. Those who survive pass on their "advantageous" genes to their offspring. Over many generations, genetic patterns that promote survival become dominant. For instance, hunters become successful seekers and killers of animals and gatherers become excellent finders of berries, roots, and fruit. Herbert Spencer (1954) asserted that the struggle for survival within the human species motivates people to compete for scarce resources. Individuals who are skillful competitors, who are fit for the struggle, will succeed and prosper. The unfit, or those who lack the motivation to compete, will fail. Life is unjust, but who says it should be? (Summer, 1970). Survival needs can be individual and collective. Baldwin (1991), for example, suggested that the principle of collective survival is part of the psychology of African people. Continued existence of the group—and not necessarily individual survival—is closely linked to the collective responsibility and interdependence of Africans. Perhaps this explanatory principle is applicable not only to African culture, but also to most social and ethnic groups that have been oppressed or continue to live under oppression.

2. The topic of paragraph 2 is _____,
   and the main idea is _____
   _____.

3   The sociobiological approach to human motivation generally fails to explain the diversity of human needs and overlooks the influence of social, cultural, and religious factors. For example, personal wealth and birth rate are negatively correlated: nations that have high income per capita usually have low birth rates. According to sociobiology, the more threatened people are economically, the more children they will have, hoping that some of them will survive. On the other hand, economic security guarantees that the child will live, and, therefore, people are not as motivated to have more children (Schubert, 1991). This link has been proven in many countries around the world. However, the "wealth/birth rate" correlation is not proven in rich Arab nations of the Persian basin that continue to have high birth rates.

BEFORE YOU CONTINUE READING

3. The topic of paragraph 3 is _____,

   and the main idea is _____

   _____.

THEORIES OF SOCIAL INSTINCTS

4   Theories of social instincts emphasize the universal role of basic **instincts**—relatively complex and inherited biological mechanisms, similar in humans and animals. A founder of Russian experimental psychology, V. Bekhterev (1921), wrote about the inborn "social reflexes" that determine human actions. Social reflexes are universal for all people in all cultures and cause humans to act purposefully, overthrow governments, write music, and commit crimes. G. Tarde (1903), a prominent scientist from France, suggested that everything in human behavior—envy, vanity, friendship, hatred, and love—is

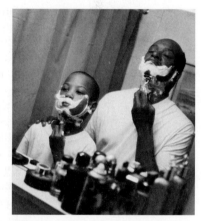

Fig. 10.2 A son imitating his father shaving

the result of the natural process of imitation. According to Tarde, different social conditions, including national traditions, customs, and norms, are maintained because of people's natural instinct of imitation. All in all, these and many other theories of social instincts attempt to offer simple and attractive explanations or analogies that could be suitable for the analysis of human motivation and behavior across cultures. Yet psychological research yields little empirical evidence of the existence of human instincts as "preinstalled" software that causes human action.

BEFORE YOU CONTINUE READING

4. The topic of paragraph 4 is _____,

   and the main idea is _____

   _____.

5   In contrast to sociobiological theories, the sociological approach emphasizes the crucial role of social factors in determining individual motivation. We illustrate the sociological approach by describing two theories.

SOCIAL SCIENCE: SEE THE SOCIETY FIRST

6   Consider, for example, the views of Max Weber (1922). Weber drew a line between two types of societies: preindustrial (traditional) and industrial (nontraditional). People in preindustrial societies are inseparable from traditions and customs. In these societies, people's desires and actions are viewed as appropriate and inappropriate on the basis of their links—or lack thereof—to the existing customs and rules. For example, married couples in traditional societies are not likely to pursue divorce. It is inappropriate behavior because it destroys the traditional family. Capitalist societies, on the contrary, endorse rationality as a pillar of human motivation. People deliberately assess the most efficient ways of accomplishing a particular goal. If two spouses decide that they cannot live together any longer, they could break up their marriage. Why? Because this act serves their best interest. In such cases, reason overcomes emotion, calculation replaces intuition, and scientific analysis eliminates superstition. The scarcity and value of their time often motivate people in modern societies, whereas in traditional cultures time is not viewed as a commodity.

7   Another prominent sociologist and economist, Karl Marx, preached that an economic condition of inequality activates human needs (Marx, 1867). Each society is divided roughly into two large and antagonistic social classes. People of the same social class, but of different ethnic groups, have much more in common than people belonging to the same ethnic or national group, but to an antagonistic social class. The oppressed want their share of resources, whereas the oppressors want to keep the status quo. Despite its attractiveness, Marxism failed to explain many other noneconomic aspects of human motivation. For example, it is easy to show that social equality, unfortunately, does not stop aggression and violence. Similarly, economic inequality does not necessarily cause hostility among people.

■ ■ ■

Checking Comprehension

TEXT ANALYSIS

Very often writers introduce a topic in the first paragraph and include sentences that outline the reading. For example, in paragraph 1, the writer states *let us briefly examine several well-established theories of motivation*. The writer further says that *a critical examination of these approaches* will be useful. The reader, therefore, can expect the author to describe a few theories of motivation and to critique them. Creating a diagram to organize this information will help you understand and remember the text.

Reread the Introductory Reading. Use the diagram below to organize the information.

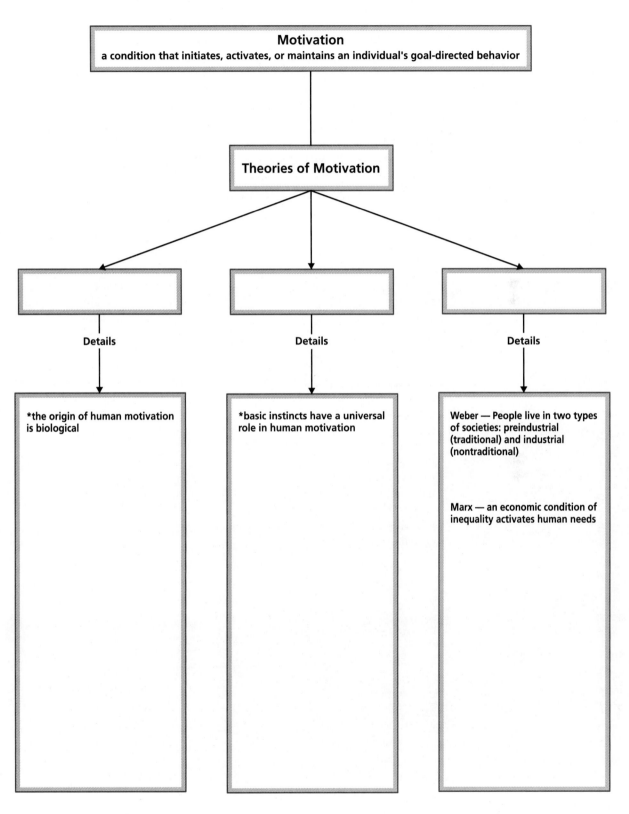

Motivation
a condition that initiates, activates, or maintains an individual's goal-directed behavior

Theories of Motivation

Details

*the origin of human motivation is biological

Details

*basic instincts have a universal role in human motivation

Details

Weber — People live in two types of societies: preindustrial (traditional) and industrial (nontraditional)

Marx — an economic condition of inequality activates human needs

SENTENCE FOCUS

Sometimes authors present theories and approaches for the reader's understanding, but then also offer an opinion or critique of them. In the Introductory Reading, the author announces that he will do a "critical examination" of several theories of motivation.

A **Reread paragraphs 3, 4, and 7. Identify the sentences in which the author critiques the theory. Write them below.**

PARAGRAPH 3

_____

_____

PARAGRAPH 4

_____

_____

PARAGRAPH 7

_____

_____

B **In the sentences you chose, underline the words or phrases which indicate a critique.**

C Identify some of the statements in the Introductory Reading on pages 259–262 that you question or do not agree with. Then write your critique of these statements. Use the chart below to organize your work. One has been done as an example.

STATEMENTS	A CRITIQUE OF THIS STATEMENT
1. (paragraph 6) Married couples in traditional societies are not likely to pursue divorce. It is inappropriate behavior because it destroys the traditional family. Capitalist societies, on the contrary, endorse rationality as a pillar of human motivation. People deliberately assess the most efficient ways of accomplishing a particular goal. If two spouses decide that they cannot live together any longer, they could break up their marriage. Why? Because this act serves their best interest. In such cases, reason overcomes emotion, calculation replaces intuition, and scientific analysis eliminates superstition. The scarcity and value of their time often motivate people in modern societies, whereas in traditional cultures time is not viewed as a commodity.	This paragraph has many problems. First, divorce doesn't always destroy traditional families. Second, people—even those in capitalist societies—who get divorced are often very emotional and are not rational at all. Third, how they view time seems unrelated to the rest of the paragraph.
2.	
3.	
4.	

VOCABULARY IN CONTEXT

Reread the paragraphs indicated from the Introductory Reading to figure out the meaning of the italicized words. Then circle the correct choice to complete the sentences.

Paragraph 1: *initiates* and *universal*

1. From this context, we can understand that *initiates* means ___.
   a. attracts
   b. forces
   c. sets in motion

2. From this context, we can understand that something *universal* ___.
   a. applies to everyone
   b. exists throughout the universe
   c. is very common

Paragraph 2: *offspring, scarce,* and *collective*

1. From this context, we can understand that *offspring* means ___.
   a. group members
   b. close friends
   c. children

2. From this context, we can understand that *scarce* means ___.
   a. very expensive
   b. in short supply
   c. complex

3. From this context, we can understand that *collective* means ___.
   a. shared by a group
   b. struggled for by individuals
   c. needed by everyone

USING THE DICTIONARY

Read the following excerpts and dictionary entries. Select the most appropriate entry for the context, and choose the best answers to the items that follow. If you choose an entry that includes subentries (for example *1a, 1b, 1c*), indicate the letter as well as the number.

EXCERPT ONE

Some sociological theories claim the nature of human motivation is social or economic. Classical psychologists have also contributed to the theory of motivation by determining major psychological mechanisms that *underlie* basic human needs.

> **un·der·lie** \-'lī\ *vt* **-lay** \-'lā\; **-lain** \-'lān\; **-ly·ing** \-'lī-iŋ\ (bef. 12c) **1** *archaic* : to be subject or amenable to **2** : to lie or be situated under **3** : to be at the basis of : form the foundation of : SUPPORT ⟨ideas *underlying* the revolution⟩ **4** : to exist as a claim or security superior and prior to (another)

1. In this context, the most appropriate definition of *underlie* is _____.

2. According to this sentence, classical psychologists study motivation and try to discover the psychological factors that _____ our basic human needs, such as the need to survive.
   a. are the real cause of
   b. are situated under
   c. are subject to

EXCERPT TWO

Personal wealth and birth rate are negatively *correlated*: nations that have high income per capita usually have low birth rates. According to sociobiology, the more threatened people are economically, the more children they will have, hoping that some of them will survive. On the other hand, economic security guarantees that the child will live, and, therefore, people are not as motivated to have more children. This link has been proven in many countries around the world. However, the "wealth/birth rate" *correlation* is not proven in rich Arab nations of the Persian basin that continue to have high birth rates.

cor·re·late \-ˌlāt\ *vb* **-lat·ed; -lat·ing** *vi* (ca. 1742) : to bear reciprocal or mutual relations: CORRESPOND ~ *vt* **1 a :** to establish a mutual or reciprocal relation between ⟨~ activities in the lab and the field⟩ **b :** to show correlation or a causal relationship between **2 :** to present or set forth so as to show relationship ⟨he ~s the findings of the scientists, the psychologists, and the mystics — Eugene Exman⟩—**cor·re·lat·able** \-ˌlā-tə-bəl\ *adj* —**cor·re·lat·or** \-ˌlā-tər\ *n*
cor·re·la·tion \ˌkȯr-ə-'lā-shən, ˌkär-\ *n* [ML *correlation-, correlatio*, fr. L *com-* + *relation-, relatio* relation] (1561) **1 :** the state or relation of being correlated; *specif* : a relation existing between phenomena or things or between mathematical or statistical variables which tend to vary, be associated, or occur together in a way not expected on the basis of chance alone ⟨the obviously high positive ~ between scholastic aptitude and college entrance—J. B. Conant⟩ **2 :** the act of correlating—**cor·re·la·tion·al** \-shnəl, -shə-nᵊl\ *adj*

Read the dictionary entries for *correlate* and *correlation*. Then read the following sentences. In which one do the two facts correlate?
   a. Every time I bring my umbrella with me, it rains.
   b. When the weather is beautiful, class attendance usually goes down.
   c. When my cat is hungry, the dog is sleeping.

WRITE A SUMMARY

In five or six sentences, write a summary of the Introductory Reading. Refer to the statements you wrote in the Before You Continue Reading sections. Remember to use your own words.

_____

_____

_____

_____

_____

INTRODUCING THE MAIN READING

Activate Your Knowledge

The reading which follows has been taken from *Introduction to Cross-Cultural Psychology: Critical Thinking and Contemporary Applications*. It discusses the concept of motivation, forces which drive motivation, and theories which help to explain human motivation. To understand the Main Reading, it will be helpful if you review what you read in Chapters 3 and 4, as well as what you read in the Introductory Reading on pages 259–262.

A **A psychologist named Abraham Maslow wrote about the innate needs of human beings. He suggested that these needs must be met in a specific order and that the most basic needs must be met before a person can move on to meet the higher needs. Work alone or with a partner. Consider the five needs Maslow identified. Put them in order, with the most basic as number 1 and the highest need as number 5.**

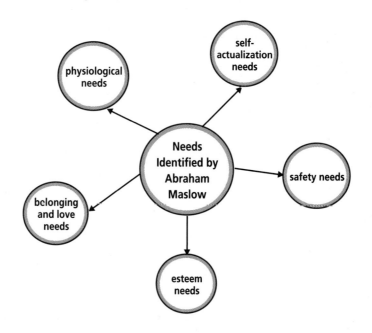

B Compare your ordered list with a classmate's. Keep in mind that you may not agree.

SCANNING AND SKIMMING

A Before you work with the Main Reading on pages 270–274, go through it and write down the headings on the lines below.

<u>   **Universal Mechanisms of Human Motivation**   </u>

_____

_____

_____

_____

B Read the following questions. Then skim through the sections of the reading under the appropriate headings to find the answers. Read quickly. Compare your answers with a classmate's.

1. What aspects of human personality do humanistic theories focus on?

_____

2. What does a self-actualizing person need?

_____

3. What are *intrinsic* and *extrinsic motivation*?

_____

C Based on the title, headings, and your brief skimming, what do you think you are going to read about in the Main Reading?

1. In a few sentences, write your predictions.

_____

_____

_____

2. Write one or two questions you expect to have answered in the Main Reading.

_____

_____

3. Go to page *v* of the Contents. Read the brief summary of this passage, then decide whether to make any changes to your predictions.

4. Compare your predictions and questions with a classmate's. Keep in mind that you may not agree.

MAIN READING

The following reading is from Introduction to Cross-Cultural Psychology: Critical Thinking and Contemporary Applications. *As you read, highlight the important ideas and the vocabulary used to express those ideas. Monitor your comprehension by completing the* Before You Continue Reading *statements. Annotate the text.*

Universal Mechanisms of Human Motivation

1   Human beings are motivated by many of the same needs. In fact, one of the central concepts of motivational theories is **need**, a motivated state caused by physiological or psychological deprivation (such as lack of food or water). The goal of behavior is to attain a state of stability or balance within the individual. Stimuli, such as hunger and pain, energize and initiate our behavior. Traditionally, needs are divided into two categories: *biological* and *social*. Biological needs are universal and direct human behavior toward self-preservation. Indeed, we all have to eat to survive. Social needs direct people toward establishing and maintaining relationships. A number of psychologists have developed theories which help explain these biological and social factors. These theories have been categorized as Humanistic.

BEFORE YOU CONTINUE READING

1. The topic of paragraph 1 is _____ , and the main idea is _____
_____ .

HUMANIST THEORIES: ABRAHAM MASLOW

2   These theories generate some interest among cross-cultural psychologists. They focus on human dignity, individual choice, and self-worth. Abraham Maslow (1970), a pioneer of Humanistic psychology, proposed that humans have a number of innate needs that are arranged in a hierarchy in terms of their potency, or power.

ABRAHAM MASLOW'S HIERARCHY OF NEEDS	
Level 5	Self-Actualization Needs
Level 4	Esteem Needs
Level 3	Belonging and Love Needs
Level 2	Safety Needs
Level 1	Physiological Needs

Based on A. Maslow, Motivation and Personality, 1970

Maslow grouped these needs into five categorical levels: physiological, safety, love, esteem, and self-actualization. Once an individual has satisfied the cluster of needs at a particular level, he or she is able to progress to the next hierarchical level. Thus, for example, people typically are not prompted to seek acceptance and esteem until they have met their needs for food, water, and shelter.

3   Maslow noted that as one ascends the hierarchy of needs, one becomes less animal-like and more humanistic. If the person has been able to satisfy adequately the needs in the first four levels, he or she is in a position to fulfill the highest order needs, namely to actualize one's unique potential. According to Maslow, once a person enters the realm of **self-actualization**, he or she becomes qualitatively different from those who are still attempting to meet their more basic needs. The self-actualizing person's life is governed by the search for "being-values" (B-values), such as Truth, Goodness, Beauty, Wholeness, Justice, and Meaningfulness.

4   Although the structure of needs presented by Maslow may be appropriate for individuals of all cultures, the relative strengths of the needs are culture specific. Self-preoccupation could be seen as a Western characteristic not so dominant in some other cultures. The Chinese hierarchy of values, for instance, includes the promotion of interconnectedness, in contrast to the emphasis on self-development in Maslow's version. In one study, Nevis (1983) revised Maslow's hierarchy of needs, and argued that one of the most basic needs of people in communist China is the need to belong, rather than physiological needs. Moreover, self-actualization could manifest as a devoted service to community. If a person self-actualizes by means of contributing to the group, this individual is realizing the value of collectivist self-actualization!

BEFORE YOU CONTINUE READING

2. The topic of paragraphs 2–4 is _____,
and the main idea is _____
_____.

INTRINSIC AND EXTRINSIC MOTIVATION

5   Cognitive theories maintain that people are aware of their thought patterns and therefore can control their motivation and behavior. People learn what they want and how to achieve rewards, mastery, and affiliation. There are two types of motivation: intrinsic and extrinsic. **Intrinsic motivation** engages people in various activities for no apparent reward except the pleasure and satisfaction of the activity itself. Edward Deci (1972) suggested that people engage in such behaviors for two reasons: to obtain cognitive stimulation and to gain a sense of accomplishment, competency, and mastery over the environment. In contrast, **extrinsic motivation** comes from the external environment. Examples of extrinsic rewards include praise, a high grade, or money given for a particular behavior.

Fig. 10.3 Volunteers serving Christmas dinner to the homeless. Los Angeles, California

Such rewards can strengthen existing behaviors, provide people with information about their performance, and increase feelings of self-worth. In childhood, people begin to learn about both intrinsic and extrinsic rewards. For example, in one study it was found that educated American children displayed a stronger capacity for delaying their expectations for an immediate reward than less educated children, who showed the opposite trend (Doob, 1971). Differences in gender socialization may cause different motivational outcomes. A study of American, Polish, and German children (Boehnke et al., 1989) showed that in all three samples girls preferred intrinsic motives more frequently than boys. Perhaps achievement-oriented motivation was part of the socialization of the boys in the studied nations. Emphasizing the importance of learning and rational choice, cognitive theories can be useful in cross-cultural research. Let us now examine achievement motivation.

> **BEFORE YOU CONTINUE READING**
>
> 3. The topic of paragraph 5 is _____,
> and the main idea is _____
> _____.

ACHIEVEMENT MOTIVATION

6   People constantly strive for achievement and excellence. Take a look at masterpieces of human creativity such as the pyramids in Egypt and the Eiffel tower in Paris. Turn to a sports channel on television and see how athletes of different national, religious, and ethnic backgrounds compete for excellence. Read the poetry of Nizami, the great son of Persia, and any novel written by literary genius Gabriel García Márquez of Colombia. People try to achieve what others could not. **Need for achievement** is a social need that directs people to constantly strive for excellence and success, influence and accomplishment. Activities not oriented toward these goals are not motivating and are usually performed without commitment. Are we born with such motivation to achieve?

> **BEFORE YOU CONTINUE READING**
>
> 4. The topic of paragraph 6 is _____,
> and the main idea is _____
> _____.

7   One of the early leaders in early studies of achievement motivation, David McClelland (1958), gave a categorical "no" to this question. He demonstrated that achievement motivation is learned during childhood. It might be acquired from parents who stress excellence and display affection and emotional rewards to their children for high levels of achievement. During the individual's life, a wide range of social and psychological factors could further influence achievement motivation. If there is no such example set for the child, he or she will not develop the need for achievement.

8   Particular social norms may be linked to this motivation. In a classic research study on motivation, McClelland (1987) analyzed children's stories in 22 cultures with respect to the degree to which the stories showed themes of achievement motivation. He then related these

levels of motivation to measures of economic development in the studied countries. Achievement motivation scores were highly correlated with economic growth of the children's countries. In other words, the greater the emphasis placed on achievement in the stories told to children in various nations, the more rapid the economic development in these nations as the children grew up.

9 In a cross-national project that involved more than 12,000 participants, Furnham et al. (1994) also showed a strong relationship between individual achievement motivation and economic growth. In particular, economic growth correlated with attitudes toward competitiveness. The stronger these attitudes, the higher the achievement motivation. The higher the achievement motivation, the greater the rate of economic growth. It shouldn't take much imagination to realize that any two individuals may develop two different types of achievement motivation: low and high. One strives for excellence and success, the other is happy doing what is required and does not need recognition from others. What definitely is intriguing is the idea of cultural differences in motivation. Do the results of the studies mentioned previously suggest that there are high- and low-achievement-oriented nations and cultures?

BEFORE YOU CONTINUE READING

5. The topic of paragraphs 7–9 is _____,
   and the main idea is _____
   _____.

SUCCESS MOTIVATION

10 This question brings the debate about cultural differences in achievement motivation to a new level. The key to the answer is that achievement or success can be understood in several ways. So-called **individualist-success motivation**—the type of motivation measured in most studies cited so far—affects one's attitudes and actions and is directed to the attainment of personal goals. On the contrary, **collectivist-success motivation** directs a person to connect with other people; the individual's contribution is seen as beneficial to the members of a particular group or society in general (Parsons & Goff, 1978).

Fig. 10.4 Winner of a spelling bee with his trophy

11 Each society chooses standards for excellence and always determines what type of goals—individual or collective—a person is expected to achieve. The individualist type prevails among people in Western cultures, such as the United States, France, and Germany. The collectivist type is more common in Eastern cultures, such as India, Korea, and Japan (Maehr & Nicholls, 1983). In Japan, for

Fig. 10.5 A group of sixteen blind hikers from Japan, South Korea, and Taiwan celebrate after reaching the peak of Jade Mountain in Taiwan (1999)

example, striving for success is motivated more often by a concern for the reaction of others than by the pursuit of personal satisfaction (Gallimore, 1974). Within Chinese culture, collective achievement orientation is regarded as most valuable (Yand, 1986). In Korea, Thailand, and China, there is a special kind of work ethic, according to which future-oriented and harmonious interpersonal networks are essential for business success (Cho & Kim, 1993). It was also found that Australian Aboriginal students placed greater emphasis on collectivist intentions, compared with non-Aboriginal students (Fogarty & White, 1994). Cross-cultural psychologists continue to study a range of cultures, and to learn more about the nature of human motivation.

■ ■ ■

Checking Comprehension

TEXT ANALYSIS

A As you learned throughout this book, charts, diagrams, outlines, and flow charts can help you organize and understand information. Reread paragraph 1. On a separate piece of paper create a chart, diagram, outline, or flow chart to organize the information.

B Answer the following questions in complete sentences.

1. How do biological needs and social needs differ?

_____

_____

2. As people progress through Maslow's hierarchy of needs, how do they change?

_____

_____

3. Are human beings born with the motivation to achieve, or is it a learned behavior? Explain your answer.

_____

_____

4. What is the basic difference between individualist-success motivation and collectivist-success motivation?

_____

_____

C Read the following statements. Indicate which actions represent *intrinsic motivation* (IM) and which represent *extrinsic motivation* (EM).

1. ___ A child receives a toy for cleaning up her room.

2. ___ A student studies for an exam and earns a grade of A.

3. ___ An employee receives a bonus of $500 for his hard work.

4. ___ A student figures out a difficult math calculation even though it was not assigned.

5. ___ A child spends hours building a house of cards.

6. ___ A man takes up painting and paints a landscape.

SENTENCE FOCUS

Certain verbs and expressions in a text indicate whether the author is presenting information as an established theory or research that supports a theory.

A Read the list of words and phrases below. Decide whether they indicate theory or research that supports theory. Place them in the correct box in the chart on the next page.

according to	could + *verb*	maintain	propose
argue that	demonstrate	may + *verb*	show
correlate	find	perhaps	suggest

Words / Phrases That Indicate a Theory	Words / Phrases That Indicate Supporting Research

B Read the sentences below. Mark them *theory* (T) or *supporting research* (SR). Underline the clues in the sentence that helped you decide. The first one has been done as an example.

1. T Abraham Maslow (1970), a pioneer of Humanistic psychology, <u>proposed</u> that humans have a number of innate needs that are arranged in a hierarchy in terms of their potency, or power.

2. _____ David McClelland (1958) demonstrated that achievement motivation is learned during childhood.

3. _____ In one study, Nevis (1983) revised Maslow's hierarchy of needs, and argued that one of the most basic needs of people in communist China is the need to belong, rather than physiological needs.

4. _____ In a cross-national project that involved more than 12,000 participants, Furnham et al. (1994) also showed a strong relationship between individual achievement motivation and economic growth.

5. _____ Edward Deci (1972) suggested that people engage in such behaviors for two reasons: to obtain cognitive stimulation and to gain a sense of accomplishment, competency, and mastery over the environment.

6. _____ In Furnham et al.'s (1994) study, economic growth correlated with attitudes toward competitiveness.

7. _____ In one study, it was found that educated American children displayed a stronger capacity for delaying their expectations for an immediate reward than less educated children, who showed the opposite trend (Doob, 1971).

8. _____ Particular social norms may be linked to achievement motivation.

9. _____ A study of American, Polish, and German children (Boehnke et al., 1989) showed that in all three samples girls preferred intrinsic motives more frequently than boys.

10. _____ Perhaps achievement-oriented motivation was part of the socialization of the boys in the studied nations (Boehnke et al., 1989).

Learning Vocabulary

VOCABULARY IN CONTEXT

Reread the paragraphs indicated from the Main Reading to figure out the meaning of the italicized words. Then write or circle the correct choice to complete the sentences.

Paragraph 1: *deprivation*

From this context, we can understand that *deprivation* refers to ___.
    a. food and water
    b. the lack of something
    c. hunger and pain

Paragraph 3: *ascends* and *actualize*

1. From this context, we can understand that *ascends* means ___.
    a. rises through
    b. controls
    c. motivates

2. In this paragraph, a synonym for *actualize* is _____.

Paragraph 5: *cognitive*

From this context, we can understand that *cognitive* refers to ___.
    a. control
    b. pattern
    c. thought

USING THE DICTIONARY

Read the following excerpts and dictionary entries. Select the most appropriate entry for the context. Then choose the best answer to complete the sentence that follows. If you choose an entry that includes subentries (for example *1a, 1b, 1c*), indicate the letter as well as the number.

EXCERPT ONE
Need for achievement is a social need that directs people to constantly strive for excellence and success, influence, and accomplishment. Activities not oriented toward these goals are not motivating and are usually performed without commitment. Are we born with such motivation to achieve?

One of the early leaders in early studies of achievement motivation, David McClelland (1958), gave a *categorical* "no" to this question. He demonstrated that achievement motivation is learned during childhood.

cat·e·gor·i·cal \ˌka-tə-ˈgȯr-i-kəl, -ˈgär-\ *also* **cat·e·gor·ic** \-ik\ *adj* [LL *categoricus*, fr. Gk *katēgorikos*, fr. *katēgoria*] (1588) **1 :** ABSOLUTE, UNQUALIFIED ⟨a ~ denial⟩ **2 a :** of, relating to, or constituting a category **b :** involving, according with, or considered with respect to specific categories — **cat·e·gor·i·cal·ly** \-i-k(ə-)lē\ *adv*

1. In this context, the most appropriate definition of the word *categorical* is ___.

2. David McClelland's answer to the question was ___.
   a. an unsure "no"
   b. in a negative category
   c. absolutely not

EXCERPT TWO

In a *classic* research study on motivation, McClelland (1987) analyzed children's stories in 22 cultures with respect to the degree to which the stories showed themes of achievement motivation. He then related these levels of motivation to measures of economic development in the studied countries. Achievement motivation scores were highly correlated with economic growth of the children's countries. In other words, the greater the emphasis placed on achievement in the stories told to children in various nations, the more rapid the economic development in these nations as the children grew up.

clas·sic \ˈkla-sik\ *adj* [F or L; F *classique*, fr. L *classicus* of the highest class of Roman citizens, of the first rank, fr. *classis*] (ca. 1604) **1 a :** serving as a standard of excellence : of recognized value ⟨~ literary works⟩ **b :** TRADITIONAL, ENDURING ⟨~ designs⟩ **c :** characterized by simple tailored lines in fashion year after year ⟨a ~ suit⟩ **2 :** of or relating to the ancient Greeks and Romans or their culture : CLASSICAL **3 a :** historically memorable ⟨a ~ battle⟩ **b :** noted because of special literary or historical associations ⟨Paris is the ~ refuge of expatriates⟩ **4 a :** AUTHENTIC, AUTHORITATIVE **b :** TYPICAL ⟨a ~ example of chicanery⟩ **5** *cap* : of or relating to the period of highest development of Mesoamerican and esp. Mayan culture about A.D. 300–900

We can understand from this context that anyone who wishes to do research on achievement motivation ___.
   a. will study McClelland's research first
   b. will not study McClelland's research first
   c. will try to disprove McClelland's research findings

WRITE A SUMMARY

In five or six sentences, write a summary of the Main Reading. Refer to the statements you wrote in the Before You Continue Reading sections. Remember to use your own words.

_____

_____

_____

_____

_____

_____

LEARN AND USE WORD FORMS

A Study the word forms in the chart below. If you are not sure about the meaning of a word, reread the text, highlight the words and any of their forms, and try to understand them from context.

VERB	NOUN	ADJECTIVE	ADVERB
achieve	achievement/achiever	achieved/achieving	
fulfill	fulfillment	fulfilled/fulfilling	
imitate	imitation	imitative	imitatively
initiate	initiation	initiated/initiating	
motivate	motivation/motivator	motivated/motivating	
self-actualize	self-actualization	self-actualized/self-actualizing	
socialize	socialization	socialized/socializing	
diversify	diversity	diverse	
stimulate	stimulus (*plural* stimuli)	stimulated	
survive	survival		

B Read the sentences below. Choose the appropriate word from the following sets and complete each sentence. Be sure to use the correct tense of verbs in either the affirmative or the negative and the singular or plural of nouns. Use each word only once.

| achieve | imitate | survive |
| diversity | self-actualize | |

1. Cross-cultural psychologists sometimes observe considerable _____ in motivational factors among individuals even within homogeneous cultures.

2. The _____ rate of individuals in some environments often depends on their ability to interact successfully with members of their group.

3. The value of individual _____ varies depending on the individualistic or collectivistic nature of the person's culture.

4. People _____ everyone's behavior, only that of people they want to be like.

5. According to Maslow, for people to reach the _____ stage, they must first pass through all the earlier stages.

| fulfill | initiate | motivate | socialize | stimulate |

6. Even within a homogeneous culture, individuals may respond very differently to the same _____.

7. The extrinsic and intrinsic factors that _____ a person's behavior may change over that person's lifetime.

8. Biological needs and social needs _____ different types of behavior as people respond to each need.

9. Children become _____ into their culture at a very early age.

10. A _____ or satisfying life may be defined very differently by different people, even within the same culture.

FOLLOW-UP ASSIGNMENTS

Before you begin any of the assignments, review the content-specific vocabulary and academic vocabulary below, and look over the vocabulary in the word form chart on page 279. If you are still unsure what any words or terms mean, go back through the chapter and review. As you complete the follow-up assignments, be sure to incorporate the appropriate vocabulary.

Content-Specific Vocabulary

Abraham Maslow	individualist-success	self-actualization
achievement	motivation	sociobiological
motivation	industrial society	approach
collectivist-success	instincts	sociological
motivation	intrinsic	approach
extrinsic	motivation	
motivation	natural selection	
hierarchy of needs	preindustrial	
humanistic	society	
theories		

Academic Vocabulary

correlation	offspring	survival
diversity	promote	theory
fulfillment	scarce	underlie
imitate	stimulus	universal
initiate	(*plural* stimuli)	

Writing Activities

1. Consider your own culture in light of the motivational theories presented here. Write three paragraphs. In the first paragraph, describe your culture. In the second paragraph, describe the theory of success motivation. In the third paragraph, interpret your cultural group's behavior with regard to either individualist-success motivation or collectivist-success motivation. Give examples to support your interpretation.

2. Review the four situations described on page 257. Select one. Write three paragraphs. In the first paragraph, review the situation you have chosen. In the second paragraph, outline the human motivation theory you will use to interpret the individual's behavior. In the third paragraph, interpret the individual's behavior in light of the theory you have selected, and give your reasons for your choice.

3. Think about either Max Weber's or Karl Marx's social science theories. Write three paragraphs. In the first paragraph, describe this person's theory. In the second paragraph, outline the main points of his theory that you agree with, and explain why you agree. In the third paragraph, explain the points you disagree with, and explain why you disagree.

Extension Activities

1. Research one of the individuals whose actions are described on page 257. Use the Internet, periodicals, and books. Find out more about this person. Think about what may have motivated this person's behavior. Prepare an oral report, a written report, or a poster, and present your findings to the class.

2. Research two of the cultures mentioned in Chapter 10. Compare them in light of one of the theories presented. Prepare an oral report, a written report, or a poster, and present your findings to the class.

3. Find out more about one of the studies cited in the Chapter 10. Prepare an oral report, a written report, or a poster, and present your findings to the class. Be sure to include a critique of the research in your report.

4. Conduct research on the Internet. Go online. Use a search engine such as Google, AltaVista, Yahoo, About, or Dogpile. Investigate a topic related to the information you read about in Chapter 10. Choose a topic that especially interests you. You may wish to follow up on one of the questions you wrote on page 259 or page 269. Use key words such as: *motivational theory, humanistic theory, Abraham Maslow, hierarchy of needs, intrinsic motivation, extrinsic motivation, collectivism, V. Bekhterev, Max Weber,* and *Karl Marx*. Prepare an oral report, a written report, or a poster, and present your findings to the class.

INDEX OF KEY WORDS AND PHRASES

CREDITS

Photo Credits: **Page 1,** left: © David Aubrey/Corbis. right: © Kevin Fleming/Corbis. **Page 2,** © Peter Johnson/Corbis. **Page 9,** Hulton Archive/Getty Images. **Page 10,** Paul McCormick/The Image Bank/Getty Images. **Pages 11, 21,** Enger, et al., *Concepts in Biology 9e.* © 2000 McGraw-Hill. Reproduced with permission of the McGraw-Hill Companies. **Page 22,** © Niall Benvie/Corbis. **Page 24,** Courtesy Sybille Kalas. **Page 31,** Enger, et al., *Concepts in Biology 9e.* © 2000 McGraw-Hill. Reproduced with permission of the McGraw-Hill Companies. **Page 33,** top: © Royalty-Free/Corbis. bottom: © Dean Conger/Corbis. **Page 37,** © Michael & Patricia Fogden/Corbis. **Page 44,** © Dion Ogust/The Image Works. **Page 47,** © D. Robert & Lorri Franz/Corbis. **Page 48,** © Harry Rogers/Photo Researchers, Inc. **Page 59,** left: The Bridgeman Art Library/Getty Images. right: Manned Spacecraft Center, NASA. **Page 60,** left: © Royalty-Free/Corbis. right: © Larry Kolvoord /The Image Works. **Page 64,** Andrew Mounter/Taxi/Getty Images. **Page 66,** Photodisc Blue/Getty Images. **Page 74,** © Staffan Widstrand/Corbis. **Page 77,** © Robert van der Hilst/Corbis. **Page 78,** © D. Robert & Lorri Franz/Corbis. **Page 80,** © Bettmann/Corbis. **Page 88,** © Corbis. **Page 94,** © Earl & Nazima Kowall/Corbis. **Page 102,** Courtesy, National Museum of the American Indian, Smithsonian Institution [Specimen 23/2171 and 22/5562Neg. 31183]. Photo by Carmelo Guadagno. **Page 108,** © Corbis. **Page 117,** © Reuters/Corbis. **Page 118,** © Bettmann/Corbis. **Page 119,** © Archivo Iconografico, S.A./Corbis. **Page 123,** © Bettmann/Corbis. **Page 125,** © Bettmann/Corbis. **Page 136,** From Kishlansky, et al., *Civilization in the West, Volume B, 4e.* © 2001 Addison Wesley Longman. **Page 137,** © Bettmann/Corbis. **Page 146,** left: Scala/Art Resource, NY. right: © Roger Ressmeyer/Corbis. **Page 147,** top left: © Royalty-Free/Corbis. top right: © Craig Aurness/Corbis. bottom left: Digital image © 1996 Corbis; Original image courtesy of NASA/Corbis. bottom right: © Topham/Photri/The Image Works. **Page 150,** Taxi/Getty Images. **Page 151,** From Kishlansky, et al., *Civilization in the West, Volume B, 4e.* © 2001 Addison Wesley Longman. **Page 159,** NASA nova. **Page 160,** Ann Ronan Picture Library/HIP/The Image Works. **Page 161,** © Bettmann/Corbis. **Page 164,** © Bettmann/Corbis. **Page 173,** From Kishlansky, et al., *Civilization in the West, Volume B, 4e.* © 2001 Addison Wesley Longman. **Page 175,** top: © Freelance Consulting Services Pty Ltd/Corbis. bottom: © Bettmann/Corbis. **Page 176,** Scala/Art Resource, NY. **Page 177,** Scala/Art Resource, NY. **Page 187,** top: © Archivo Iconografico, S.A./Corbis. bottom: Scala/Art Resource, NY. **Page 188,** left: © North Carolina Museum of Art/Corbis. right: © Archivo Iconografico, S.A./Corbis. **Pages 190, 192, 193, 195, 197,** Scala/Art Resource, NY. **Page 205,** © Arne Hodalic/Corbis. **Page 206,** top left: © Adam Woolfitt/Corbis. bottom left: © Massimo Listri/Corbis. right: © Christie's Images/Corbis. **Page 214:** left, Scala/Art Resource. **Pages 214,** right, and **216,** The Nelson-Atkins Museum of Art, Kansas City, Missouri (Purchase: Nelson Trust) 47-71. Photo by Robert Newcombe. **Page 217,** © Archivo Iconografico, S.A./Corbis. **Page 220,** Xia Gui, Chinese, late 12th early 13th century. *Sailboat in Rainstorm.* Chinese, Southern Song dynasty, about 1189-94. Object Place: China. Ink and light color on silk. 23.9 x 25.1 cm (9 7/16 x 9 7/8 in.). Museum of Fine Arts, Boston. Special Chinese and Japanese Fun, 12.891. Photograph © 2004 Museum of Fine Arts, Boston. **Page 229,** top: © Peter Johnson/Corbis. bottom: © John Heseltine/Corbis. **Page 230,** © David Turnley/Corbis. **Page 234,** © Macduff Everton/Corbis. **Page 235,** © Horace Bristol/Corbis. **Page 243,** top: © Bettmann/Corbis. bottom: © Lindsay Hebberd/Corbis. **Page 246,** © Vince Streano/Corbis. **Page 256,** © Bryan F. Peterson/Corbis. **Page 260,** © Royalty-Free/Corbis. **Page 261,** © George Simian/Corbis. **Page 271,** © Joseph Sohm; ChromoSohm Inc./Corbis. **Page 273,** ©LWA-Dann Tardif/Corbis. **Page 274,** © Reuters/Corbis.

Text Credits: **Pages 8, 20, 36, 43,** Enger, et al., *Concepts in Biology 9e.* © 2000 McGraw-Hill. Reproduced with permission of the McGraw-Hill Companies. **Pages 64, 74, 92, 101,** Michael Alan Park, *Introducing Anthropology: An Integrated Approach.* © 2000 McGraw-Hill. Reproduced with permission of the McGraw-Hill Companies. **Page 123,** *Conceptual Physical Science,* 2nd ed. by Paul G. Hewitt, John Suchocki, and Leslie A. Hewitt. Copyright © 1999 by Paul G. Hewitt, John Suchocki, and Leslie A. Hewitt. Reprinted by permission of Pearson Education, Inc. and Kishlansky, et al., *Civilization in the West, Volume B, 4e.* © 2001 Addison Wesley Longman. Reproduced with permission of Addison Wesley Longman. **Pages 134, 149, 158,** Kishlansky, et al., *Civilization in the West, Volume B, 4e.* © 2001 Addison Wesley Longman. Reproduced with permission of Addison Wesley Longman. **Pages 180, 190, 208, 216,** *Art Past, Art Present, 4e* by Wilkins/Schultz/Linduff, © Reprinted by permission of Pearson Education, Inc., Upper Saddle River, NJ. **Pages 233, 242, 259, 268, 270,** From Eric Shiraev & David Levy. *Introduction to Cross-Cultural Psychology: Critical Thinking and Contemporary Applications,* © 2001. Published by Allyn and Bacon, Boston, MA. Copyright © 2001 by Pearson Education. Reprinted by permission of the publisher.